Journal of Consciousness Studies
controversies in science & the humanities

Vol. 17, No. 11–12, November–December 2010

5   About Authors

The Victorian's Guide to Consciousness
Essays Marking the Centenary of William James (1842–1910)
Guest Editor: Allan Combs

8   Dedication to the late David Fontana

9   Editor's Foreword — *Allan Combs*

11 A Psychological Commentary on the Essays — *Eugene Taylor*

19 Nineteenth Century Pioneers in the Study of Dissociation: William James and Psychical Research — *Carlos S. Alvarado & Stanley Krippner*

44 The Ever-New Flow of Time: Henri Bergson's View of Consciousness — *G. William Barnard*

62 Consciousness Already There Waiting to be Uncovered: William James's Mystical Suggestion as Corroborated by Himself and His Contemporaries — *Jonathan Bricklin*

93 Neurology & the Mind at the Turn of the Century — *Allan Combs*

100 Is there Awareness Outside Attention? A Psychological Perspective — *Allan Combs, Stanley Krippner & Eugene Taylor*

116 William James, Conversion and Rapid, Radical Transformation — *Arthur Hastings*

121 William James and the Search for Scientific Evidence of Life After Death: Past, Present, and Possible Future — *Gary E. Schwartz*

153 Who Was Frederic William Henry Myers? — *Eugene Taylor*

Continued overleaf

Contents continued

Continuing Debate

173 The Content of Olfactory Experience   *Christopher Mole*

Wit and Wisdom

180 Consciousness Puzzle Page   *Ed Subitzky*

Conference Report

181 Nature & Human Nature   *Graham Horswell*

Book Reviews

189 **Michael Tye,**
 Consciousness Revisited   *Bruno Mölder*

195 **Michael N. Marsh,**
 Out of Body and Near-Death Experiences   *Chris Nunn*

198 **Maxine Sheets-Johnstone,**
 The Corporeal Turn   *Steve Torrance*

202 **Charles Tart,**
 The End of Materialism   *Charles Whitehead*

207 Books Received

Annual Index

208 Index of Titles 2010

211 Index of Authors 2010

Published in the UK and USA by Imprint Academic, PO Box 200, Exeter EX5 5YX, UK

World Copyright © Imprint Academic, 2010. No part of any contribution may be reproduced in any form without permission, except for the quotation of brief passages in criticism and discussion. The opinions expressed in the articles and book reviews are not necessarily those of the editors or the publishers.

JCS is indexed and abstracted in: *Social Sciences Citation Index*®, *ISI Alerting Services* (includes *Research Alert*®), *Current Contents*®: *Social and Behavioral Sciences, Arts and Humanities Citation Index*®, *Current Contents*®: *Arts & Humanities Citation Index*®, *Social Scisearch*®, *PsycINFO*® and *The Philosopher's Index*.

ISSN 1355 8250

Journal of Consciousness Studies

Editor
Valerie Gray Hardcastle, Dean of McMicken College of Arts and Sciences, University of Cincinnati. *valerie.hardcastle@uc.edu*

Managing Editors (address for submissions)
Anthony Freeman, Imprint Academic, PO Box 200, Exeter EX5 5YX, UK. Tel: +44 1392 851550. *Anthony.jcs@gmail.com*
Graham Horswell (Assistant): *Graham.jcs@gmail.com*

Book Reviews Editor (address for books for review)
Julian Kiverstein, Department of Philosophy, University of Edinburgh, George Sqare, Edinburgh, EH8 9JX, UK. *J.Kiverstein@ed.ac.uk*

Associate Editors
Jean Burns: *jeanbur@earthlink.net*; **Ivo Mosley** (Poetry):*ivomosley@aol.com*
Chris Nunn: *cmhnunn@btinternet.com*

Founding Editors
Joseph A. Goguen (1941–2006), **Robert K.C. Forman**: *Forman@TheForge.org*
Jonathan Shear: *jcs@infionline.net*, **Keith Sutherland**, Publisher: *keith@imprint.co.uk*

Editorial Advisory Board
Bernard J. Baars, Neurosciences Institute; **David Chalmers**, Australian National University; **Ewert Cousins**, Fordham University; **Daniel Dennett**, Tufts University; **Margaret Donaldson**, Edinburgh University; **Peter Fenwick**, Maudsley Hospital; **Stuart Hameroff**, University of Arizona; **Erich Harth**, Syracuse University; **Basil Hiley**, Birkbeck College; **Nicholas Humphrey**, London School of Economics; **Piet Hut**, Institute for Advanced Studies; **Robert Kentridge**, University of Durham; **Christof Koch**, CalTech; **George Lakoff**, UC, Berkeley; **Philip Merikle**, University of Waterloo; **Mary Midgley**, University of Newcastle; **Raimon Panikkar**, UC, Santa Barbara; **Roger Penrose**, Oxford University; **Geraint Rees**, Institute of Cognitive Neuroscience, **Eleanor Rosch**, UC, Berkeley; **David Rosenthal**, CUNY, **John Searle**, UC, Berkeley; **Huston Smith**, Syracuse University; **Susan Leigh Star**, Santa Clara University; **Roger Walsh**, UC, Irvine; **Arthur Zajonc**, Amherst College.

Manuscript Submissions
For style guide and other directions for authors go to the journal's website, imprint-academic.com/jcs

---

Subscription and Ordering Information

Annual Subscription Rates for 2010 (12 monthly issues):

Individuals: $150/£75   **Institutions**: $520/£260

Prices for print journal and include accelerated delivery (UK/USA), surface mail rest of world, and free access to the journal online at Ingenta.com

Orders to : Imprint Academic, PO Box 200, Exeter EX5 5YX, UK.
Tel: +44 1392 851550; Fax: 851178; *Email: sandra@imprint.co.uk*

Cheques (£ or $US 'Imprint Academic'); VISA/AMEX/MASTERCARD

ia imprint-academic.com

TSC Stockholm, Sweden, May 2–8, 2011

www.consciousness.arizona.edu

SPECIAL CALL FOR PAPERS

Special Sessions

marking Anthony Freeman's forthcoming retirement
from the managing editorship of *JCS*

To honour and celebrate Anthony's distinguished accomplishments and stewardship of the *Journal of Consciousness Studies* since its foundation in 1994, special concurrent sessions will be held at the upcoming conference:

Toward a Science of Consciousness
Brain, Mind and Reality
May 2–8, 2011
Stockholm, Sweden

♦ **To contribute**, please submit an abstract though the conference website www.consciousness.arizona.edu and add a notation that the submission is intended for the Anthony Freeman/JCS session.

♦ **Topics** may relate to specific articles, issues, themes and overall directions in Consciousness Studies overseen by Anthony Freeman.

♦ **The deadline** for abstracts for the Anthony Freeman/JCS sessions is December 31, 2010.

Stuart Hameroff

Christer Perfjell

Conference co-chairs

ABOUT AUTHORS

Carlos S. Alvarado has a PhD in psychology from the University of Edinburgh. Many of his published papers have focused on the history of mesmerism, parapsychology, and psychology. In addition, he has conducted survey research on out-of-body experiences and other psychic experiences. Alvarado is currently Scholar in Residence and Faculty at Atlantic University, Assistant Professor of Research at the University of Virginia, and Adjunct Research Faculty at the Institute of Transpersonal Psychology. He is in the editorial boards of the Journal of Near-Death Studies, the Journal of the Society for Psychical Research, and the Journal of Scientific Exploration.

G. William Barnard, (BA Antioch University; MA Temple University; PhD University of Chicago) is currently an Associate Professor of Religious Studies, as well as a University Distinguished Teaching Professor. His primary areas of research interest are the comparative philosophy of mysticism, consciousness studies, religion and the social sciences, contemporary spirituality, and religion and healing. Professor Barnard is the author of the book *Exploring Unseen Worlds: William James and the Philosophy of Mysticism.* He is also co-editor of *Crossing Boundaries: Essays on the Ethical Status of Mysticism*, and has just completed a monograph, *Living Consciousness: Reclaiming the Metaphysical Vision of Henri Bergson*, soon to be published by State University of New York Press. Professor Barnard has also written many journal articles and book chapters on a variety of topics, such as pedagogy in religious studies, the nature of religious experience, and issues in the psychology of religion. He is currently researching the Santo Daime tradition, a syncretistic religious movement in Brazil.

Jonathan Bricklin is the editor of the anthology *Sciousness* (Eirini Press, 2007). Previous publications with *JCS* include 'A Variety of Religious Experience: WIlliam James and the Non-Reality of Free Will' (1999), a translation of James' 'La Notion De Conscience', (2005), and 'Switched-Off Consciousness: Clarifying What It Cannot Mean' (2006). His essay 'Sciousness and *Con*sciousness: William James and the Prime Reality of Non-Dual Experience' was published by the *Journal of Transpersonal Psychology* (2003). Jonathan is a Program Director at the New York Open Center.

Allan Combs is a consciousness researcher, neuropsychologist, and systems theorist. He holds appointments at The California Institute of

Integral Studies, the Saybrook Graduate School, and is Professor Emeritus at the University of North Carolina-Asheville. He is the author of over 100 articles, chapters, and books on consciousness and the brain, including *The Radiance of Being*, winner of the best-book award of the *Scientific and Medical Network of the UK*, *Mind in Time: The Dynamics of Thought, Reality, and Consciousness*, with Mark Germine and Ben Geortzel; and *Consciousness Explained Better: Towards an Integral Understanding of the Multifaceted Nature of Consciousness*. Professor Combs is co-founder The Society for Chaos Theory in Psychology and the Life Sciences, a member of The General Evolution Research Group, and the one-hundred member Club of Budapest.

Arthur Hastings is professor and Director of the William James Center for Consciousness Studies at the Institute of Transpersonal Psychology, Palo Alto, CA. He holds a PhD in communication from Northwestern University. He is the author of *With the Tongues of Men and Angels*, a book on the psychology of channeling, and articles and books on transpersonal psychology, bereavement, argumentation, holistic health, hypnosis, and paranormal phenomena.

Stanley Krippner, PhD, professor of psychology at Saybrook University, San Francisco, is a Fellow in four American Psychological Association (APA) divisions, and past-president of two divisions. Formerly, he was director of the Kent State University Child Study Center, Kent OH, and the Maimonides Medical Center Dream Research Laboratory, Brooklyn NY. He is co-author of *Extraordinary Dreams, Personal Mythology, Dream Telepathy,* and *Haunted by Combat: Understanding PTSD in War Veterans*, and co-editor of *Healing Tales, Healing Stories, Mysterious Minds, Debating Psychic Experience, The Psychological Impact of War on Civilians: An International Perspective,* and *Varieties of Anomalous Experience: Examining the Scientific Evidence*. He received the APA Award for Distinguished Contributions to the International Development of Psychology in 2002, the Society for Psychological Hypnosis Award for Distinguished Contributions to Professional Hypnosis in 2002, the Ashley Montagu Peace Award in 2003, and lifetime achievement awards from the Association for the Study of Dreams and the Parapsychological Association. He also holds Fellow status in several additional organizations including, the Association for Psychological Science, the Society for the Scientific Study of Religion, and the Society for the Scientific Study of Sexuality.

Christopher Mole is Assistant Professor in the Department of Philosophy and in the Program in Cognitive Systems at the University of British Columbia, Vancouver. His work is mainly concerned with the philosophy and psychology of attention and he is co-editor of the forthcoming book *Attention: Philosophical and Psychological Essays* (Oxford University Press, 2011).

Ed Subitzky is a humour writer and cartoonist with a philosophical bent, whose work has appeared in the *New York Times* and the *New Yorker*. He has a lifelong interest in consciousness and the mind.

Gary E. Schwartz is Professor of Psychology, Medicine, Neurology, Psychiatry, and Surgery at the University of Arizona, Tucson, and director of the Laboratory for Advances in Consciousness and Health (formerly the Human Energy Systems Laboratory). He received his PhD in psychology from Harvard University in 1971 and was an assistant professor there before serving as a professor of psychology and psychiatry at Yale University, until moving to Arizona in 1988. He has published more than four hundred and fifty scientific papers, co-edited eleven academic books, and is the author of *The Energy Healing Experiments* (2007), *The G.O.D. Experiments* (2006), *The Afterlife Experiments* (2002), *The Truth about Medium* (2005), and is co-author of *The Living Energy Universe* (1999). Gary is a Fellow of the American Psychological Association, the American Psychological Society, the Society for Behavioral Medicine, and the Academy for Behavioral Medicine Research.

Eugene Taylor holds a PhD in the History and Philosophy of Psychology. Currently, he is Professor of Psychology, Saybrook University; Lecturer on Psychiatry at Harvard Medical School; and Senior Psychologist on the Psychiatry Service at the Massachusetts General Hospital. Among other works, he is the author of *William James on Exceptional Mental States* (1983/2010); *William James on Consciousness Beyond the Margin* (1996); *The Mystery of Personality: A History of Psychodynamic Theories* (2009); and *William James and the Spiritual Roots of American Pragmatism* (forthcoming).

This special issue of the *Journal of Consciousness Studies*
is dedicated to

David Fontana (1934–2010)

whose death was announced as the journal
was being prepared for printing.

David was professor of transpersonal psychology at Liverpool's John Moores University and had worked tirelessly to bring transpersonal psychology and the study of evidence for conscious existence beyond the physical world into the mainstream of academic life.

It was a major achievement when in 1996, together with Ingrid Slack and Martin Treacy, he established a Transpersonal Psychology Section within the British Psychological Society. The publication of his aptly subtitled book *Is There An Afterlife?: A Comprehensive Overview of the Evidence* (2005) was another landmark in the scientific study of consciousness in all its aspects, pioneered by William James whose centenary we celebrate in this issue.

Allan Combs

Editor's Foreword to
The Victorian's Guide to Consciousness

The essays included in this collection, and introduced in the following psychological commentary by Eugene Taylor, present some of the basic ideas about the nature of consciousness as understood by theorists of the turn of the twentieth century. Several of the essays compare these notions with modern views. Except for the sophistication of the research design, the investigation reported here by Gary Schwartz, on William James and mediumship, could actually have been published in the late nineteenth century. The main intention in most of the essays, however, is to explore the dominant thinking of that time in comparison to contemporary thought on similar problems.

To gain the broadest perspective let me reflect on the fact that there seems to be a rough but recognizable mythopoetic cycle in the overall cultural history of the West, a cycle that is sometimes mirrored in shorter periods of time as well. It involves a transition from something like magical thinking to mythic thought, then on to mental or rational thinking. These purported stages in western cultural history were identified by the twentieth century German historian and poet Jean Gebser (1986). Here I want to suggest something of this nature across the past century of the study of the consciousness. The turn of the twentieth century might be thought of as a kind of mythical era, suggestive of Giambattista Vico's *age of heroes* (Bergin and Fisch, 1948), characterized by wondrously profound theories of consciousness and human nature by larger-than-life figures such as William James,

Correspondence:
Allan Combs, California Institute of Integral Studies   *Email: ACombs@ciis.edu*

Frederic Myers, Henri Bergson, Carl Jung, and Sigmund Freud, each creating a legacy still very much alive.

This period was followed by almost a century of rationalistic approaches to consciousness in psychology and philosophy. During the second half of the twentieth century the cognitive sciences in particular have created an almost hyper-rational approach. Daniel Dennett's *Consciousness Explained* is perhaps the most celebrated and highly refined example of the latter, and is consistent with neurological thinking exemplified by theorists such as Pat Churchland and Francis Crick, names familiar to the readers of these pages.

Gebser believed that following this hyper-rational era there would come an 'integral' age that could enfold the past gains of both the mythical and rational periods, incorporating them both into a unified and expanded worldview. Perhaps these essays will play a small but significant role in the opening of this age of scholarship.

References

Bergin, T.G. & Fisch, M.G. (trans. & ed.) (1948) *Scienza Nuova Seconda (1730/1744): The New Science of Giambattista Vico*, Ithaca, NY: Cornell University Press.

Dennett, D.C. (1991) *Consciousness Explained*, New York: Little, Brown.

Gebser, J. (1986) *The Ever Present Origin: Foundations of the Aperspectival World*, Columbus, OH: Ohio University Press.

Eugene Taylor

A Psychological Commentary on 'The Victorian's Guide to Consciousness': Essays about William James and the Study of Consciousness at the Turn of the 20th Century and Today

In our opening article by Alvarado and Krippner, the authors have dug out most of James's cases pertaining to psychic phenomena between 1867 and 1910 in service of the idea that psychical research played a major role in reshaping scientific investigation of the spiritualists and mental healers, particularly with regard to the development of such new fields as experimental psychopathology. I would go further, suggesting that the early committees of the American Society for Psychical Research, an independent body between 1885 and 1889 and then a branch of the Society for Psychical Research in England until 1905, made major contributions not only to psychopathology but also to the revolution in psychotherapeutics after 1900 in the US. In addition, in James's hands psychical research put an emphasis on the growth oriented dimension of personality such that, yes, illness might be healed. But the primary focus was actually on the spiritual self-realization of the person, where psychic phenomena were seen as guideposts of one's progress along the way. Character development in the normal personality was just as important as returning the sick to health, a point that still eludes both psychology and psychiatry today.

Correspondence:
Eugene Taylor, Saybrook University, 747 Front Street, 3rd floor, San Francisco, CA, 94111-1920   Email: Etaylor@saybrook.edu

William Barnard, who marches through Henri Bergson's major works, introduces us to the concept of consciousness as Bergson understood it. *Durée real*, the duration of our experience, the flow of time consciousness, remains the bedrock of our experience, according to Bergson, but we remain cut off from it by living too much out in the world and not enough in our interiors. As a result our experience is cut up into bits and we struggle through reason and logic to make sense out of it all. As I see it, it is an idea that appears remarkably similar to James's conception of the stream of consciousness and in such parallels we have the foundation for their letters and their relationship, although Bergson felt the parallelism was probably not as close as James was wont to make it. Nevertheless, when James officiated at arranging for the publication of the English version of Bergson's *Creative Evolution*, Bergson reciprocated by arranging for the translation of a number of James's works, including his *Pragmatism*, into French. Indeed, Bergson was likely the major route by which James's work became known to the later French existentialists. Certainly helped by their relationship, Bergson, though an acclaimed philosopher and not a scientist, was a world-wide figure of veneration at the time that James died, particularly in the United States. In 1912, a ticker-tape parade in New York City was held in his honour when he came to visit. And because his focus was experiential he was understood by the general public rather than applauded by those who cleaved to a strict deterministic materialism. Within each person's creative intuition, Bergson said, and Barnard affirms, is the source of freedom.

Jonathan Bricklin has produced possibly one of the most significant papers of the collection. Making his points judiciously, and cleaving closely to what James himself had actually said, Bricklin points out, for instance, the major difference between James and Bergson, in that Bergson focused almost exclusively on the flow of time, while James considered it an artificial construction. What James was getting at in *The Varieties of Religious Experience* (1902) and elsewhere, Bricklin suggests, was that mystical states of consciousness, because they are time transcendent, are a veridical revelation of a larger reality beyond linear time. Bricklin achieves this understanding by a close review of James's involvement with Shadworth Hodgson; by drawing specific parallels with Einstein's idea of veridical revelation; through a study of James's complicated relationship with theorists such as Benjamin Paul Blood, Frederic Myers, and Sir Oliver Lodge; and then through a curious section on 'The Witness', in which Bricklin makes some likely conjectures about James's commitment to a Vedantic or Theosophic view of the universe, going so far in the beginning of the paper as to label some evidence he found in James as constituting James's allegiance to the doctrine of nondualism. While the paper overall contributes striking new evidence to the corpus of James scholarship, I would quibble with Bricklin's use of the term nondualism with regard to James. The term nondualism is certainly incorrect when applied to James's metaphysics of radical empiricism, for two reasons.

The first reason is that James, after all, proclaimed himself a pluralist because monism could always be one of his options. A monist cannot do this because every argument must be finally reduced to his monistic frame of reference. James also said nearly in the same breath that in order to adopt the position of the pluralist, he did not mind contradicting himself, because life was like that and because this was his answer to one of the arch criticisms of the monists against his metaphysics. A monist, however, can only deal with the single focus of their reality. They are able to entertain the dualist's position, but only by posing something that is the opposite of their original stance, such as good versus evil, free will versus determinism, or nature versus nurture, or the mind and the body. In the end, the dichotomy is always reduced to a monistic stance as the superior choice. The monist cannot handle the pluralists' position, however. A pluralist can still champion rational thought, but also differentiate between the irrational and the non-rational, while the monist cannot. Further, nondual is a term classically applied to the monism of Advaita Vedanta, a position popularized in the US by the folk psychologist, Ken Wilber, and one who influenced him, Sri Aurobindo Ghose.

Second, Bertrand Russell had coined a phrase that has created one hundred years of misunderstanding with regard to James's metaphysics; namely that James was a 'neutral monist'. This diagnosis has been almost universally adopted by the analytic philosophers throughout the Twentieth century, all of whom themselves have been reductionistic monists, thus contributing to a colossal misreading of James by that branch of philosophy even today.

Allan Combs surveys the general state of neurology and brain science in the second half of the nineteenth century and does a credible job of representing the main lines of development in the mainstream of science and medicine. To this picture must be added, however, the rather late development of the modern neuron theory focusing on the individual nerve cells, their cell bodies, their axons and dendrites, and how they function. There were also major advances in our understanding of the autonomic nervous system. Regarding this last point, the New York neurologist, George Miller Beard, had made a detailed study of medical electricity and its palliative effects on the body in the 1860s, then launched investigations into the phenomena of hypnosis in the 1870s, as well as the trance states of 'enebriates', people in shock after a natural disaster, and cases of sexual neurasthenia and nervous exhaustion. Long before other investigators began to conceptualize the action of all the branches of the nervous system, he was studying what he called the vegetative nervous system. William James took a keen interest in these subjects when he published 'What is an Emotion?' in 1884, effectively taking the study of the emotions out of philosophy and placing it squarely in physiology. James's work had an important effect on Theodule Ribot's essays on diseases of the will, diseases of the emotions, and diseases of personality, in addition to spurring increased scientific study of the emotions in such undergraduate students as Walter Bradford Cannon. Cannon, of course, went on to identify the fight or flight response and to outline the effects of the autonomic nervous system, particularly the chemistry and action of adrenalin and noradrenalin, in *Bodily Emotions in Hunger, Fear, Rage and Pain* (1915). Noting these developments helps to round out Professor Combs' review of the status of neurology in the late nineteenth century.

In their chapter, Combs, Krippner, and Taylor attempt to link modern chaos theory with James's conception of consciousness and do a fair job of indicating certain important parallels. Historians of the late nineteenth century, however, lack a certain sophistication with regard to the actual arguments at the time between philosophers and scientists regarding what is consciousness. Can it be scientifically studied? And what were precisely the major arguments defining the mind–body problem during that period? Part of the problem has been that the chroniclers of depth psychology were largely captured by the Freudocentric view in the early histories of depth psychology, as if there were no other views on consciousness except those of Charcot in 1881 and Freud at the Clark University Conference of 1909. In fact, there was a flourishing, cross cultural dynamic psychology of the subconscious well established before Freud came out of his early period of creative isolation. Historians of psychology and psychiatry, up until the more recent scholarship of Henri Ellenberger, remained enamoured with this more Freudocentric point of view. A case in point which the present authors take up concerns the differing terms used to refer to dynamic unconscious processes back then.

As well, historians in general take the history of psychology in the late nineteenth century to be about the creation myth started by the experimental psychologists back in 1950, reciting that scientific psychology began with the founding of Wilhelm Wundt's laboratory at Leipzig in 1879 (William James actually started the first laboratory in 1875 at Harvard). The history of the laboratory, however, is incompatible with the history of depth psychology, a fact still unrecognized by general historians today, so the picture remains completely muddled. Views about modern neuroscience put forward by Combs, Krippner, and Taylor, however, only make sense when the actual events and ideas of the nineteenth century period become finally reconstructed. In any event, Combs, Krippner, and Taylor spend the main body of their text on themes in the neurosciences, suggesting parallels between contemporary developments in the scientific study of consciousness today and the scientific study of the same concept one hundred years ago. The comparison makes much more sense when the early development of dynamic theories of the subconscious are reconstructed and then factored into the comparison.

Arthur Hastings presents us with a cogent argument in favour of interpreting James's emphasis on the immediate transformation of consciousness as a phenomenon of quantum change. Implied altered states of consciousness in which there is a hierarchy from higher to lower he equates with James on differing systems of energy within the person and notes that this approach is comparable today to the ideas of various transpersonal theorists such as Stanislav Grof.

The discussion of consciousness, however, I maintain, also implies an embedded conception of the person. James himself posited that we are not one unified self but an ultimate plurality of selves, one or the other being dominant in waking consciousness at different times and sometimes with conscious splitting, where two halves share the field. His point about different levels of consciousness is well taken, nonetheless. James was familiar with this idea one hundred years ago from Swedenborg's doctrine of discrete degrees — that waking consciousness is not the same as transcendent awareness in the sense of just more of it. Rather, states of consciousness are separated from each other by discrete degrees. States of consciousness are not continuous from one to the next. To move up requires non-rational experiences of insight and transcendence, not logic and reason.

Hastings presumes that to achieve higher states of consciousness 'neural systems have to be rewired'. Writing in the passive voice as he does, it still seems like he is saying one would have to rewire one's own systems, as if the process was really under the conscious control of one's rational faculties. It could be that an opening to wider experience and the possibility of surrender to whatever the higher power might be is what leads to the rewiring, not the other way around. Hastings takes up the question of deliberately inducing such states, which James says and Hastings agrees, can possibly facilitate such a transformation but do not guarantee them. I would say that in Hastings' summary of such deliberate acts, it is not the act itself that precipitates the transformation but the attitude of the person within which the transformation takes place. Michel Murphy, founder of Esalen Institute, once asked Arnold Schwarzenegger if he ever meditated. Schwarzenegger's reply was 'ya, one pump with it is worth ten pumps without it' (personal communication, quote from Michael Murphy). My take on it is expressed by the Japanese phrase: *tongu zen shu*, instant realization followed by a lifetime of gradual achievement.

Gary Schwartz poses a question that will immediately disturb the normative scientist on several counts. The most important insult to one's scientific sensibilities must be the very act of bringing up the subject of psychic phenomena and its attendant question of life after death as general topics of legitimate scientific interest. Indeed, to identify oneself as a so-called real scientist, one must subscribe to the belief that no such phenomena actually exist. The operative term here is 'real', implying that reality as defined by the scientist is the only one possible. Waking rational consciousness thus becomes the *sine qua non* of human evolution — last to come in evolutionary development but usually the first to go whenever there is a serious insult to the brain. This is why in the emergency room or the ambulance, the attendant says to the patient: 'Do you know your name? Do you know where you are?' — a primitive but simple test to ascertain if the rational and reflective capacities are still intact. The question is a good and important one pragmatically, but it also has embedded within it the dual assumptions that reality is defined by the attachment of the senses to objects in the external material world in either a pleasurable or painful way and that, moreover, the scientist can gain some measure of control over this reality through the particularly pervasive method of the rational ordering of sense data alone. In very Kantian fashion this view implies that all we can know are data that come to waking consciousness from the senses and the application of the rules of logic to their classification, storage, and retrieval at some later time, when large enough data bits can be organized into higher levels of abstraction. All we can know in reductive, positivist science, is what we can hear, feel, taste, touch, and smell. Communication independent of the five senses is absolutely ruled out.

The second insult Prof. Schwartz presents that will be equally off-putting to the mainstream scientist is his presumption that we have, in fact, established communication with the dead, such that it is possible to infer what the environment on the other side must be like. Schwartz's position is that William James is still alive and well on the other side and in this manner continues to influence us today. This is a common idea with parapsychologists, as are other such phenomena such as retroactive intentional influence — the idea that, time being relative on the other side, personalities beyond the grave in the future can influence events in the present. Personally, I am not sure what this means, but it does appear perfectly logical from their point of view. I should point out two truisms, however. James declared he was not very interested in the question of life after death, though for him it remained an open hypothesis. James would not likely be in complete agreement with Prof. Schwartz's point of view that James himself is still on the other side as we remembered him, still influencing us today, for the great question that James put before us in his own time — and still relevant — was the conundrum of how waking consciousness could study states of consciousness beyond itself. James would, however, agree with Prof Schwartz's correct assumption that in so far as the purview of all scientific inquiry must embrace the full spectrum of human experience, science was duty bound to apply the methods of science to it, if we are to have a legitimate and objective science in the first place.

Finally, the identity is revealed of none other than Frederik William Henry Myers, poet, classist, and psychical researcher, who was at the centre of developments in scientific psychotherapy in the English-speaking world in the closing decades of the nineteenth century. Through his studies of mediumship, clairvoyance, telepathy, and dynamic models of the subliminal consciousness, he contributed to what at that time was legitimately called experimental psychology. Though hardly recognized except for such distinguished figures as William James and Carl Jung at the time, and long forgotten for over more then a century, his reputation is being revived in modern consciousness studies.

In general, we have tried to survey the status of what can only be called the precursors to modern developments in the neurosciences. Any statement on the scientific investigation of consciousness, however, then or now, must perforce comment on William James, largely because all thought in the Western world with regard to the mind–body problem culminates in James's work between 1865 and 1910. This is appropriate, given that 2010 is the centenary of his passing. One can say in this regard that we are only beginning to approach conclusions he had previously already come to. In fact, experiences in the transformation of personality and consciousness on which he wrote so authoritatively 'link with contemporary themes'. However, in my opinion, James was then 150 years ahead of his time, meaning that after just 100 years, he is still 50 years ahead of us.

Carlos S. Alvarado &
Stanley Krippner

Nineteenth Century Pioneers in the Study of Dissociation

William James and Psychical Research

Abstract: *Following recent trends in the historiography of psychology and psychiatry we argue that psychical research was an important influence in the development of concepts about dissociation. To illustrate this point, we discuss American psychologist and philosopher William James's (1842–1910) writings about mediumship, secondary personalities, and hypnosis. Some of James's work on the topic took place in the context of research conducted by the American Society for Psychical Research, such as his early work with the medium Leonora E. Piper (1857–1950). James's work is an example of the influence of psychical research on several aspects of psychology such as early models of the unconscious and of dissociation.*

Keywords: William James, dissociation, mediumship, hypnosis, psychical research

There has been a rise of interest in the concept of dissociation in the last few decades, as well as in the history of this construct and the intellectual factors that permeated these discussions (e.g. Crabtree, 1993; 2007; Gauld, 1992; Hacking, 1995). In this paper we focus on the writings of the well-known American philosopher and psychologist William James (1842–1910), as well as the field of psychical research, of which James was a pioneer.

Our discussion of psychical research follows fairly recent historiographical trends in which a variety of authors have argued that movements such as spiritualism and psychical research that have been considered marginal in the historical development of psychology and psychiatry were in fact influential in the construction of certain aspects of these disciplines (e.g. Alvarado, 2002; Crabtree, 1993; Plas, 2000; Shamdasani, 1993; Taylor, 1996). In fact, an investigation of the work of influential nineteenth century figures in psychology shows that some of them were involved in one way or another with psychical research.[1] One of them was William James, who, according to Eugene Taylor (1996), 'was informed by early studies in experimental neuropathology, physiological psychology, and psychical research, which, in turn, significantly contributed to the development of the new field of experimental psychopathology' (p. 10).

Historians such as Régina Plas (2000) have argued that the study of psychic (or parapsychological) phenomena was an influential part in the beginnings of empirical psychology. A pioneer in this line of thinking was Henri F. Ellenberger (1905–1993) who, in his monumental book *The Discovery of the Unconscious* (1970), defended the importance of the investigation of mesmerism and spiritualism for the development of ideas about the unconscious, a trend followed by many others (e.g. Alvarado, Machado, Zangari and Zingrone, 2007; Crabtree, 1993; Plas, 2000; Shamdasani, 1993). But there is no doubt that many psychologists of this era were sceptical of the phenomena, suspecting that it represented nothing but conventional psychological functioning or even fraud (e.g. Carpenter, 1877; Janet, 1889; Jastrow, 1889).[2]

In this paper we will summarize James's writings on dissociation, with particular attention to those related to psychical research and, specifically, mediumship and hypnosis. While most of his writings on the subject were published during the nineteenth century, a few appeared in the early years of the twentieth century.

---

[1] This was the case of Ambroise August Liébeault (1823–1904; Alvarado, 2009a), Frederic W.H. Myers (1843–1901; Hamilton, 2009), Sigmund Freud (1856–1939; Fodor, 1971), Carl G. Jung (1875–1961; Fodor, 1971), Pierre Janet (1859–1947; Le Maléfan, 1993), Charles Richet (1850–1935; Wolf, 1993), and Théodore Flournoy (1854–1920; Shamdasani, 1994).

[2] Such rejection of psychic phenomena has been documented by several historians (e.g. Brown, 1983; Coon, 1992; Le Maléfan, 1999; Oppenheim, 1985).

James's Outlook

The study of William James has become an industry. This is obvious when one inspects the number of studies available today about his life and work (e.g. Johnson and Henley, 1990; Proudfoot, 2004; Richardson, 2006; Taylor 1996). Born in 1842 William James studied painting and other topics in Europe. He graduated with an M.D. degree in 1869 from the Harvard School of Medicine. Between 1872 and 1907 he taught, at Harvard, comparative anatomy and physiology, philosophy, and psychology (Courses, n.d.). Over the years James became known for such writings as *The Principles of Psychology* (1890b), *Psychology: Briefer Course* (1892a), *The Will to Believe, and Other Essays in Popular Philosophy* (1897), *Human Immortality* (1898a), *Talks to Teachers on Psychology* (1899), *The Varieties of Religious Experience* (1902), *Pragmatism* (1907), and *A Pluralistic Universe* (1909b) (for writings by and about James see Medd, 2010; Perry, 1920).

James had a clear empirical approach to psychological problems, something related to his well-known interests in pragmatism, radical empiricism, and pluralism. The American psychologist Gardner Murphy (1895–1979) saw James as a pioneer trying to be empirical in his quests in the context of the 'new scientific world of the evolutionary period' (Murphy, 1960, p. 4). This empirical outlook, and one attempting to present psychology to a great extent as a metaphysically-free enterprise, was evident in *The Principles of Psychology* (1890b). As James wrote: 'This book..., assuming that thoughts and feelings exist and are vehicles of knowledge, thereupon contends that psychology when she has ascertained the empirical correlation of the various sorts of thought or feeling with definite conditions of the brain, can go no farther — can go no farther, that is, as a natural science. If she goes farther she becomes metaphysical' (*ibid.*, Vol. 1, p. vi). But some years later James changed his mind. For example, he stated in his Presidential Address to the American Psychological Association that metaphysical and epistemological considerations should not be kept out of books about psychology (James, 1895, p. 124).

Replying to the belief that James abandoned psychology for philosophy after 1890, Taylor (1996) has argued that what James rejected was a positivist epistemology and that his work in areas such as psychopathology and psychical research, as well as the concept of the unconscious, shows he still operated as a psychologist. Taylor also stated that James defined psychology as a 'person-centered' field, one connected to different fields such as philosophy and the natural sciences, a perspective that could be seen in parts of *The Principles of*

Psychology. This stance gave metaphysics a place in the new psychology. As Taylor wrote: 'His new position acknowledged the reality of consciousness as an ultimate plurality of states; it shed significant light on then current scientific studies of personality disintegration; it admitted the iconography of the transcendent as a crucial determinant of personality transformation; and it provided James with an analytical tool powerful enough to critique the unexamined assumptions of radical materialism in experimental science' (*ibid.*, p. 5; see also Lamberth, 1999).

Even in his early writings, James (1879, 1884) discussed aspects of consciousness. In *The Principles of Psychology*, he wrote that consciousness 'does not appear to itself chopped up in bits. Such words as "chain" or "train" do not describe it fitly as it presents itself in the first instance. It is nothing jointed; it flows. A "river" or a "stream" are the metaphors by which it is most naturally described' (1890b, Vol. 1, p. 239). In a later book, *Talks to Teachers on Psychology*, he referred to 'a succession of states, or waves, or fields... of knowledge, of feeling, of desire, of deliberation, etc., that constantly pass and repass, and that constitute our inner life' (James, 1899, p. 15). However, James also noted that there were some disruptions in the flow of consciousness and one of these was dissociation.

Dissociation for James was part of a larger issue, that of consciousness and personality. This is clear in the following statements written as part of an introduction to Boris Sidis' (1867–1923) book *The Psychology of Suggestion*:

> What are the limits of the consciousness of a human being? Is 'self' consciousness only a part of the whole consciousness? Are there many 'selves' dissociated from one another? What is the medium of synthesis in a group of associated ideas? How can certain systems of ideas be cut off and forgotten? Is personality a product, and not a principle? Such are the questions now being forced to the front — questions now asked for the first time with some sense of their concrete import, and questions which it will require a great amount of further work, both of observation and of analysis, to answer adequately. (James, 1898b, pp. v–vi)

Dissociation and Psychical Research

By the time that James had become a well-known scholar, studies of dissociation were well underway. Representing this interest, the French physician Jules Héricourt wrote an overview article in the *Revue Scientifique* entitled 'La Activité Inconsciente de l'Esprit' (1889). He argued that separate from conscious processes there were also unconscious ones that could produce an 'apparent doubling of the normal conscious personality' (*ibid.*, p. 258; this, and other translations, are ours). Early studies of hypnotic procedures had demonstrated the existence of state specific memories, as argued by authors who identified themselves with Mesmerism (e.g. Deleuze, 1813). Years later the French physiologist Charles Richet induced personality changes in hypnotized participants (Richet, 1883), and other investigators reported cases of hypnotically-induced changes of personality (Azam, 1887), as well as ambulatory dissociations (Hodgson, 1891; Ladame, 1888), indicating that the human psyche had a number of levels of consciousness, many with apparently different memory records.

Many relevant hypnotic observations — state-specific memory, changes of personality — were reported by Pierre Janet in several influential publications (Janet, 1886; 1887; 1888; 1889). In his first paper Janet (1886) referred to hypnotic experiments with his patient Lucie, who, when re-hypnotized, continued talking about the same topic she was conversing about in her previous hypnotic condition (p. 579). In his view hypnotic suggestion was accompanied by 'some degree of unconsciousness or rather... of some doubling of consciousness' (*ibid.*, p. 592). Many fascinating observations were reported by Janet in his classic book *L'automatisme psychologique* (1889), such as one with Lucie in which her writing appeared to be childish after Janet 'suggested that she was not herself, but that she was a little seven year old child...' (p. 412).

The celebrated clinician Jean-Martin Charcot (1825–1893) reported a case in which a woman, designated as Hab, showed a 'particular state that we call a *secondary state*, or her B state... broken only by rare returns, both spontaneous and induced, and in any case of short duration, to the previous state, the *primary state* A' (Guinon, Blocq, Souques and Charcot, 1893, p. 172). When recollecting details about her life in her primary state Hab appeared to know about her life prior to 1885, but had no recollections about events that took place between 1885 and 1890. The '*secondary B state*' only could recall memories of some incidents from recent times. The A state could be induced by asking for its appearance, and had less 'hysterical stigmata' (such as anaesthesia and visual problems) associated with it than symptoms manifested during the B state.

During this period there were several general discussions of these phenomena that prompted some authors to argue for the existence of an unconscious mind (sometimes referred to as a 'subconscious mind') and for the reality of various dissociative manifestations such as secondary personalities (e.g. Héricourt, 1889; James, 1890a;

Newbold, 1896; Prince, 1890). Writing in *Scribner's Magazine* in an article entitled 'The Hidden Self' James (1890a) stated: 'It seems to me a very great step to have ascertained that the secondary self, or selves, coexist with the primary one, the trance-personalities with the normal one, during the waking state. But just what these secondary selves may be, and what are their remoter relations and conditions of existence, are questions to which the answer is anything but clear' (p. 373).

In addition to the study of dissociation, and other problems of the emerging fields of psychology and psychiatry, the nineteenth century saw the development of what was later called psychical research. The germs of systematic research were present in the movements of mesmerism and spiritualism, which included investigations of phenomena such as apparitions, clairvoyance, healing, and mediumship (Inglis, 1992; Podmore, 1902). But not all of the early works on these topics included serious research efforts; in an attempt to correct this practice, James wrote a book review (1869/1960) in which he made a call for the systematic investigation of these phenomena. In his view, 'The present attitude of society on this whole question is as extraordinary and anomalous as it is discreditable to the pretensions of an age which prides itself on enlightenment and the diffusion of knowledge' (*ibid.*, p. 21).

The Society for Psychical Research (SPR) was established in London in 1882, an organization having an ambitious programme of research (Gauld, 1968). The purpose of the SPR was to pursue 'an organized and systematic attempt to investigate that large group of debatable phenomena designated by such terms as mesmeric, psychical, and spiritualistic' (Objects of the Society, 1882, p. 3). The agenda of the SPR included studies of telepathy, consisting of both experiments (e.g. Guthrie and Birchall, 1883) and analyses of cases taking place in daily life, as seen in one of the central classics of the period, *Phantasms of the Living* (Gurney, Myers and Podmore, 1886). In this study, Gurney argued that visual, auditory, and tactile experiences, as well as impressions corresponding to events such as illness and accidents taking place at a distance, were the result of telepathic messages. Such telepathic 'phantasms' or hallucinations soon became a well-known explanation for such experiences.

Some of the SPR's other work relevant to dissociation were Edmund Gurney's (1847–1888) studies of the stages of hypnosis as well as state-specific hypnotic memory (Gurney, 1884; 1887a,b; 1888). Regarding the latter, Gurney reported the following observation with a person he had hypnotized: 'In this condition he was able to read... After reading a paragraph... he was then [awakened] completely as usual. But only one word of what he had read could be recalled, and he was very uncertain about that; he recollected distinctly, however, a paragraph that he had recently read in the normal state, and felt satisfied that that was the last one read. Again hypnotized, he had full recollection of the paragraph read in the hypnotic state with open eyes' (Gurney, 1888, p. 10).

Others reported observations about mediumistic trance, including the psychical researcher Richard Hodgson (1855–1905; Hodgson, 1892; 1898) who worked with the Boston medium Leonora E. Piper (1857–1950). Initially the medium showed what seemed to be an initial stage in which she was 'dreamily conscious of the sitter, and dreamily conscious of "spirits"' (Hodgson, 1898, p. 397). This state was followed by the manifestation of what Hodgson referred to as the subliminal consciousness of the medium 'which is in direct relation... not so much with our ordinary physical world as with "another world"' (*ibid.*, p. 397). The latter was followed by a state conceptualized as one in which the 'subliminal consciousness withdraws completely from the control of her body and takes her supraliminal consciousness with it' (*ibid.*, p. 398). Hodgson also noticed that Mrs. Piper came out of trance, reversing the order of appearance of the above mentioned states.

The work of the classical scholar Frederic W.H. Myers was also very important for the SPR as well as for psychical research and for psychology in general. In his early writings Myers (1884; 1885; 1889) called attention to both sensory and motor automatisms (e.g. hallucinations and automatic writing) as a way in which the subliminal (unconscious) mind communicated. Myers later stated: 'I suggest... that the stream of consciousness in which we habitually live is not the only consciousness which exists in connection with our organism. Our habitual or empirical consciousness may consist of a mere selection from a multitude of thoughts and sensations, of which some at least are equally conscious with those that we empirically know' (Myers, 1892, p. 301). He connected the subliminal mind with a variety of dissociative phenomena. Some were what he referred to as phenomena generally accepted by psychology — such as automatisms, hypnosis, and alterations of personality. But he also included manifestations such as telepathy and mediumship that still had not gained general scientific acceptance (Myers, 1903).

As discussed in various historical studies, psychical research was also cultivated in countries other than England. They included France (Plas, 2000), Germany (Treitel, 2003), Italy (Biondi, 1988), and the

United States (Moore, 1977). In France the physiologist Charles Richet (1884) explored what the French and others referred to as 'mental suggestion'. In the United States, an organization similar to the SPR, the American Society for Psychical Research (ASPR), was organized in Boston (Formation of the Society, 1885; see also Moore, 1977). The society was part of the SPR until 1906, when it became independent. During its early period its members conducted research on topics such as thought-transference and mediumship (e.g. Bowditch *et al.*, 1886; James, 1886).

James became involved with the SPR, and was its president in 1896. His Presidential Address was published in the opening page of the June 19, 1896 issue of *Science* (James, 1896a).[3] He pointed out that the field had few active workers and that its phenomena were 'fortuitous and occasional' (*ibid.*, p. 882). Regardless of this, James believed that the SPR had a record of significant achievements. Among them were the results of its work with hallucinations and mediumship, and the general tendency of the SPR to discuss subject matter using first-hand evidence, something that he believed had not always been the case in previous work. James also praised Myers' writings about automatisms and the subliminal self. He wrote that 'thanks to his genius, we begin to see for the first time what a vast interlocked and graded system these phenomena, from the rudest motor automatisms to the most startling sensory apparition, form. Mr. Myers' methodical treatment of them by classes and series is the first great step towards overcoming the distaste of orthodox science to look at them at all' (*ibid.*, p. 885).[4]

But regardless of these developments James believed in caution and wrote in the same Presidential Address: 'We must... be satisfied for many a year to go without definitive conclusions, confident that if we only keep alive and heap up data, the natural types of them (if there are any) will surely crystallize out; whilst old material that is baffling will

---

[3] *Science* had already a track record of publishing news and reviews of the work of the SPR (e.g. American Society for Psychical Research, 1887; Mrs. Sidgwick and the Mediums, 1886). James's psychical research has been discussed in books (e.g. Blum, 2006; Richardson, 2006; Taylor, 1996), as well as in introductions to James's collected papers (McDermott, 1986; Murphy, 1960), in articles (Gitre, 2006; Gondra Rezola, 2000; Knapp, 2001), and in a dissertation on the topic (Knapp, 2003). For a compilation of the relevant psychical research writings see James (1986).

[4] James (1901; 1903) wrote much about Myers and was influenced by him (Taylor, 1996). See also James (1902, pp. 511–512), and some of his correspondence (H. James, 1920, Vol. 2, pp. 57, 141). His attitude, sometimes critical, is reflected in the fact that he said he had a high opinion of 'of Myers's constructive gifts, but on the whole a lower opinion of the objective solidity of the system. So many of the facts which form its pillars are still dubious' (H. James, 1920, Vol. 2, p. 186).

get settled as we proceed, through its analogy with new material that will come with the baffling character removed' (*ibid.*, p. 886).

James was also involved with the founding of the ASPR in the United States, where we find him on the initial organizing committee (Formation of the Society, 1885, p. 1) and as part of the organization's council (Council of the Society, 1885; Hodgson, 1889, p. 286). In addition, he wrote on a variety of topics in the ASPR's *Proceedings* (James, 1886; 1889a,b; James and Bowditch, 1885), including mediumship and hypnosis.

In his book *Human Immortality*, James (1898a) briefly referred to psychic phenomena in relation to his discussion of the production and transmission models of consciousness. That is, he contrasted the idea that the brain produced or created consciousness with the possibility that it was merely an instrument that channeled consciousness, which was basically an independent principle. As he stated:

> A medium... will show knowledge of his sitter's private affairs which it seems impossible he should have acquired through sight or hearing, or inference therefrom. Or you will have an apparition of some one who is now dying hundreds of miles away. On the production-theory one does not see from what sensations such odd bits of knowledge are produced. On the transmission-theory, they don't have to be 'produced' — they exist ready-made in the transcendental world, and all that is needed is an abnormal lowering of the brain-threshold to let them through. (James, 1898a, p. 26)

It is also important to acknowledge James's contributions to the popularization and defence of psychical research. This is clear in discussions of the field published in popular reviews such as *Forum* and *American Magazine* (James, 1892b; 1909a), in specialized publications such as *Science* and the *Psychological Review* (e.g. James, 1896a,b), and in his reviews of many published works on the topic.[5]

It is clear that James accepted the existence of some extraordinary phenomena. However, he stated at the end of his life: 'I am theoretically no "further" than I was at the beginning...' (James, 1909a, p. 580). James believed psychical researchers had expected too much and that instead they should 'mark progress not by quarter-centuries but by half-centuries or whole centuries' (*ibid.*, p. 580).

---

[5] An example was a review of *Phantasms of the Living* published in *Science* (James, 1887a). James also published several book and article reviews about psychic phenomena in the *Psychological Review* (Alvarado, 2009c).

James, Mediumship, and Hypnosis

Mediumship

In one of his articles James (1890a) disagreed with Janet's (1889) view that hypnotically induced secondary selves were pathological. Trances, he believed, were too complex to be able to reduce all of them to a simple explanation, such as Janet's. Furthermore, James wrote: 'I know a non-hysterical woman who, in her trances, knows facts which altogether transcend her *possible* normal consciousness, facts about the lives of people whom she never saw or heard of before. I am well aware of all the liabilities to which this statement exposes me, and I make it deliberately, having practically no doubt whatever of its truth' (James, 1890a, p. 373).

This was a reference to the above-mentioned Boston medium Leonora E. Piper, who James (1886; 1890c) studied.[6] James first saw Mrs. Piper in 1885, after his mother and sister-in-law had reported having veridical communications from her. Interested, he went to see the medium with his wife, experiencing firsthand the medium's French 'spirit control', an entity who described himself as a 'Dr. Phinuit'. He wrote about his experience:

> The medium... when entranced, repeated most of the names of 'spirits' whom she had announced on the two former occasions and added others. The names came with difficulty, and were only gradually made perfect. My wife's father's name of Gibbens was announced first as Niblin, then as Giblin. A child Herman (whom we had lost the previous year) had his name spelt out as Herrin. I think that in no case were both Christian and surnames given on this visit. But *the facts predicated* of the persons named made it in many instances impossible not to recognize the particular individuals who were talked about. We took particular pains on this occasion to give the Phinuit control no help over his difficulties and to ask no leading questions... My impression after this first visit was, that Mrs. P. was either possessed of supernormal powers, or knew the members of my wife's family by sight and had by some lucky coincidence become acquainted with such a multitude of their domestic circumstances as to produce the startling impression which she did. My later knowledge of her sittings and personal acquaintance with her has led me absolutely to reject the latter explanation, and to believe that she has supernormal powers. (James, 1890c, p. 652)

James (1886) authored a report of his investigation of Piper as a member of the ASPR's Committee on Mediumistic Phenomena. He

---

[6] Mrs. Piper was the first mental medium the SPR investigated systematically and at length. Reports about her performances during the nineteenth century were published by the SPR (e.g. Hodgson, 1892; 1898; Leaf, 1890; Lodge, 1890). For more information about Mrs. Piper see her daughter's biography (Piper, 1929) and Sage (1902/1904).

mentioned having testimony from 25 sitters, five of whom had verbatim stenographic reports. In addition, James wrote:

> Fifteen of the sitters were surprised at the communications they received, names and facts being mentioned at the first interview which it seemed improbable should have been known to the medium in a normal way. The probability that she possessed no clue as to the sitter's identity was, I believe, in each and all of these 15 cases, sufficient. But of only one of them is there a stenographic report; so that, unfortunately for the medium, the evidence in her favor is, although more abundant, less exact in quality than some of that which will be counted against her. (James, 1886, p. 103)

James was convinced of Piper's honesty and that she presented genuine trance phenomena. Furthermore, he believed her 'to be in possession of a power as yet unexplained' (*ibid.*, p. 104). Such an emphasis in the veridical content of mediumship was consistent with the interest of psychical researchers in 'supernormal' knowledge as well as the topic of survival of death, concerns that guided psychical investigations during the nineteenth century.[7] This led James to conduct tests of thought-transference with the medium in hypnosis and out of it, but with no success.

But James was interested in other aspects of Piper's mediumship as well, aspects consistent with the writings of Myers (1884; 1885) on the topic. 'What science wants', James (1886, p. 104) wrote, 'is a *context* to make the trance-phenomena continuous with other physiological and psychological facts.' To explore this James hypnotized Mrs. Piper. After two failed attempts he suggested that her 'spirit control' assist in making Mrs. Piper a more 'mesmeric' research participant. James wrote in his 1886 report:

> She became partially hypnotized on the third trial; but the effect was so slight that I ascribe it rather to the effect of repetition than to the suggestion made. By the fifth trial she had become a pretty good hypnotic subject, as far as muscular phenomena and automatic imitations of speech and gesture go: but I could not affect her consciousness, or otherwise get her beyond this point. Her condition in this semi-hypnosis is very different from her medium-trance. The latter is characterized by great muscular unrest, even her ears moving vigorously in a way impossible to her in her waking state. But in hypnosis her muscular relaxation and

---

[7] For examples of interest in what James called 'supernormal phenomena' see studies that have discussed telepathy and clairvoyance (Luckhurst, 2002; Plas, 2000). The interest in survival of death shown by psychical researchers was a direct inheritance from the movement of spiritualism (Podmore, 1902), and reflected the crises of faith typical during the nineteenth century, as seen in Great Britain (Gauld, 1968; Turner, 1974). On the influence of the concept of survival of death on psychical research see Alvarado (2003).

weakness are extreme. She often makes several efforts to speak ere her voice becomes audible; and to get a strong contraction of the hand, for example, express manipulation and suggestion must be practised. The automatic imitations I spoke of are in the first instance very weak, and only become strong after repetition. Her pupils contract in the medium-trance. Suggestions to the 'Control' that he should make her recollect after the trance what she had been saying were accepted, but had no result. (pp. 104–105)

James wrote about Dr. Phinuit's communications both to him and his wife about their own personal shortcomings during which time he was 'very different in style from his more usual talk, and probably superior to anything that the medium could produce in the same line in her natural state' (James, 1890c, p. 655). He also noticed that Dr. Phinuit could not understand French but that nonetheless he served as the master of ceremonies in Mrs. Piper's communications with other 'spirits'. Furthermore, James mentioned some instances of direct control of the medium by alleged spirits other than Dr. Phinuit.

In a review of Hodgson's (1898) report James (1898c) commented on Mrs. Piper's trance memory being capable of conversing about topics related to earlier communications even if they had taken place a while back. James wrote: 'Mrs. Piper's trance-memory... is no ordinary human memory; and we have to explain its singular perfection either as the natural endowment of her solitary subliminal self, or as a collection of distinct memory-systems, each with a communicating "spirit," as its vehicle' (James, 1898c, p. 423).

In addition to his initial sittings in the 1880s, James held many séances with Piper in later years. For example, in an important report about her mediumship Richard Hodgson mentioned several sittings arranged by James held in his home at Cambridge between 1893 and 1895 (Hodgson, 1898, pp. 482, 494, 525, 526, 528, 534). Years later James (1909c) reported on communications Piper produced purporting to be from Hodgson, who had died in 1905. He considered the content of the communications was 'supernormal' but was not sure of the source of the information obtained. In his view: 'The active cause of the communications is on any hypothesis a will of some kind, be it the will of R.H.'s spirit, of lower supernatural intelligences, or of Mrs. Piper's subliminal..., yet the major part of it is suggestive of something quite different — as if a will were there, but a will to say something which the machinery fails to bring through' (James, 1909c, p. 116).

James seemed to incline towards an outside will, but speculated on the interaction of many factors in the communications. He wrote: 'The sitter, with his desire to receive, forms, so to speak, a drainage-opening or sink; the medium, with her desire to personate, yields the nearest lying material to be drained off; while the spirit desiring to communicate is shown the way by the current set up, and swells the latter by its own contributions' (*ibid.*, p. 120).

James's openness to different influences affecting mental mediumship was clear in speculations about psychological factors influencing the communications he presented in *The Principles of Psychology* (1890b). He wrote:

> One curious thing about trance-utterances is their generic similarity in different individuals. The 'control' here in America is either a grotesque, slangy, and flippant personage ('Indian' controls, calling the ladies 'squaws,' the men 'braves,' the house a 'wigwam,' etc., etc., are excessively common); or, if he ventures on higher intellectual flights, he abounds in a curiously vague optimistic philosophy-and-water, in which phrases about spirit, harmony, beauty, law, progression, development, etc., keep recurring. It seems exactly as if one author composed more than half of the trance-messages, no matter by whom they are uttered. Whether all sub-conscious selves are peculiarly susceptible to a certain stratum of the *Zeitgeist*, and get their inspiration from it, I know not; but this is obviously the case with the secondary selves which become 'developed' in spiritualist circles. There the beginnings of the medium trance are indistinguishable from effects of hypnotic suggestion. The subject assumes the role of a medium simply because opinion expects it of him under the conditions which are present; and carries it out with feebleness or vivacity proportionate to his histrionic gifts. (James, 1890b, Vol. 1, p. 394)

Interestingly, James (1889b) reported on other cases of apparent mediumship in his paper 'Notes on Automatic Writing', published in the ASPR *Proceedings*. He started his essay by saying that Janet (1886; 1887) had reported anaesthesia of the arm used by a participant to produce automatic writing and that he had made similar observations himself. In James's words: 'I have actually tested three automatic writers for anaesthesia. In one of them, examined between the acts of writing, no anaesthesia was observed, but the examination was superficial. In the two others, both of them men, the anaesthesia to pricking and pinching, and possibly to touch, seemed complete' (James, 1889b, p. 549).

One of these cases was that of a 21-year-old student who produced writing via a planchette and his hand. While the participant claimed he did not experience the pinchings done by James, his written messages did. James wrote:

> Here... we have the consciousness of a subject split into two parts, one of which expresses itself through the mouth, and the other through the hand, whilst both are in communication with the ear. The mouth-consciousness is ignorant of all that the hand suffers or does; the hand-consciousness is ignorant of pin-pricks inflicted upon other parts of the body — and of what more remains to be ascertained. If we call this hand-consciousness the automatic consciousness, then we also perceive that the automatic consciousness may transfer itself from the right hand to the left, and carry its own peculiar store of memories with it. (*ibid.*, p. 551)

James felt these observations had some similarity with Gurney's (1887a) experiments in post-hypnotic suggestion, in which he believed consciousness was split-off and automatically communicated through the participant's hand. This led James to comment: 'This dissociation of the consciousness into mutually exclusive parts is evidently a phenomenon destined, when understood, to cast a light into the abysses of Psychology' (James, 1889b, p. 551).

Hysteria and Secondary Consciousness

Like several other American psychologists (e.g. Newbold, 1896; Sidis, 1898), James (1890a,b) was interested in those influential cases of double personality that did much to popularize the concept of unconscious personalities or trains of thought. We are referring to cases such as those of Mary Reynolds (1785–1854), Louis Vivet (b. 1863), Félida X. (b. 1843), and Janet's hypnotized patients.[8] Regarding Léonie (b. 1837), one of Janet's patients, James (1890b, Vol. 1, p. 388) wrote: 'Léonie 1 knows only of herself; Léonie 2, of herself and of Léonie 1; Léonie 3 knows of herself and of both the others.' Consistent with this, James was of the opinion that 'in certain persons at least, the total possible consciousness may be split into parts which coexist, but mutually ignore each other and share the objects of knowledge between them, and — more remarkable still — are complementary' (James, 1890a, p. 369).

Another interesting but less well known case showing divided consciousness was that of Anna Windsor, who suffered from hystero-epilepsy.[9] James (1889b) reported the case using notes written by Dr. Ira Barrows (1804–1882). Barrows' notes suggested the existence of a second consciousness in Windsor involving different actions and

---

[8] For more information on these cases see Carroy (1991), Crabtree (1993), Hacking (1995), and Kenny (1986).

[9] This case also deserves study in terms of how it has been cited. Some citations of the case include Myers (1903, Vol. 1, pp. 355–360), Newbold (1896), Prince (1890), and Sidis (1898, pp. 285–288).

creative endeavours. The record cited by James started on September 17, 1860 with the observation that, in delirium, the patient tore her hair with the left hand while her right hand prevented those actions. On September 29, according to Barrows' notes: 'Complains of great pain in right arm, more and more intense, when suddenly it falls down by her side. She looks at it in amazement. Thinks it belongs to some one else; positive it is not hers. Sees her right arm drawn around upon her spine. Cut it, prick it, do what you please to it, she takes no notice of it' (*ibid.*, p. 552). Barrow added a note about events five years later stating: 'She believes her spine is her right arm, and that her right arm is a foreign object and a nuisance. She believes it to be an arm and a hand, but treats it as if it had intelligence and might keep away from her. She bites it, pounds it, pricks it, and in many ways seeks to drive it from her. She calls it "Stump; Old Stump"...' (*ibid.*, p. 552).

Other phenomena included apparent writing in her sleep, with no recollection on awakening of having done so. The notes continue:

> February 1 to 11 — Under the influence of magnetism writes poetry; personates different persons, mostly those who have long since passed away. When in the magnetic state, whatever she does and says is not remembered when she comes out of it. Commences a series of drawings with her right paralyzed hand, 'Old Stump.' Also writes poetry with it. Whatever 'Stump' writes, or draws, or does, she appears to take no interest in; says it is none of hers, and that she wants nothing to do with 'Stump' or 'Stump's.' I have sat by her bed and engaged her in conversation, and drawn her attention in various ways, while the writing and drawing has been uninterrupted... (*ibid.*, p. 552)

Barrow recorded on January 19, 1862 that the right hand was rational and responded to questions in writings, and continued to prevent the patient from tearing clothes and her hair by holding the left hand. The right hand continued to be active during sleep, carrying on conversations, writing poetry, and rapping on the bed's headboard to signal the patient's mother if spasms or other phenomena ensued. The rest of the notes read as follows:

> January, 1863 — At night, and during her sleep, 'Stump' writes letters, some of them very amusing; writes poetry, some pieces original. Writes 'Hasty Pudding,' by Barlow, in several cantos, which she had never read; all correctly written, but queerly arranged, as, *e.g.*, one line belonging in one canto would be transposed with another line in another canto. She has no knowledge of Latin or French, yet 'Stump' produces... rhyme of Latin and English...
>
> 'Stump' writes both asleep and awake, and the writing goes on while she is occupied with her left hand in other matters. Ask her what she is

writing, she replies, '*I* am not writing; that is "Stump" writing. I don't know what he is writing. I don't trouble myself with "Stump's" doings.' Reads with her book upside down, and sometimes when covered with the sheet. 'Stump' produces two bills of fare in French... (*ibid.*, pp. 553–554)

James pointed out that he did not have the records of Windsor's manifestations for the later period of her life. In the rest of the paper he discussed other cases of automatism in which there were some indications of veridical information being presented.

In 1896 James gave his celebrated Lowell lectures on exceptional mental states (Taylor, 1984). In these presentations he included such topics as hysteria, hypnotism, automatisms, and multiple personality. At the beginning of the lecture on the latter topic James stated: 'From the ordinary focus and margin, from the ordinary abstraction, we shade off into phenomena that look like consciousness *beyond the margin*' (Taylor, 1984, p. 73).

Hypnosis

James reminded us that 'in the earlier stages of hypnotism the patient remembers what has happened, but with successive sittings he sinks into a deeper condition, which is commonly followed by complete loss of memory' (1890b, Vol. 2, p. 602). Referring to the hypnotic participant when he or she had been suggested to commit crimes he wrote: 'His spontaneity is lost only for those systems of ideas which *conflict* with the suggested delusion. The latter is thus "systematized"; the rest of consciousness is shut off, excluded, dissociated from it. In extreme cases the rest of the mind would seem to be actually abolished and the hypnotic subject to be literally a changed personality...' (*ibid.*, p. 605).

James also mentioned in *The Principles of Psychology* the abolition of pain, and other sensations, as well as perceptions that were not consciously registered. He wrote: 'Messrs. Gurney, Janet, and Binet have shown that the ignored elements are preserved in a split-off portion of the subjects' consciousness which can be tapped in certain ways, and made to give an account of itself' (*ibid.*, p. 609). Similarly, some of these authors were said to have demonstrated that suggestions to perform acts were 'stored up in consciousness; not simply organically registered, but that *the consciousness which thus retains it is split off, dissociated from the rest of the subject's mind*' (*ibid.*, p. 614).

Earlier on James had experimented with hypnosis in his work for the ASPR's Committee of Hypnosis. In their first report (James and Carnochan, 1886) there were some demonstrations using Harvard students. The arm of two subjects (Mrs. Piper being one of them) was made anaesthetic. This led the authors of the report to ask: 'Is the anaesthesia ... produced by suggestion, due to an abolition of sensation or an abolition of "apperception"? Does the subject not *feel*? or [has] he become incapable of *noticing* what he feels? or is his state something more peculiar still?' (*ibid.*, p. 96). Several perceptual and hallucinatory tests were conducted. A puzzling effect was that 'the hallucination of a colored patch on a real white ground will sometimes be followed by a negative after-image when the gaze is transferred to another place' (*ibid.*, p. 98).

In another short paper James (1887b) reported on the effect of hypnosis on reaction time. However, he concluded, 'it is clear that there is no simple hypnotic state which can be quoted as having a determinate effect on the reaction-time. There are hypnotic and post-hypnotic *states* which vary very much, and some of which retard, whilst others quicken, the reactions' (*ibid.*, p. 248).

James used hypnosis with the Reverend Ansel Bourne (1826–ca 1910) to recover forgotten memories.[10] Bourne, from Greene, Rhode Island, disappeared after withdrawing money from a bank on January 17, 1887. On March 14 a man called A.J. Brown woke up at Norristown, Pennsylvania, where he had been tending a shop for six weeks. Brown did not know where he was and said he was Bourne and the last he remembered was being in a bank withdrawing money. In 1890 James hypnotized him:

> I induced Mr. Bourne to submit to hypnotism, so as to see whether, in the hypnotic trance, his 'Brown' memory would not come back. It did so with surprising readiness; so much so indeed that it proved quite impossible to make him whilst in the hypnosis remember any of the facts of his normal life. He had heard of Ansel Bourne, but 'didn't know as he had ever met the man.' When confronted with Mrs. Bourne he said that he had 'never seen the woman before,' etc. On the other hand, he told of his peregrinations during the lost fortnight,... and gave all sorts of details about the Norristown episode. The whole thing was prosaic enough; and the Brown-personality seems to be nothing but a rather shrunken, dejected, and amnesic extract of Mr. Bourne himself. He gives no motive for the wandering except that there was 'trouble back there' and he 'wanted rest'... I had hoped by suggestion, etc., to run the two personalities into one, and make the memories continuous, but no artifice would avail to accomplish this, and Mr. Bourne's skull today still covers two distinct personal selves. (James, 1890b, Vol. 1, pp. 392; for more details see Hodgson, 1891)

---

[10] For an overview of the Bourne case see Kenny (1986). See also Bourne (1858), Hodgson (1891), and James (1890b, Vol. 1, pp. 391–393).

Hypnosis was also mentioned by James in the Lowell 1896 lectures on exceptional mental states. In his view suggestibility 'is due to the narrowness of the field of consciousness' (Taylor, 1984, p. 27).

Beyond Dissociation

McDermott (1986) has argued that James learned about the margins of consciousness and the artificial separation of experience through psychical research and psychopathology. This is seen in James's (1890b) exploration of consciousness in terms of flow and expansion.

James later emphasized higher dimensions of consciousness, or at least speculated about them. He stated his belief that 'our lives are like islands in the sea, or like trees in the forest' (1909a, p. 589). Using the images of islands and trees James argued that their separation from the rest was illusory due to 'subterranean connections'. In this paper, he went to speculate on the possible collective nature of consciousness and the illusory separation of minds for adaptation purposes (see also James, 1898c; 1909b).

In *The Varieties of Religious Experience* (1902) he speculated on the involvement of 'the higher faculties of our hidden mind' (p. 513) with religious experience. He went on to write: 'The whole drift of my education goes to persuade me that the world of our present consciousness is only one out of many worlds of consciousness that exist, and that those other worlds must contain experiences which have a meaning for our life also; and that although in the main their experiences and those of this world keep discrete, yet the two become continuous at certain points, and higher energies filter in' (*ibid.*, p. 519). This statement suggests that James's initial interest and more mundane concept of dissociation expanded in a transpersonal way.

Conclusion

James's ideas were congruent with his philosophy of radical empiricism and his concept of pluralism. But our emphasis here has not been on his intellectual evolution in relation to other aspects of his thought (as seen in Lamberth, 1999; Taylor, 1996). Instead we have focused on his case as an exemplar illustrating the influence of unorthodox phenomena on the study of dissociation.

We are referring to the influence and interaction of psychical research with James's studies of dissociation, a state of affairs that he shared with other figures such as Flournoy, Gurney, Myers, and Richet. The work of these men was nurtured by the conceptual agenda of psychical research. Furthermore, like the influence of hysteria and the performances of specific hysterics (Alvarado, 2009b; Ellenberger, 1970), the phenomenon of mediumship and the performances of particular mediums provided a 'laboratory' and a catalyst for the development of ideas and the recording of observations, a topic discussed elsewhere (Alvarado *et al.*, 2007).

Unlike Janet and others, James did not use dissociation to explain mediumship and related phenomena in the sense of reducing everything to suggestion and the workings of a secondary consciousness. Instead he adapted ideas, such as Myers', that assumed the existence of a secondary consciousness and that were not only relevant to pathology, but to the 'supernormal' and the transcendental. James's acceptance of the 'supernormal' in the case of Mrs. Piper represents a break with Janet and other conventional explorers of dissociation. It was in fact a plea to study and accept the possibility that dissociation and consciousness in general could transcend bodily limitations, as argued by other psychical researchers. Such an approach was never widely accepted and remains to this day confined to the field of parapsychology and similar movements.

While we have mentioned the writings of several authors who have 'rescued' the contributions of psychical research to psychology and psychiatry from oblivion, there are unfortunately many modern histories in these fields today that still do not acknowledge such influences. Many of these histories have been concerned only with distinguishing psychology from pseudoscience, and with labelling psychical research as a discredited discipline (e.g. O'Boyle, 2006), while others do not even mention psychical research, as seen in discussions of James (e.g. Mandler, 2007).

Regardless of the above cited body of work much remains unexplored about the history of the interface between dissociation — and psychology and psychiatry in general — and psychical research. It is our hope that future studies will explore this literature in more detail so as to expand the scope of the historiographies of psychology and psychiatry to include wider currents of influence, as well as the work of neglected individuals such as those uniquely gifted research participants cited in this essay.[11]

---

[11] Additional figures deserving study include those who wrote later studies of Mrs. Piper (Sidgwick, 1915; Tanner, 1910), and the writings of many others (e.g. Morselli, 1908; Sudre, 1926).

Acknowledgement

The authors gratefully acknowledge the support of Saybrook University's Chair for the Study of Consciousness in the preparation of this paper.

References

Alvarado, C.S. (2002) Dissociation in Britain during the late nineteenth century: The Society for Psychical Research, 1882–1900, *Journal of Trauma and Dissociation*, **3**, pp. 9–33.

Alvarado, C.S. (2003) The concept of survival of bodily death and the development of parapsychology, *Journal of the Society for Psychical Research*, **67**, pp. 65–95.

Alvarado, C.S. (2009a) Ambroise August Liébeault and psychic phenomena, *American Journal of Clinical Hypnosis*, **52**, pp. 111–121.

Alvarado, C.S. (2009b) Nineteenth-century hysteria and hypnosis: A historical note on Blanche Wittmann, *Australian Journal of Clinical and Experimental Hypnosis*, **37**, pp. 21–36.

Alvarado, C.S. (2009c) Psychical research in the Psychological Review, 1894–1900: A bibliographical note, *Journal of Scientific Exploration*, **23**, pp. 211–220.

Alvarado, C.S., Machado, F.R., Zangari, W. & Zingrone, N.L. (2007) Perspectivas históricas da influência da mediunidade na construção de idéias psicológicas e psiquiátricas, *Revista de Psiquiatria Clínica*, **34** (supp. 1), pp. 42–53.

American Society for Psychical Research (1887) *Science*, **9**, pp. 50–51.

Azam, E.E. (1887) *Hypnotisme, double conscience et altérations de la personnalité*, Paris: J.B. Baillière et Fils.

Biondi, M. (1988) *Tavoli e Medium: Storia dello Spiritismo in Italia*, Rome: Gremese.

Blum, D. (2006) *Ghost Hunters: William James and the Search for Scientific Proof of Life After Death*, New York: Penguin Press.

Bourne, A. (1858) *Wonderful Works of God: A Narrative of the Wonderful Facts in the Case of Ansel Bourne*, Irvington, NJ: Moses Cummings.

Bowditch, H.P., Pickering, E.C., Watson, W.M., Hall, E.H., Minot, C.M., Jackson, C.C. & Peirce, J.M. (1886) Report on the Committee of Thought-Transference, *Proceedings of the American Society for Psychical Research*, **1**, pp. 106–116.

Brown, E.M. (1983) Neurology and spiritualism in the 1870s, *Bulletin of the History of Medicine*, **37**, pp. 563–577.

Carpenter, W.B. (1877) *Mesmerism and Spiritualism, &c., Historically and Scientifically Considered*, London: Longmans, Green and Co.

Carroy, J. (1991) *Hypnose, Suggestion et Psychologie: L'invention de Sujets*, Paris: Presses Universitaires de France.

Coon, D.J. (1992) Testing the limits of sense and science: American experimental psychologists combat spiritualism, 1880–1920, *American Psychologist*, **47**, pp. 143–151.

Council of the Society (1885) *Proceedings of the American Society for Psychical Research*, **1**, p. 4.

Courses (n.d) *Courses William James taught at Harvard*, [Online], http://www.des.emory.edu/mfp/JamesTeachingSchedule.html [14 April 2010].

Crabtree, A. (1993) *From Mesmer to Freud*, New Haven, CT: Yale University Press.

Crabtree, A. (2007) Automatism and secondary centers of consciousness, in Kelly, E.F., Kelly, E.W., Crabtree, A., Gauld, A., Grosso, M. & Greyson, B. (eds.) *Irreducible Mind*, pp. 301–365, Lanham, MD: Rowman & Littlefield.
Deleuze, J.P.F. (1813) *Histoire Critique du Magnétisme Animal*, (vol. 1), Paris: Mame.
Ellenberger, H.F. (1970) *The Discovery of the Unconscious: The History and Evolution of Dynamic Psychiatry*, New York: Basic Books.
Fodor, N. (1971) *Freud, Jung and Occultism*, New Hyde Park, NY: University Books.
Formation of the Society (1885) *Proceedings of the American Society for Psychical Research*, **1**, pp. 1–2.
Gauld, A. (1968) *The Founders of Psychical Research*, London: Routledge & Kegan Paul.
Gauld, A. (1992) *A History of Hypnotism*, Cambridge: Cambridge University Press.
Gitre, E.J.K. (2006) William James on divine intimacy: Psychical research, cosmological realism and a circumscribed re-reading of *The Varieties of Religious Experience*, *History of the Human Sciences*, **19**, pp. 1–21.
Gondra Rezola, J.M. (2000) William James y la investigación psíquica, *Revista de Historia de la Psicología*, **21**, pp. 567–573.
Guinon, G., with Bloc, [no initial], Souques, [no initial] & Charcot, J.B. (eds.) (1893) *Clinique des Maladies du Système Nerveux: M. le Professeur Charcot: Leçons du Professeur, Mémoires, Notes et Observations*, (vol. 2), Paris: Bureaux du Progrès Médical.
Gurney, E. (1884) The stages of hypnotism, *Proceedings of the Society for Psychical Research*, **2**, pp. 61–72.
Gurney, E. (1887a) Peculiarities of certain post-hypnotic states, *Proceedings of the Society for Psychical Research*, **4**, pp. 268–323.
Gurney, E. (1887b) Stages of hypnotic memory, *Proceedings of the Society for Psychical Research*, **4**, pp. 515–531.
Gurney, E. (1888) Recent experiments in hypnotism, *Proceedings of the Society for Psychical Research*, **5**, pp. 3–17.
Gurney, E., Myers, F.W.H. & Podmore, F. (1886) *Phantasms of the Living*, (2 vols.), London: Trübner.
Guthrie, M. & Birchall, J. (1883) Record of experiments in thought-transference, *Proceedings of the Society for Psychical Research*, **1**, pp. 263–283.
Hacking, I. (1995) *Rewriting the Soul: Multiple Personality and the Sciences of Memory*, Princeton, NJ: Princeton University Press.
Hamilton, T. (2009) *Immortal Remains: F.W.H. Myers and the Victorian Search for Life After Death*, Exeter: Imprint Academic.
Héricourt, J. (1889) L'activité inconsciente de lesprit, *Revue Scientifique*, **44**, pp. 257–268.
Hodgson, R. (1891) A case of double consciousness, *Proceedings of the Society for Psychical Research*, **7**, pp. 221–255.
Hodgson, R. (1892) A record of observations of certain phenomena of trance, *Proceedings of the Society for Psychical Research*, **8**, pp. 1–167.
Hodgson, R. (1898) A further record of observations of certain phenomena of trance, *Proceedings of the Society for Psychical Research*, **13**, pp. 284–582.
Hodgson, R. (1889) Meetings of the Society, *Proceedings of the American Society for Psychical Research*, **1**, pp. 285–286.
Inglis, B. (1992) *Natural and Supernatural: A History of the Paranormal from Earliest Times to 1914*, (rev.), London: Prism.

James, H. (ed.) (1920) *The Letters of William James*, (2 vols.), Boston, MA: Atlantic Monthly Press.
James, W. (1869/1960) Review of Planchette, in Murphy, G. & Ballou, R.O. (eds.) *William James on Psychical Research*, pp. 19–23, New York: Viking Press.
James, W. (1879) Are we automata?, *Mind*, **4**, pp. 1–22.
James, W. (1884) What is an emotion?, *Mind*, **9**, pp. 188–205.
James, W. (1886) Report of the Committee on Mediumistic Phenomena, *Proceedings of the American Society for Psychical Research*, **1**, pp. 102–106.
James, W. (1887a) Phantasms of the living, *Science*, **9**, pp. 18–20.
James, W. (1887b) Reaction-time in the hypnotic trance, *Proceedings of the American Society for Psychical Research*, **1**, pp. 246–248.
James, W. (1889a) Note on the foregoing report, *Proceedings of the American Society for Psychical Research*, **1**, pp. 285–286.
James, W. (1889b) Notes on automatic writing, *Proceedings of the American Society for Psychical Research*, **1**, pp. 548–564.
James, W. (1890a) The hidden self, *Scribner's Magazine*, **7**, pp. 161–173.
James, W. (1890b) *The Principles of Psychology*, New York: Henry Holt.
James, W. (1890c) A record of observations of certain phenomena of trance Part III, *Proceedings of the Society for Psychical Research*, **6**, pp. 651–659.
James, W. (1892a) *Psychology: Briefer Course*, New York: Henry Holt.
James, W. (1892b) What psychical research has accomplished, *Forum*, **13**, pp. 727–742.
James, W. (1895) The knowing of things together, *Psychological Review*, **2**, pp. 105–124.
James, W. (1896a) Address of the President before the Society for Psychical Research, *Science*, **3**, pp. 881–888.
James, W. (1896b) Psychical research, *Psychological Review*, **3**, pp. 649–651.
James, W. (1897) *The Will to Believe and Other Essays in Popular Philosophy*, New York: Longmans, Green.
James, W. (1898a) *Human Immortality*, Boston, MA: Houghton Mifflin.
James, W. (1898b) Introduction, in Sidis, B. (ed.) *The Psychology of Suggestion*, pp. v–vii, New York: D. Appleton.
James, W. (1898c) Review of A Further Record of Observations of Certain Phenomena of Trance, by R. Hodgson, *Psychological Review*, **5**, pp. 420–424.
James, W. (1899) *Talks to Teachers on Psychology*, New York: Henry Holt.
James, W. (1901) Frederic Myers' service to psychology, *Proceedings of the Society for Psychical Research*, **17**, pp. 13–23.
James, W. (1902) *The Varieties of Religious Experience*, New York: Longmans, Green.
James, W. (1903) Review of Human Personality and Its Survival of Bodily Death, *Proceedings of the Society for Psychical Research*, **18**, pp. 22–33.
James, W. (1907) *Pragmatism: A New Name for Some Old Ways of Thinking*, New York: Longmans, Green.
James, W. (1909a) The confidences of a 'psychical researcher', *American Magazine*, **68**, pp. 580–589.
James, W. (1909b) *A Pluralistic Universe*, New York: Longmans, Green.
James, W. (1909c) Report on Mrs. Pipers Hodgson-control, *Proceedings of the Society for Psychical Research*, **23**, pp. 2–121.
James, W. (1986) Essays in psychical research, in Burkhardt, F.H. (ed.) *The Works of William James, vol. 16*, Cambridge, MA: Harvard University Press.
James, W. & Bowditch, H.P. (1885) Circular No. 2 issued by the Committee on Work, *Proceedings of the American Society for Psychical Research*, **1**, pp. 5–6.

James, W. & Carnochan, G.M. (1886) Report of the Committee on Hypnotism, *Proceedings of the American Society for Psychical Research*, **1**, pp. 95–102.
Janet, P. (1886) Les actes inconscientes et la dédoublement de la personnalité pendant le somnambulisme provoqué, *Revue Philosophique de la France et de L'étranger*, **22**, pp. 577–592.
Janet, P. (1887) L'anesthésie systématisée et la dissociation des phénomènes psychiques, *Revue Philosophique de la France et de L'étranger*, **23**, pp. 449–472.
Janet, P. (1888) Les actes inconscients et la mémoire pendant le somnambulisme, *Revue Philosophique de la France et de L'étranger*, **25**, pp. 238–279.
Janet, P. (1889) *L'automatisme psychologique*, Paris: Félix Alcan.
Jastrow, J. (1889) The problem of 'psychic research', *Harpers New Monthly Magazine*, **79**, pp. 76–82.
Johnson, M. & Henley, T.B. (eds.) (1990) *Reflections on The Principles of Psychology*, New York: Earlbaum.
Kenney, M.G. (1986) *The Passion of Ansel Bourne: Multiple Personality in American Culture*, Washington, DC: Smithsonian Institution Press.
Knapp, K.D. (2001) WJ, spiritualism, and unconsciousness beyond the margin, *Streams of William James*, **3** (2), pp. 1–5.
Knapp, K.D. (2003) *To the Summerland: William James, Psychical Research and Modernity* (Ph.D. dissertation, Boston College).
Ladame, D. (1888) Observation de somnambulisme hystérique avec dédoublement de la personnalité, guéri par la suggestion hypnotique, *Revue de L'hypnotisme Expérimental et Thérapeutique*, **2**, pp. 257–262.
Lamberth, D.C. (1999) *William James and the Metaphysics of Experience*, Cambridge, MA: Cambridge University Press.
Leaf, W. (1890) A record of observations of certain phenomena of trance, part II, *Proceedings of the Society for Psychical Research*, **6**, pp. 558–646.
Le Maléfan, P. (1993) Pierre Janet, le spiritisme et les délires spirites, *L'evolution Psychiatrique*, **58**, pp. 445–452.
Le Maléfan, P. (1999) *Folie et Spiritisme: Histoire du Discourse Psychopathologique sur la Pratique du Spiritisme, Ses Abords et Ses Avatars (1850–1950)*, Paris: L. Hartmattan.
Lodge, O. (1890) A record of observations of certain phenomena of trance, part I, *Proceedings of the Society for Psychical Research*, **6**, pp. 443–557.
Luckhurst, R. (2002) *The Invention of Telepathy 1870–1901*, Oxford: Oxford University Press.
Mandler, G. (2007) *A History of Modern Experimental Psychology: From James and Wundt to Cognitive Science*, Cambridge, MA: MIT Press.
McDermott, R.A. (1986) Introduction, in Burkhardt, F.H. (ed.) *Essays in Psychical Research*, (The Works of William James, Vol. 16), pp. xiii–xxxvi, Cambridge, MA: Harvard University Press.
Medd, J. (2010) *William James Cybrary*, [Online], http://wjcybrary.net/index.htm [16 April 2010].
Moore, R.L. (1977) *In Search of White Crows: Spiritualism, Parapsychology, and American Culture*, New York: Oxford University Press.
Morselli, E. (1908) *Psicologia e 'Spiritismo'*, (2 vols.), Turin: Fratelli Bocca.
Mrs. Sidgwick and the mediums (1886) *Science*, **7**, pp. 554–555.
Murphy, G. (1960) Introduction, in Murphy, G. & Ballou, R.O. (eds.) *William James on Psychical Research*, pp. 3–18, New York: Viking Press.
Myers, F.W.H. (1884) On a telepathic explanation of some so-called spiritualistic phenomena: Part I, *Proceedings of the Society for Psychical Research*, **2**, pp. 217–237.

Myers, F.W.H. (1885) Automatic writing: Part II, *Proceedings of the Society for Psychical Research*, **3**, pp. 1–63.
Myers, F.W.H. (1889) Automatic writing: The daemon of Socrates, *Proceedings of the Society for Psychical Research*, **5**, pp. 522–547.
Myers, F.W.H. (1892) The subliminal consciousness: Chapter I. General characteristics of subliminal messages, *Proceedings of the Society for Psychical Research*, **7**, pp. 298–327.
Myers, F.W.H. (1903) *Human Personality and Its Survival of Bodily Death*, (2 vols.), London: Longmans, Green.
Newbold, W.R. (1896) Double personality, *Appleton's Popular Science Monthly*, **50**, pp. 67–79.
Objects of the Society (1882) *Proceedings of the Society for Psychical Research*, **1**, pp. 3–6.
O'Boyle, C.G. (2006) *History of Psychology: A Cultural Perspective*, Mahwah, NJ: Lawrence Erlbaum.
Oppenheim, J. (1985) *The Other World: Spiritualism and Psychical Research in England, 1850–1914*, Cambridge: Cambridge University Press.
Perry, R.B. (1920) *Annotated Bibliography of the Writings of William James*, New York: Longmans, Green.
Piper, A.L. (1929) *The Life and Work of Mrs. Piper*, London: K. Paul, Trench, Trubner.
Plas, R. (2000) *Naissance d'une Science Humaine: La Psychologie: Les Psychologues et le 'Merveilleux Psychique'*, Rennes: Presses Universitaires de Rennes.
Podmore, F. (1902) *Modern Spiritualism: A History and a Criticism*, London: Methuen.
Prince, M. (1890) Some of the revelations of hypnotism: Post-hypnotic suggestion, automatic writing and double personality, *Boston Medical and Surgical Journal*, **122**, pp. 493–495.
Proudfoot, W. (ed.) (2004) *William James and a Science of Religions: Re-experiencing The Varieties of Religious Experience*, New York: Columbia University Press.
Richardson, R.D. (2006) *William James: In the Maelstrom of American Modernism*, Boston, MA: Houghton Mifflin.
Richet, C. (1883) La personnalité et la memoire dans le somnambulisme, *Revue Philosophique de la France et de L'étranger*, **15**, pp. 225–242.
Richet, C. (1884) La suggestion mentale et le calcul des probabilités, *Revue Philosophique de la France et de L'étranger*, **18**, pp. 609–674.
Sage, M. (1902/1904) *Mrs. Piper and the Society for Psychical Research*, New York: Scott-Thaw.
Shamdasani, S. (1993) Automatic writing and the discovery of the unconscious, *Spring*, **54**, pp. 100–131.
Shamdasani, S. (1994) Encountering Hélène: Théodore Flournoy and the genesis of subliminal psychology, *From India to the Planet Mars: A Case of Multiple Personality with Imaginary Languages*, pp. xi–li, Princeton, NJ: Princeton University Press.
Sidgwick, E. (1915) A contribution to the study of the psychology of Mrs. Piper's trance phenomena, *Proceedings of the Society for Psychical Research*, **28**, pp. 1–657.
Sidis, B. (1898) *The Psychology of Suggestion*, New York: D. Appleton.
Sudre, R. (1926) *Introduction à la Métapsychique Humaine*, Paris: Payot.
Tanner, A. E. (1910) *Studies in Spiritism*, New York: D. Appleton.

Taylor, E. (1984) *William James on Exceptional Mental States: The 1896 Lowell Lectures*, Amherst, MA: University of Massachusetts Press.

Taylor, E. (1996) *William James on Consciousness Beyond the Margin*, Princeton, NJ: Princeton University Press.

Treitel, C. (2003) *A Science for The Soul: Occultism and the Genesis of the German Modern*, Baltimore, MD: Johns Hopkins University Press.

Turner, F.M. (1974) *Between Science and Religion: The Reaction to Scientific Naturalism in Late Victorian England*, New Haven, CT: Yale University Press.

Wolf, S. (1993) *Brain, Mind and Medicine: Charles Richet and the Origins of Physiological Psychology*, New Brunswick, NJ: Transaction Publishers.

Paper received June 2010.

G. William Barnard

The Ever-New Flow of Time

Henri Bergson's View of Consciousness[1]

Abstract: Henri Bergson created a rich and detailed theory of consciousness beginning with the publication of Time and Free Will *in 1889 and continuing through the publication of* The Two Sources of Morality and Religion *in 1932. His theory had much in common with William James's views in that both emphasized consciousness as a continuous process. James's famous 'stream of consciousness' is strikingly similar to Bergson's early notion of duration (durée), even if Bergson more strongly emphasized the temporal qualities of consciousness. Bergson later modified his understanding of consciousness, creating a metaphysical vision that he hoped might not only overcome determinism and materialism, but also offer a sophisticated way to understand parapsychological phenomena such as telepathy and clairvoyance (topics of concern to many major theorists of the time). During his life, Bergson's ideas were widely celebrated in the United States and in Europe.*

Key words: Henri Bergson, consciousness, time, duration, durée, freedom, perception, memory

This essay introduces Henri Bergson's essential ideas on the nature of consciousness. Perhaps no philosopher was more admired and respected in his own time than Bergson was at the turn of the twentieth century, and yet his work has since been almost entirely eclipsed by

Correspondence:
G. William Barnard, Department of Religious Studies, Southern Methodist University, P.O. Box 750202, Dallas, TX 75275-0202, USA
Email: bbarnard@smu.edu

---

[1] Portions of this article were abstracted with permission from 'Vital Intuitions: Henri Bergson and Mystical Ethics' in G. William Barnard and Jeffrey Kripal, *Crossing Boundaries: Essays on the Ethical Status of Mysticism* (2002; Seven Bridges Press).

the positivistic and analytic trends in science and philosophy that followed closely on the First World War. Nonetheless, in the early part of the twentieth century, Bergson's thought was well known and highly esteemed. For instance, upon first reading Bergson's *Creative Evolution*, William James wrote him a letter exclaiming, 'Oh, my dear Bergson, you are a magician and your book is a miracle' (Bankov, 2000, p. 36).

It is not surprising that James would express such admiration for Bergson's work. The thinking of the two men on the nature of consciousness was remarkably similar, both stressing its fundamental character as a continuously flowing process. Echoes of Bergson's process view can also be found in sources as widely scattered as Bohmian physics and Dzogchen Buddhism; and Bergson's metaphysical reflections are reminiscent of contemporary theories such as Ervin Laszlo's (2007) akashic field and Rupert Sheldrake's (2009) morphogenetic field.

The original seed of Bergson's entire corpus can be found in his first publication, *Time and Free Will*. Rooted in a profound introspective examination of the nature of consciousness (hence its original title in French: *Essai Sur Les Données Immédiates de la Conscience*, i.e. *An Essay on the Immediate Data of Consciousness*) this text asks: What do we discover when we become conscious of our own consciousness?

According to Bergson, what we will find when we reflect on the nature of our consciousness is an inner life that is ceaselessly changing — an inner world in which one state of consciousness seamlessly flows into the next. For instance, at this moment, let's say that I am aware of feeling sad. But, whether or not I am conscious of it, in the very next moment that feeling will have changed ever so subtly into something else. Perhaps I have shifted the position of my body, or have shifted what I am seeing or hearing or thinking. All of these new experiences in this new moment combine with the memory of the original feeling of sadness; they come together to produce a different 'note' in the ongoing melody of my consciousness. As time passes, these changes in my consciousness continue to multiply. In fact, for Bergson, the passage of time *is itself* the changing of our consciousness. Ultimately, these changes, reverberating throughout my being, become so evident that I have to acknowledge that I am no longer feeling the way I once was; I am no longer 'sad'; now I am, let's say, 'content'.

The prism of our linguistic structure fragments our experience, splitting the dynamic flux of our consciousness into unchanging, self-contained parts (i.e. 'states' of consciousness such as 'sadness' or 'contentment'). Since words are separate, unchanging units ('contentment', as a word, always stays the same and is always a different word than 'sadness'), we tend to assume that as time passes within us one 'nugget' of consciousness (e.g. 'sadness') is replaced by another 'nugget' of consciousness (e.g. 'contentment'), almost as if these moments of consciousness were beads of different colours lined up next to each other. This type of tacit spatial symbolism (each bead is solid, separate, measurable) makes it extremely difficult to recognize that, in reality, our feelings are continually in flux, and that while it is possible to distinguish different 'tones' to our inner experience, there are, in actuality, no distinct boundaries within consciousness.

In a later text published in 1934 (*The Creative Mind*) Bergson used another metaphorical image to explain that we tend to think of our inner experience as if it were captured on a roll of movie film, essentially turning the undivided flux of our consciousness into a linear series of static snapshots, one frozen 'moment' followed by another (Bergson, 1934/1946). In this 'cinematographic' perspective each thought, each memory, each feeling, is tacitly understood to exist separately, each having its own discrete identity, each taking up just so much 'space' in our psyche, each static snapshot lined up and unrolling on the underlying homogenous substance of the film of time.

But as Bergson points out, if we look carefully we will discover the 'moments' of our consciousness are not separate from each other. Instead, within the flux of our consciousness, there is nothing static, there are no snapshots cut off from the rest, there is simply the continuous flow of our awareness, each state of consciousness interpenetrating the others, 'a spectrum of a thousand shades, with imperceptible gradations leading from one shade to another' (*ibid.*, p. 193).

This indivisible fusion of manyness and oneness, this ongoing, dynamic, temporal flux of our consciousness, this flowing that is ever-new and always unpredictable, this continual, seamless, interconnected, immeasurable movement of our awareness is what Bergson calls 'durée', or in English, 'duration'. In the English language, the term 'duration' is inevitably linked with notions of 'endurance' and has connotations of grimly and stoically 'enduring' something painful or difficult. But the term as Bergson uses it is intended to represent the temporal flux of our consciousness, a lived awareness which is 'durable', i.e. it persists (while always changing), it is always present (and always moving), it endures, in time, as time. This duration, for Bergson, is that which we experience within ourselves through an intuitive introspective awareness — not as something that exists separate from us, but instead, as the dynamic essence of who we really are.

Unfortunately, as Bergson was so fond of pointing out, experiencing ourselves as a continuous, dynamic, interconnected, conscious flux is extremely difficult. In order to do so, we have to battle against deeply ingrained ways of understanding ourselves and our relationship to life. One of the most fundamental obstacles to introspective clarity is that we typically do not pay any attention to what takes place within us. As Bergson puts it, 'we have no interest in listening to the uninterrupted humming of life's depths' (*ibid.*, p. 176). Instead, what matters to us is the external world that seems to surround us, a world populated with material objects (e.g. cars, trees, chairs, dogs, other humans, etc.) that seem to exist separate from each other, that seem to possess well-defined boundaries, that seem to remain relatively stable.

Bergson claims that in order to survive as a species most of our attention has focused on manipulating the external objects that seem to surround us. Inevitably, however, this practical, pragmatic mode of interaction with the external world (a mode of interaction that is greatly assisted by the structure of our language with its distinct and sharply defined words and concepts) affects the quality of our inner experience as well. Our need to portion out, measure, and dominate the external world, our tendency to see ourselves surrounded by objects that are static and external to ourselves and each other, objects that exist in a neutral, homogenous space, creates a predisposition to view our inner temporal experience through a corresponding type of spatial template. Seeing ourselves through this distorting lens we lose touch with the 'indivisible and indestructible continuity' of the 'melody of our experience'; we divide this melody into distinct notes that can be set out, side by side to each other in a two-dimensional, paper thin existence (*ibid.*, p. 83). Whereas in actuality our inner world is a 'melody where the past enters into the present and forms with it an undivided whole which remains undivided and even indivisible in spite of what is added at every instant', instead we experience an inner life that is tightly controlled, where every feeling has a label, and every idea is carefully weighed and considered (*ibid.*, p. 83). Whereas in actuality there is the seamless, dynamic onrush of our awareness in time, instead we live in a time that is measured and parceled out, split up into seconds, minutes, hours — the efflorescence of ceaseless novelty and inner continuity pulverized into units of sameness, each counted and accounted for.

Bergson stresses that understanding ourselves through the distorting funhouse mirror of our interactions with the external world leads, almost inevitably, to a specific philosophical stance: determinism. Physical determinism is a set of beliefs which argues that 'the external world yields to mathematical laws'; physical determinism claims that 'a superhuman intelligence which would know the position, the direction, and the speed of all the atoms and electrons of the material universe at a given moment could calculate any future state of the universe as we do in the case of an eclipse of the sun or the moon' (*ibid.*, p. 108).

Bergson emphasizes that if we believe that the activities of the external world are completely predetermined and if we see our inner reality as a reflection of the outer world in which our consciousness, like matter, is split up into tiny self-contained atoms, then it only makes sense to believe that our inner experience is also predetermined (especially if we think that our consciousness is reducible to the actions of physical atoms in the human organism). From this perspective, our current state of consciousness is said to be the inevitable, predictable result of the actions of prior 'atoms' of consciousness (e.g. my anger is the direct and predetermined result of my prior conviction that my friend insulted me). This type of psychical determinism, in a manner similar to physical determinism, claims that a 'mathematician who knew the position of the molecules or atoms of a human organism at a given moment, as well as the position and motion of all the atoms in the universe capable of influencing it, could calculate with unfailing certainty the past, present and future actions of the person to whom this organism belongs, just as one predicts an astronomical phenomenon' (Bergson, 1910, p. 144). Clearly, if consciousness is understood in this way, free will is non-existent.

In *Time and Free Will*, Bergson is willing, at least temporarily, to grant that the external world is governed by natural laws and that the behaviour of inert matter may well be predetermined and predictable. But one of the primary thrusts of his analysis of the nature of our consciousness in this text is to demonstrate that philosophical attacks on free will are based on a mistaken understanding of the nature of the human psyche. If Bergson's conception of duration is an accurate account of our human consciousness, then the notion of the atomistic self (which is assumed by those who attack free will and, ironically, by many of those who support it) is undercut at its very roots. Bergson presents a number of persuasive arguments supporting the reality of free will, but each of these arguments is, in the final analysis, grounded in his claim that the nature of consciousness is fundamentally different than the nature of external reality. The external world (at least inert matter) is, to all appearances, a collection of separate, self-contained objects external to each other, which interact with each other in pre-determined, mechanical ways. Consciousness, however, is a dynamic, ever-new, ceaselessly changing, flowing temporal reality, an interconnected whole in which each 'element' permeates and interpenetrates all the rest. Bergson concedes that advocates of philosophical determinism are, therefore, perhaps correct about the activities of inert matter, but they are radically mistaken when it comes to the nature of our psyche in that its very essence is freedom and unforeseeable creativity. He does not mince words; for him, 'freedom is… a fact, and among the facts which we observe there is none clearer' (ibid., p. 221).

To Bergson's credit, however, while he strenuously argues for the reality of free will, he also realizes that this freedom 'is not absolute… [rather], it admits of degrees' (ibid., p. 166). Bergson acknowledges that a sizeable amount of our behaviour does seem to have a striking resemblance to the mechanical, non-conscious, repetitive activity of inert matter. In fact, according to Bergson, most of our actions are little more than automatic reactions to outer stimuli, reactions which 'though conscious and even intelligent, have many points of resemblance with reflex acts' (ibid., p. 168). When we act on the instigation of solidified and encrusted habits and ideas that have remained on the surface of our psyches, we often behave in many ways like a type of 'conscious automaton' (ibid., p. 168). As Bergson puts it, when we identify with our 'superficial ego', with its clearly defined social roles, its rigidly held dogmas, its tightly controlled postures, 'we live outside ourselves, hardly perceiving anything of ourselves but our own ghost… we live for the external world rather than for ourselves; we speak rather than think; we "are acted" rather than act ourselves' (ibid., pp. 125, 231).

Nonetheless, according to Bergson, we do have the capacity to act differently. We can push aside the 'independent growths' which 'form and float' on the surface of our psyche 'like dead leaves on the water of a pond' (ibid., pp. 166, 135); we can turn within ourselves and melt the 'clear-cut crystals' of the 'ideas which we receive ready made, and which remain in us without ever being properly assimilated' (Bergson, 1934/1946, p. 192; 1910, pp. 135–136). If we accomplish this task through an intensive introspective effort, it then becomes possible to discover deep within our psyche that aspect of our being which is 'the most uniformly, the most constantly and durably' ourselves, that 'continuity of flow comparable to no flowing' we have ever seen; we can once again 'get back into pure duration' and thereby 'recover possession' of ourselves (Bergson, 1934/1946, p. 192; 1910, p. 232).

According to Bergson, actions that spring forth from this fluid, ever creative 'deep-seated self' are indeed truly free. Unfortunately, we rarely act from our depths in such a way that our whole personality vibrates (Bergson, 1910, p. 125). Instead, we prefer to relinquish our freedom, even in moments of crisis. We listen to the advice of others, we consult the rulebooks, we write down lists of pros and cons, we seek the approval of others, we cling to old patterns of behaviour that worked in the past, we struggle to stay safely within our comfort zone. Much of the time this strategy works. We have learned how to live our lives on automatic pilot, how to avoid our depths. Fortunately, however, there are also moments in our lives in which something different takes place, moments where, in the struggle to make a decision, just when we think we have made up our minds, something unexpected occurs:

> At the very minute when the act is going to be performed, *something* may revolt against it. It is the deep-seated self rushing up to the surface. It is the outer crust bursting, suddenly giving way to an irresistible thrust. Hence in the depths of the self, below this most reasonable pondering over most reasonable pieces of advice, something else was going on — a gradual heating and a sudden boiling over of feelings and ideas, not unperceived, but rather unnoticed. If we turn back to them and carefully scrutinize our memory, we shall see that we had ourselves shaped these ideas, ourselves lived these feelings, but that, through some strange reluctance to exercise our will, we had thrust them back into the darkest depths of our soul whenever they came up to the surface. (Bergson, 1910, pp. 169–170)

At moments such as these, it may appear as if we are acting irrationally. But Bergson claims that this is not actually the case. When this sort of unexpected decision surges up within us, when we act spontaneously, seemingly without thought (a type of action that is very different from impulsive action, which is rooted in habitual emotional/motor reactions), we may not be able to give a precise, easily articulated, and justified reason for our actions, but we are actually acting out of the depths of who we are at that moment — the dynamic sum total of our most profound convictions, feelings, and aspirations. Our decision could not have been worked out in advance; it could not have been made by anyone but ourselves, by anyone except who we were in that very moment.

Bergson claims that most of us implicitly want an algorithm or formula that will automatically give us the answer as to how we should act, especially in moments of difficult decisions. We want life to be predictable; we want it to obey the comforting logic of mathematics, where if we start with an initial set of premises, then certain conclusions inevitably follow — no matter who we are or when we work on the problem. But as Bergson points out, unfortunately (or fortunately!), our personal life does not follow mathematical rules. Because human beings are constantly changing, learning, and growing, 'the same reasons may dictate to different persons, or to the same person at different moments, acts profoundly different, although equally reasonable. The truth is that they are not quite the same reasons, since they are not those of the same person, nor of the same moment' (Bergson, 1911, p. 7). Since life is constantly in flux, Bergson advises that we learn to know and to trust our depths, to attune ourselves to what is most deeply and fundamentally real within us: the ever-flowing, ever-new, yet ever-connected, stream of our own consciousness.

Unfortunately, in *Time and Free Will*, Bergson is less helpful than he might be as to how we can learn to act more frequently and easily from our deep-seated self and not from the superficial ego. He is clear that genuinely free actions that are attuned to the depths of our being are possible as the result of rigorous introspective work, but he does not really give us any clues as to what factors might block access to the depths of our being, how we might overcome these inner barriers, or (at least in any detail or depth) how these mental and/or emotional obstacles might distort our decision-making process. Bergson also does not explore in *Time and Free Will* the nature of the relationship between our deeper self and reality as a whole, or the ways in which it might be possible to be attuned to levels of inspiration and guidance that transcend the boundaries of our personality — even if Bergson does address these issues in later works.

A Matter of Spirit

In *Time and Free Will*, Bergson offers a forceful defence of the freedom and creativity of human consciousness. In many ways, this text is his sustained argument against those thinkers who claim that our actions are, in the end, simply the predetermined result of a complicated, yet predictable, dance of electro-chemical interactions. However, in his attempts to underscore the reality of free will, Bergson ends up creating a yawning chasm between matter and consciousness.

According to *Time and Free Will*, matter is a collection of discrete, relatively stable objects, each of which can be measured and counted, objects that interact with each other automatically, in ways that are utterly predictable (a type of interaction that causes chemistry experiments to produce the same results every time they are performed). Consciousness, however, in Bergson's analysis, is a dynamic flux of interconnected and interpenetrating states of awareness that never repeat themselves; our consciousness is always new, always creative. The problem is, given this radical distinction between matter and consciousness, how could they possibly interact? Yet this interaction appears to be a basic and ongoing fact of experience. For instance, I make a decision (e.g. to sit down on a chair) and my body responds by sitting down. How is this decision communicated if my mind is utterly different from my physical body? Bergson's next book, *Matter and Memory* (e.g. 1991), delves into this dilemma.

In *Matter and Memory*, Bergson argues that we are continually juggling two basic levels of experience. On the one hand, we seem to live in a stable, objective world, a world that is shared by everyone, a world in which objects interact with each other in determined, invariable ways, according to fixed natural laws, a world that does not seem to depend upon anyone's conscious perceptions (e.g. the furniture in my study exists, regardless of whether anyone is present in the room to perceive this furniture). On the other hand, according to Bergson, another world of experience also demands our attention. Equally present, equally real, is the world of our conscious perceptions, a level of experience in which the outer world does seem to vary, moment to moment, depending upon the subjective perspective of the individual (e.g. if I shut my eyes, the furniture in the room disappears; if I spin around, it seems to move; if I like oak furniture, then my perception comes suffused with subtle feelings of fondness, and so on). In *Matter and Memory*, Bergson attempts to reconcile these two seemingly estranged realities.

Our normal, common sense understanding of how we come to know the objective world around us is that physical stimuli from this external world impacts our sense organs, and these organs then send signals to our brain via the nervous system. Our brain, receiving these signals, promptly translates them into our conscious perceptions. This understanding of the process of perception leads us to assume that we are, in a sense, taking photographs of the universe, using our sense organs as the camera, and developing a picture of the external world by an elaborate chemical process in the brain. The problem with this common sense understanding, however, is that there still remains a big chasm between the world of matter and consciousness itself. Our consciousness is nothing like a photograph; it is not a physical piece of paper coated with chemicals. Our consciousness is not made of matter, so how can it be the product of purely physical interactions? Bergson's solution is ingenious, if perhaps difficult at first to grasp.

Bergson begins by positing a universe that is, below the level of appearances, a pulsating, interconnected field of 'images'. These images, according to Bergson, possess qualities that are similar to both matter and consciousness. Like matter, these images are dynamic patterns of energy, vortices of vibrations that radiate outward, contacting and affecting other complexly patterned vortices of energy. This transmission of energy-information is, moment to moment, passed on to other images, automatically, fully, without hesitation. This measurable, predictable, lawful interaction is the basis for the stable, objective world of matter, a world rooted in the dependable, repeatable patterns of cause and effect studied by the natural sciences.

Understood in this way, the universe of images acts identically to the way matter is typically thought to behave. However, the universe of images posited by Bergson is dissimilar to our typical understanding of matter in two ways. First, this universe of images is not inherently divided into a collection of separate objects possessing clear cut boundaries. The world of separate objects that we normally perceive is not the true nature of matter. Instead, according to Bergson, it is, like our consciousness, an interconnected, dynamic continuum of becoming, in which 'numberless vibrations, all linked together in uninterrupted continuity' travel 'in every direction like shivers through an immense body' (Bergson, 1991, p. 208).

The second way in which the universe of images posited by Bergson is different than our usual understanding of matter is that we normally think of matter (e.g. a stone) as inert, or non-aware. However, Bergson's universe of images is essentially a type of virtual consciousness. He would argue that consciousness, in a latent form, is already present in the universe of images. The job of the sense organs, nervous system, and the brain (which are themselves images) is not to create our conscious perceptions. Instead, perception occurs when our bodies (as well as the bodies of other organisms) receive the pulses of virtually-conscious vibrations from the other images of the universe. From this infinitely complex, interpenetrating field of latent consciousness, we then select out and actualize only those vibrations which serve the needs of our particular organism, letting the rest of the information from the universe pass through unimpeded.

According to Bergson, our 'pure perceptions' (i.e. the raw data of perception — perceptions minus most of the influence of memory) are a filtrate from the totality of the universal flux of potential consciousness in which we find ourselves. Our pure perceptions are, therefore, the result of a radical truncation, a culling process by which we ignore most of what we might potentially know. As a result, we perceive only the 'external crust' or the 'superficial skin' of what actually surrounds us (*ibid.*, p. 36).

However, while our pure perceptions, in relation to the universe of images, are in this way simply a small part of the greater whole, Bergson claims that they are also neither relative, nor illusory. While our pure perceptions may not reveal to us all that there is to know in the world around us, this 'raw data' of perception is, nonetheless, not subjective. (As we will see below, the subjectivity of our concrete perceptions comes from the superimposition of memory onto our pure perceptions.) Our pure perceptions, according to Bergson, are not 'in our heads'; they are not created by our brains. Instead, this 'raw data' of our perceptions is a part and parcel of the world around us. When we see a tree, we are actually there with that tree as an objective reality in our pure perceptions. Bergson does not shy away from the implications of this unique epistemology. As he puts it, 'we are really present in everything we perceive'. In reality, therefore, our body is not limited to the small physical organism we typically identify with (although that body always remains the vital centre of our world). We also possess a massive body made up of the totality of our conscious perceptions, a body that, in a very real sense, 'reaches to the stars' (Bergson, 1932/1977, p. 258).

However, while we might, unknown to us, be part of this huge, quasi-universal body, our smaller body, the 'inner and central body' remains vitally important (*ibid.*, p. 258). Without our physical body we would have no pure perceptions. Bergson stresses that our senses, nervous system, and brain do not somehow magically change inert material vibrations into consciousness. Instead, acting as a type of dynamic filter, they continually screen out the vast majority of the information we receive from the mass of potential consciousness that surrounds us in order that we might act effectively and flourish as a physical organism.

Bergson goes on to point out that it is crucial for our physical body to play this role. If we were to perceive, and consequently act upon, the world as it exists at its most basic, subatomic vibratory level; if, for example, we no longer saw an oak table as a solid structure of wood, but instead consciously perceived and responded to the flux of almost infinite energetic patterns that underlie the table, we would become incapacitated, lost in the 'moving immensity' of what previously had been a motionless, rectangular solid object (Bergson, 1934/1946, p. 69). One of the most basic functions of our physicality is, therefore, to carve out manageable islands of stability in the onrush of universal becoming by choosing to focus only on that level of experience that best serves our needs. In essence, we create our experience of the world moment by moment through the power of our choices. Consequently, as Bergson notes:

> [N]othing would prevent other worlds, corresponding to another choice, from existing with [our world], in the same place and the same time: in this way twenty different broadcasting stations throw out simultaneously twenty different concerts which coexist without any one of them mingling its sounds with the music of another, each one being heard, complete and alone, in the apparatus which has chosen for its reception the wave-length of that particular station. (*ibid.*, pp. 69–70)

Bergson's fascinating theory of how different worlds might well exist that correspond to different levels of perception was not explicitly developed with mystical traditions in mind. Instead, Bergson was primarily interested in providing a viable explanation for psychical phenomena such as clairvoyance and telepathy. Nonetheless, this theory does have crucial implications for the genesis of mystical experience. If, as Bergson speculated, the 'mechanisms' which are 'expressly designed to screen' the enormous flood of information we receive from the universal flux of potentially conscious images were to 'get out of order', then the 'door which they kept shut' would be partially opened, thereby letting in levels of information that would normally be excluded from our more mundane awareness (Bergson, 1932/1977, p. 315).

If Bergson is correct, then this explanation of the origin of telepathic and clairvoyant knowledge might well also account for certain types of mystical experiences. If we are continually connected with the entire universe, if the apparent clearcut separation between objects is not real, but instead is created by the filtering mechanisms of the brain, perhaps different spiritual disciplines work to open up the floodgates. Perhaps they prepare us to absorb and respond effectively to more of the universal information than we are typically capable of receiving. From this perspective, if a mystic experiences a loss of egoic boundaries and the consequent sense of merger with the surrounding universe world, this experience would not be the deluded hallucinations of madness, but rather would be the result of a profound contact with a deeper, but usually unperceived, level of reality.

In addition, Bergson's claim that we filter out the vast majority of the information we receive from the universe might well account for a wide range of more prosaic levels of intuitive awareness as well. Perhaps we really do know, on some level, that someone is sexually attracted to us; perhaps we really can get an accurate sense of danger or 'wrongness' from someone; perhaps our empathetic awareness of the feelings of another is not a subjective projection of our feelings onto someone else, but instead is rooted in something real, in the flow of subliminal information that we constantly receive from the universe around us, but which we, for a variety of reasons, choose to ignore.

Further, Bergson speculates that there might well be another source for intuitive, non-ordinary experiences. Our brain does not just filter out the mass of information we continually receive from the universe of images around us. It also screens out the vast majority of the memories that we possess — an equally valuable function, since, according to Bergson, we have within us, on a subconscious level, memories of every moment of our life. If this enormous fund of recollections from the past were actively present in our consciousness, we would be overwhelmed and unable to function effectively. But Bergson claims that, fortunately for us, most of our memories are kept from our consciousness by the body's insistent need to give attention only to that which helps it respond to the requirements of the present. Most of our memories — at least the specific recollections we have of definite events in our past — are of no use to us and so are relegated to subconscious levels of our being.

Bergson theorizes that non-ordinary experiences may take place not only when the floodgates of our personal past are opened, but also when we open ourselves to other types of mental phenomena which are also blocked from our consciousness, such as telepathic information received from others. From Bergson's perspective, the sharp divisions that seem to separate physical objects do not necessarily apply to the mind. If this is the case, then there is a good possibility that our minds extend beyond the boundaries of our physical bodies (in fact, he quite explicitly argues that our memories are not stored in our brains), and that our minds are continually blending with other minds in a reciprocal flow of mental information below the surface of our awareness. Bergson notes that 'if such intercommunication exists, nature will have taken precautions to render it harmless, and most likely certain mechanisms are specially charged with the duty of throwing back, into the unconscious, images so introduced' (Bergson, 1991, p. 97). However, Bergson goes on to suggest that it is possible that certain thoughts, memories, images, or feelings from other minds might occasionally manage, for various reasons, to slip past this mechanism. If so, then these incursions might well be another, equally viable, source of telepathic and clairvoyant knowledge.

In reality, the 'matter-like' source of subliminal information from the universe of images as well as the more explicitly 'mental' source (i.e. memories, thoughts, and images from other streams of consciousness) are simply two ends of a single spectrum of universal becoming. While in *Matter and Memory*, Bergson maintains a strong functional dualism between matter and consciousness, the sharp edges of that dualism increasingly soften and blur as he notes the variety of ways in which matter and consciousness (especially its primary instantiation, memory) interact and interpenetrate during every concrete moment of perception.

For Bergson, memory in its most basic form, memory which is operative in, and interwoven with, perception, is not memory as we normally understand the term. Instead, memory at its most fundamental level is simply the continuity of our consciousness; it is the automatic and ongoing connection of our past to the present. It is this type of memory that, according to Bergson, ties together the enormous quantity and range of the vibrations of matter and condenses them into the perceived moments of our consciousness. (For example, drawing upon information from the science of his time, Bergson explains that, if we perceive a pulse of red light for a single second, during that time our consciousness has condensed 400 billion vibrations of that spectrum of light.)

Bergson suggests that this most basic modality of memory is operative even below the level of our conscious sense perceptions. He points out that this level of memory, in which the past is automatically carried into the present, is present even at the vibratory level of matter itself. These vibrations are not, according to Bergson, flashes of inert, utterly pre-determined energy taking place in a discrete, ceaselessly repeated present. Instead, these vibrations are, even at the atomic and molecular level, bound together by an impersonal substratum of memory, a type of proto-consciousness; they are simply a different degree or 'frequency' of duration — the duration of matter.

According to Bergson, the universe as a whole consists of a wide spectrum of different levels of duration, ranging from the quasi-necessity of the duration of matter, through the largely instinctive duration of various rudimentary organisms, up to the highly conscious, flexible (if at times habitual) duration of human consciousness. Bergson even speculates that it is possible, and is indeed likely, that there exists a duration of consciousness with a 'higher degree' of 'tension' (or perhaps 'at-tention'?) than our own — one that is able to condense the entire history of humanity into a very short period of its own duration in the same way that we condense the 'history' of the vibrations of matter into the ongoing flux of the perceptions of our conscious experience in any moment (Bergson, 1991, p. 207).

Bergson's own focus, however, was not always quite so speculative and cosmic in scope. His explorations of memory are often prosaic and down to earth. He recognized that the task of memory is not just to bind one moment of experience to the next by connecting the past to the present or to condense the potentially conscious vibrations of matter into our everyday conscious perceptions. Memory is also operative within us either in the form of specific recollections of past events (e.g. remembering one's first time riding a bicycle) or more frequently in the form of impersonal, bodily-based distillations of past events (e.g. the set of internalized motor skills it takes to ride a bicycle well). According to Bergson, these more personal forms of memory help to create the fullness of our concrete, lived experience by interweaving themselves into each 'pure perception' so seamlessly that 'we are no longer able to discern what is perception and what is memory' (*ibid.*, p. 103). For Bergson, every moment of our experience is a fusion of perception and memory. Indeed, as he notes, it is only because memory is added to perception that the objective, externalized moments of pure perception (which actually take place 'outside of us', among the objects themselves) are converted into experiences that seem to be subjective and internal; i.e. it is memory that makes it appear that our experience takes place 'inside our heads'.

In fact, although Bergson never explicitly argues this point, even the process of pure perception itself, which theoretically takes place without the activity of memory, could never occur without the help of a highly condensed form of personal memory. As was pointed out above, a pure perception occurs when, out of a universe of potentially conscious images, only a fraction — those which interest us — are selected. Could this variety of interests exist without memory? Without memory, would we be able to choose from a wide range of responses, instead of reacting automatically, as matter would, to the universal influx of information? It is memory that is the source of these choices and hence of our freedom. It is this form of memory — the digest of our past, embodied in the present, and concerned with our future, that shapes our perception of the world at its most basic level.

Clearly, memory serves a far more important role in the actual moments of our experience than we often realize. According to Bergson, in the final analysis, perception is simply 'an occasion for remembering' (*ibid.*, p. 66). A pure perception by itself is rather thin — it is simply a type of schematic outline, or sketch, which in order to be most effective, needs to be filled in with a wide range of memories. These memories, which are typically not specific memory images of past events, but rather, are pre-conscious, highly distilled, internalizations of cultural and psychological patterns of belief, merge with the raw perceptual data, and by doing so, shape these perceptions, giving them order, structure, and meaning. This interpretive overlay from memory is so extensive that we end up 'constantly creating or reconstructing' our present experience based on the sum total of our past (*ibid.*, p. 103).

To illustrate the role that memory plays in our perceptions, Bergson notes that if we are in a room with someone speaking a language we do not know (e.g. Italian) our ears hear the same sounds as native speakers from Italy who are also in the room. Nonetheless, our experience is quite different than that of the Italians. This is so because their past experiences of learning Italian have been condensed within their consciousness, have been compressed into a highly fluid and useful distillation of memory that can superimpose itself upon the sounds of the language being spoken, thereby enabling them to hear meaningful words and sentences, while we hear nothing but a confused mass of noise.

The memory that enables individuals who know a language to make sense of various sounds is itself a fusion of different types of memory. For instance, I have numerous specific memories of times in which I went to Spanish class in high school and did grammar and pronunciation drills. However, most of my somewhat rudimentary Spanish language skills are not rooted in my concrete recollections of specific times spent learning this or that Spanish phrase. Instead, when I hear certain words or sentences in that language, I simply comprehend them, almost literally in my flesh and bones. Each language drill session instilled learned patterns of behaviour that have become ingrained in my bodily tone, stance, breathing, and so on. This type of memory — a highly embodied, quasi-automatic, habitual reaction to the promptings of the present moment — is very different from my mental recollections of specific moments of my past.

Bergson argues that these two types of memory (recollections and habit memory) are always actively present within us, fusing with each moment of perception. However, different individuals will typically respond to life's demands drawing upon different 'percentages' of these two types of memory. On the one extreme, there are those people who react habitually and quasi-automatically to the perceived needs of the present instant. These individuals rarely reflect on their actions, preferring instead to parrot catch phrases and to mimic the behaviour of others in their group. They act on impulse, driven by ingrained, reactive patterns of behaviour that are rarely, if ever, questioned. On the other extreme, there are those individuals who are almost completely cut off from the demands of daily life and from the promptings of their body. Overly intellectual, obsessively ruminating about their past mistakes or anxiously rehearsing their future actions, they live in their 'heads', trapped in a mental world, out of touch with their feelings, their bodily sensations, and the world around them.

Bergson points out, however, that there are people who have been able to harmonize these two types of memories, individuals who are 'well-balanced', or 'nicely adapted to life' (*ibid.*, p. 153). Reflective and self-aware, they are neither mired in habitual, rigid, unreflective patterns of behaviour, nor attached to beliefs that they have not made their own. Instead, they are able to draw freely upon the wisdom of past experience and can remain fluidly responsive to the changing needs of the present.

Bergson's description of these types of quasi-ideal individuals in *Matter and Memory* are, at best, rudimentary sketches; they are skeletal outlines that are fleshed out in later works. On the whole, Bergson's focus in *Matter and Memory* is not normative — instead, it is a rigorous, densely textured, closely reasoned, complex analysis of the mind–body interaction. However, in much of the work that followed *Matter and Memory* (and indeed, in parts of *Time and Free Will* as well), the threads of Bergson's abstract philosophical analyses of the nature of consciousness and the world around us are increasingly interwoven with lyrical allusions to the transformative possibilities of human life.

For example, in 'The Perception of Change' (an essay published originally in 1911, now found in *Creative Mind*), we can see hints of Bergson's normative vision of humanity. In this essay, Bergson suggests that we are most completely ourselves when we recognize and joyously give ourselves to the ceaseless change that is going on both within us and around us. He claims that if we can cultivate within ourselves an ongoing experience of the flux of universal becoming, then our rigid and frozen perception of life can be melted, and in doing so, 'everything comes to life around us, everything is revivified in us. A great impulse carries beings and things along. We feel ourselves uplifted, carried away, borne along by it' (Bergson, 1934/1946, p. 186). He points out that if we can let go of our fears that we will 'drown in the torrent-like flow' of the movement of life; if we can release our anxiety that the world we have so carefully constructed will disintegrate if we give up our continual, and often desperate, attempts to keep things the same; if we can soften the rigid walls of our habitual patterns of reactivity and melt the frozen labels that we superimpose upon others and ourselves; we will discover, perhaps to our surprise, that we have gained a 'feeling of greater joy and strength' than we might have imagined possible (*ibid.*, pp. 177, 124). Bergson claims that we will feel increased joy 'because the reality invented before our eyes will give each one of us, unceasingly', the joy that seemingly only privileged artists possess, the joy of seeing beneath the apparent 'fixity and monotony' of our everyday lives the 'ever-recurring novelty, the moving originality of things' (*ibid.*, p. 124) We will feel greater strength because, by attuning ourselves to the ceaseless dance of creative energy that is life itself, 'we shall feel we are participating, creators of ourselves, in the great work of creation which is the origin of all things and which goes on before our eyes', becoming, therefore, conscious co-creators of our world (*ibid.*, p. 124).

References

Bankov, K. (2000) *Intellectual Effort and Linguistic Work: Semiotic and Hermeneutic Aspects of the Philosophy of Bergson*, Imatra, Finland: International Semantics Institute.
Barnard, G.W. (2002) Vital intuitions: Henri Bergson and mystical ethics, in Barnard, G.W. & Kripal, J. (eds.) *Crossing Boundaries: Essays on the Ethical Status of Mysticism*, New York: Seven Bridges Press.
Bergson, H. (1910) *Time and Free Will: An Essay on the Immediate Data of Consciousness*, Whitefish, MT: Kessinger Publishing Company.
Bergson, H. (1911) *Creative Evolution*, Lanham, MD: University Press of America.
Bergson, H. (1934/1946) *The Creative Mind*, New York: The Philosophical Library.
Bergson, H. (1932/1977) *The Two Sources of Morality and Religion*, Notre Dame, IN: University of Notre Dame Press.
Bergson, H. (1991) *Matter and Memory*, New York: Zone Books.
Laszlo, E. (2007) *Science and the Akashic Field*, Rochester, VT: Inner Traditions.
Sheldrake, R. (2009) *Morphic Resonance: The Nature of Formative Causation*, South Paris, ME: Park Street Press.

Paper received August 2010.

Jonathan Bricklin

Consciousness Already There Waiting to be Uncovered

William James's Mystical Suggestion
as Corroborated by Himself
and His Contemporaries

Abstract: *'Is... consciousness already there waiting to be uncovered and is it a veridical revelation of reality?' William James asked in one of his last published essays, 'A Suggestion About Mysticism'. The answer, he said, would not be known 'by this generation or the next'. By separating what James wanted to believe about commonsense reality, from what his 'dispassionate' insights and researches led him to believe, I show how James himself, in collaboration with a few friends, laid the groundwork for adopting his mystical suggestion as veridical. 'Consciousness already there waiting to be uncovered' — not 'generated de novo in a vast number of places' but existing 'behind the scenes, coeval with the world' — is consistent with James's 'neutral monism', his belief that Newtonian, objective, even-flowing time does not exist, and his belief that parapsychological and other transpersonal phenomena had 'broken down... the limits of the admitted order of things'. Specific parallels between James's veridical revelation and the veridical revelation of his young contemporary Einstein, are also considered.*

Keywords: William James, Shadworth Hodgson, Benjamin Paul Blood, F.H. Myers, Oliver Lodge, Einstein, Parmenides, Santayana, William Bigelow, Mrs. Titus, Leonora Piper, E.D. Fawcett, Krishnamurti, Craig

Correspondence:
Jonathan Bricklin, New York Open Center, 22 E. 30th St., NY, NY 10016
Email: jonathan@opencenter.org

Hogan, A Suggestion About Mysticism, A Pluralistic Mystic, Anaesthetic Revelation, nitrous oxide, ether, hasheesh, hashish, time, timeflow, timemask, continuum, block universe, Pluriverse, consciousness, sciousness, specious present, neutral monism, precognition, retrocognition, nondualism, witness, saksin, hologram, eternalism

Introduction

> The reality that I was in was more real, more intense, than anything in this current world of ours. It was hyper-reality.
> I was in a place. Around me was flatness and barrenness. To talk about a sequence to the experience is to distort it. There was no time there. I now know that time is a convenient fiction for this world, but it did not exist in that one. Everything seemed to be at one moment, even when 'events' seemed to occur in a sequence. What seemed to be the sky, the land, and everything was of a pale blue-gray color. It was like being on a raft in the middle of the ocean where sky and sea merge into one monochromatic world, but I felt as though I were standing on firm land. There was only the blue-gray vastness that seemed to stretch endlessly...
> The... re-experiencing of my life... was simultaneous and yet separate and distinct. There was no such thing as the sequence of events that we believe time to be. (Steven Fanning, Professor of History, University of Illinois, quoted by Huston Smith, no date)

> ...is not the notion of eternity being given at a stroke to omniscience only just another way of whacking upon us the block universe, and of denying that possibilities exist? (James, 1897, p. 553)

From the moment he adopted a belief in free will, routing a depression so severe he had identified himself with a catatonic patient (Allen, 1967, p. 166), William James championed a world that was what it seemed to be, a world of 'fresh activity-situations' (James, 1909b, p. 810n). Free will was only part of that world; the other part was time. But in the same Harvard *Ingersoll Lecture* series that first William Bigelow,[1] and later Huston Smith,[2] introduced the time-collapse of near-death experiences, James proposed that the world of 'natural

---

[1] 'Accumulated states of consciousness of a lifetime sometimes revive simultaneously in a single flash. The events of the whole past are seen down to the most minute and remote details, like a landscape under a flash of lightning' (Bigelow, 1908, pp. 14–15). Bigelow, a Victorian MD who became one of the first American Buddhists, specifically mentions James's teacher and friend, Dr. Oliver Wendell Holmes, as having 'had this experience on one occasion, just before losing consciousness altogether while drowning...' (Bigelow, 1908, p. 15). Dr. Forbes Winslow's *Obscure Diseases of the Mind* (published in 1866), cited by James in his *Principles of Psychology* (James, 1890, p. 355), also relates time-collapse experiences in relation to incidents of near-death by asphyxiation (*ibid.*, p. 285).

[2] See quote above.

experience' may be just a 'timemask, shattering or refracting the one infinite Thought which is the sole reality into those millions of finite streams of consciousness known to us as our private selves' (James, 1898, p. 1110).

It seems a bizarre assertion for him to have made, even to divinity students — the very students whom, on another occasion (see quote above; James, 1897), he had warned against such a 'static timeless perfect absolute' (James, 1909b, p. 777). But James was nothing if not true to experience, and though he declared that 'experience as a whole wears the form of a process of time' (James, 1904b, p. 1169), he questioned what, precisely, was being worn. As much as he wanted to believe that the world was being created as it went along, his introspections into the fundamental processing of consciousness, his psychical research, his experimentation with what we now call entheogenic drugs, and, most significantly, a series of profound mystical experiences that whacked upon him a version of a block universe, suggested otherwise.

James's 'masterful strategy to stay poised between... the mystically appealing unbounded unconscious and the hazards of falling into its abyss' (Bjork, 1983, p. 157)[3] was accomplished in part by his not assembling in one place all his challenges to what he called, but inconsistently defended as, 'the really real' world of common sense (Skrupskelis and Berkeley, 2002, p. 295).[4] This was especially true for the series of experiences in which that hazard was greatest, and about which James wrote in one of his last published essays, 'A Suggestion About Mysticism'. For although James confessed his 'dread to die until he settled the Universe's hash' (Skrupskelis and Berkeley, 2002), he ignored much of his own compelling evidence, gathered over a lifetime, in support of this last attempt to do so, and invoked future generations to determine whether his mystically inspired version of the universe — 'consciousness already there waiting to be uncovered' (James, 1910a, p. 1280) — was a 'veridical revelation' (*ibid.*).

In this essay we will look at some of James's own corroborations of his mystical suggestion, however much he himself ignored them (or, as in his essays on pragmatism, tried to undo them), and the

---

[3] Bjork dubbed James 'the compromised scientist'. But that is only half the story. The other half, as we will try to show here, is that James was a compromised mystic. As Barnard astutely observed: '...the Tantric and Sufi belief that a mystic could also be highly successful in the everyday work-world was never part of James's understanding of the possibilities of mysticism' (Barnard, 1997, p. 72).

[4] See, for instance, his 1908 letter to his colleague F.C.S. Schiller (Skrupskelis and Berkeley, 2003, p. 552).

corroborations of a few of his friends and colleagues. The most obvious support, from the eternalistic philosophers Royce and Bradley, is well known, as James himself frequently opposed them in essays and letters. Here we will focus on four non-adversarial colleagues — Shadworth Hodgson, Benjamin Paul Blood, Oliver Lodge, and Frederic Myers — as well as a young German physicist who anticipated James with a veridical revelation of his own.

The essay is divided into five sections as follows:

1) Introductory remarks about James's view on timeflow, emphasizing Shadworth Hodgson's influence.
2) James's mystical suggestion as a veridical revelation, with specific parallels with Einstein's veridical revelation.
3) A suggestion from the 'Anaesthetic Revelation', incorporated into James's mystical suggestion, emphasizing his complicated relationship with Blood's mysticism.
4) Psychical research related to his mystical suggestion, emphasizing the influence of Frederic Myers and Sir Oliver Lodge.
5) 'The Witness', emphasizing the variety of religious understanding and experience suggested by both James's mystical suggestion and his radical empiricism: nondualism.

1. Timeflow

…it is not so impossible or even difficult to conceive the universe as it transcends time as has been supposed. (Charles Sanders Peirce, in a letter to James; Skrupskelis and Berkeley, 2000, p. 335)

In the *Principles of Psychology*, James quotes a poet's assertion that in a closed-eyed meditative state we can 'attend exclusively to the actual passing of time… like one who wakes to hear time flowing in the middle of the night, and all things moving to a day of doom' (James, 1890, p. 583). Such pure time, as 'a kind of impalpable inner flowing' (James, 1904a, p. 1143), James believed to be fiction. Unlike his friend and most admired colleague, Henri Bergson, James did not believe in 'the flow of real time' (G. Myers, 1986, p. 155), or what he called its 'devouring tooth' (James, 1890, p. 591).[5] Time, James believed, was not an innate intuition,[6] but a 'patently artificial' 'construction' (James, 1907b, p. 564). From Newton's foundational fiat — 'Absolute, True, and Mathematical Time, of itself, and from its own

---

[5] 'Succession, time *per se*, is no force. Our talk about its devouring tooth, etc., is elliptical. Its *contents* are what devour' (James, 1890, p. 591).

[6] As Kant had asserted.

nature, flows equably without regard to anything external' (Newton, 1687/2002, p. 6) — James declared independence: 'We assume for certain purposes one "objective" Time that *aequabiliter fluit* [flows evenly], but we don't livingly believe in or realize any such equally-flowing time' (James, 1907b, p. 566).

The time flow we do realize, the '*original paragon and prototype of all conceived times*', is an experienced '*short duration*', '*immediately and incessantly sensible*', that James[7] called the '*specious present*' (James, 1890, p. 594). Following Shadworth Hodgson, whose writing he called 'the greatest mine of philosophic wealth now extant'[8] (Skrupskelis and Berkeley, 1997, p. 43), James saw this prototypical temporal feeling as itself formed from two 'sub-feelings': a growing-fainter 'goes' and a growing-stronger 'comes' (Shadworth Hodgson, quoted by James, 1890, p. 572).

With this 'specious present' as the basic unit of timeflow, James saw commonsense linearity as an amalgam: *actual* feelings, or rather 'sub-feelings', of going away and coming toward, mixed with *imaginary* spatialized representations of past and future, separated by the 'darkest in the whole series, the "present"' (Hodgson, quoted by James, 1890, p. 323). This succession of sub-feelings (the growing-fainter 'goes' of past feeling, and the growing- stronger 'comes' of future feeling) gets represented as a temporal linear landscape — past, present, future — even though the actual dynamic feeling of ongoing consciousness does not 'require that the sub-feelings come in sequence, first one, then the other; nor to know what coming in sequence means' (Hodgson, quoted by James, 1890, p. 572). Past, present and future are *concepts* which organize successive experience, just as the concept of space organizes co-existing experience. It is not, James says, that '…things come to be thought by us as past… because of any "intrinsic quality" of their own, but rather because they are associated with other things which for us signify pastness' (*ibid.*, p. 570).

We think of the past and the future as distinct domains, continuous within themselves; the most recent past, for example, however much experienced only as a 'sub-feeling' of 'fading away', is known as the nearest part of a more distant past, such as a scene from childhood. But as James emphasizes, what makes a distant past distant is not some

---

[7] After E.R. Clay.

[8] '…his method of attacking problems by asking what their terms are "known as," made Hodgson one of James' two inspirations for Pragmatism, the other being Peirce' (Skrupskelis and Berkeley, 2004, p. 401).

sort of stretching out of the near past. Beyond the nearest 'immediate consciousness of pastness' (*ibid.*, p. 611) is a past constituted in an entirely different way: not from an extension of the sub-feeling *perception* of pastness, but from a present *conception*. That is, the past beyond the perceived past of the passing moment is

> known symbolically by names, such as 'last week', '1850'; or thought of by events which happened in them, as the year in which we attended such a school, or met with such a loss. So that if we wish to think of a particular past epoch, we must think of a name or other symbol, or else of certain concrete events, associated therewithal. (*ibid.*)

The future, too,[9] beyond the perceived nearest 'sub-feeling' of 'dawning into', is conjured from symbolic markers, such as 'tomorrow', and by 'certain concrete events' conceived in present time. Often, the images of past and future are the same, or interchangeable, so that, in the absence of a symbolic marker, such as 'yesterday' or 'tomorrow', or a temporally distinguishing emotional contraction, like regret (for the past) or anxiety (for the future), there is no sensed tense. But whether past or future is sensed, perceived changes do not play out in time, James argued. Rather, time itself is derived from a hybrid of perceived changes: '...the short duration of which we are immediately and incessantly sensible', plus symbolic markers.

Elsewhere (Bricklin, 2007), I have detailed how James took special notice of the various lengths of felt durations for the same content; of how the varying speed of the same content of consciousness suggests the varying speed that can be applied to the discrete static frames of film, and of how more than one neuroscientist has suggested that 'we may find movies convincing precisely because we ourselves break up time and reality much as a movie camera does, into discrete frames, which we then reassemble into an apparently continuous flow' (Sacks, 2004). James at first rejected *discrete* sequencing in devising a metaphor for consciousness, such as the links of a 'chain' and a 'train', and settled on his linkless 'stream' (James, 1890, p. 233), a continuum, in which, as in all continua, 'its parts appear as immediate next neighbors, with absolutely nothing between' (James, 1911, p. 1077). This same rejection of discrete sequencing is found in his later writings as well. Reflecting on the failure of the kinetoscopic camera to completely close the gap between 'next neighbors' he concluded: 'you

---

[9] James himself does not complete the symmetry, since his elaboration of the distant past is in his chapter on memory. But the symmetry is explicitly emphasized in his chapter on time, where he notes how we date things by 'mentally tossing them into the past or future *direction*' (James, 1890, p. 594).

cannot make continuous being out of discontinuities' (James, 1909b, p. 736).

But James did not have to wait for the seamless flow of today's cinema to change his mind about the potential of discrete moments to 'make continuous being'. He was always ambivalent. In the *Principles*, where he had passed over the links of a chain in favour of a seamless stream, he had also claimed as indisputable Hodgson's dictum that 'the chain of consciousness is a sequence of *differents*' (James, 1890, p. 224). And even Hodgson's 'retrospective' and 'prospective' sub-feelings that make up the prototype of all duration — the specious present — do not, James believed, flow into each other, but are experienced together as a discrete moment. The 'immediately and incessantly sensible' temporal 'prototype' is not itself a duration-flow, but a 'duration-block' (*ibid.*, p. 574):

> We do not first feel one and then feel the other after it, and from the perception of the succession infer an interval of time between, but we seem to feel the interval of time *as a whole* with its two ends *embedded* in it. (*ibid.*)

Moreover, the discontinuities that disqualified the kinetoscope from representing the stream of consciousness, James himself found in the stream in the only introspection into his thought process that he appraised as meditation (*ibid.*, p. 1133).[10] Discretely constituted cinema, unlike a continuous stream, encompasses the gap between thoughts that James and other introspective psychologists, such as Karl Marbe (see Bricklin, 1999, p. 81), glimpsed, and meditation reveals.[11] And in his last years, devoted not to psychology but philosophy, responding to, or perhaps even 'fearing' (Gale, 1999, p. 290) Zeno's critique of a continuum as illogical, James openly embraced discrete sequencing:

> All our sensible experiences, as we get them immediately… change by discrete pulses of perception, each of which keeps us saying 'more, more, more', or 'less, less, less', as the definite increments or diminutions make themselves felt… They come to us in drops. Time itself comes in drops. (James, 1911, p. 734)

---

[10] The discontinuity was found in his 'meditating on the phenomenon' of free will, that seemed to him to 'contain in miniature form the data for an entire psychology of volition' (James, 1890, p. 1133).

[11] According to Krishnamurti, it is only the speed of thought that disguises this discontinuity or gap (Krishnamurti, 1954, p. 226), called 'bardo' by the Tibetans — the same word used for the gap between incarnations (Ray, 2001, pp. 330, 333). (See Bricklin, 2007, for an extended discussion of this gap.)

James's flight from a continuum-based reality paralleled the quantum revolution in physics of his day. A few years before James had rendered his stream of consciousness into drops, both heat energy and light had been revealed to be discrete pulses, rather than the continua they appeared as. 'The energy of a beam of light emanating from a certain point', wrote Einstein, in the discovery that launched the quantum revolution (Gribbin, 2002, p. 511), 'is not distributed continuously in an ever increasing volume, but is made up of a finite number of indivisible quanta of energy that are absorbed or emitted only as wholes' (*ibid.*).[12]

As he had done with the discrete frames of the kinetoscope, James might have emphasized that such discrete moments could never explain 'life... in its original coming' (James, 1909b, p. 736). But some late-life experiences with pulsing images, 'mystical in the highest degree', left him wondering whether the world was truly a world of happenings and becomings after all (James, 1910a, p.1279).

2. James's Mystical Suggestion

> 'The falling of the barriers say that there is the dual process... the hemming in, the partitioning off, the localizing, the selfing. All that is one process. Now reverse it and say the escape, the unifying, the delocalization of the soul that is nearer. Get the thought clear testifying to the existence of a whole...' Mrs. Willett, the wife of Frederic Myers' brother-in-law, and one of Lawrence LeShan's 'serious clairvoyants'. (LeShan, 1974, p. 35)[13]

In 1905, Einstein published his 'Theory of Special Relativity'; two years later, Minkowski derived the concept of space-time from it. James was not aware of the space-time revolution in physics underway[14] that culminated in 1916 with the publication of Einstein's 'General Theory of Relativity', which formally introduced time as a 'fourth dimension'; but in his 1910 essay, 'A Suggestion About Mysticism',

---

[12] The quantum revolution, which has now evolved into an uneasy co-orthodoxy with relativity, is still, like James, respectful of Zeno (see Mazur, 2007).

[13] 'A serious clairvoyant is an individual who has been shown over a period of years of intensive study to be able, under strictest laboratory conditions, to acquire information from other than known channels and about whom there has never been the slightest evidence of chicanery. Typical among these are Mrs. Piper, Mrs. Willett, and Eileen Garrett' (LeShan, 1974, p. 260).

[14] Though the year after he died, Bergson and Einstein publicly debated timeflow.

James promoted its most radical conclusion: the objective world simply *is* rather than *happens*.[15]

Four separate experiences that seemed to 'consist... in the uncovering of tracts of *consciousness*' and/or 'reality' (James, 1910a, pp. 1279, 1280) prompted James to ask 'Is... consciousness already there waiting to be uncovered?' (*ibid.*, p. 1280). James called these experiences a 'mystical paroxysm' (*ibid.*, p. 1273), and characterized them as 'very sudden and incomprehensible enlargements of the conscious field, bringing with them a curious sense of cognition of real fact' (*ibid.*, p. 1274). Three of the paroxysms 'broke in abruptly upon a perfectly commonplace situation', such as while he was engaged in conversation (*ibid.*). With his characteristic mastery of language, James found words at the very edge of the ineffable to describe them:

> What happened each time was that I seemed all at once to be reminded of a past experience; and this reminiscence, ere I could conceive or name it distinctly, developed into something further that belonged with it, this in turn into something further still, and so on, until the process faded out, leaving me amazed at the sudden vision of increasing ranges of distant fact of which I could give no articulate account. The mode of consciousness was perceptual, not conceptual — the field expanding so fast that there seemed no time for conception or identification to get in its work. There was a strongly exciting sense that my knowledge of past (or present?) reality was enlarging pulse by pulse, but so rapidly that my intellectual processes could not keep up the pace. The content was thus entirely lost to retrospection — it sank into the limbo into which dreams vanish as we gradually awake. The feeling — I won't call it belief — that I had a sudden opening, had seen through a window, as it were, distant realities that incomprehensibly belonged with my own life, was so acute that I can not shake it off to-day. (*ibid.*, pp. 1274–1275)

James compared this process of 'uncovering tracts of consciousness' to how our vision appears to uncover tracts of 'objects', the field range expanding instantaneously with the 'slightest movement of the eye', realizing what '*always stood there to be known*' (*ibid.*, p. 1274). Although he 'prefer[ed] not to set any definite bonds' to the 'extent' of such a 'transmarginal' field (*ibid.*, p. 1273), and only at the end, as we shall see, introduced the future into its extent, such a field would clearly account for the conversions of vast temporal successions into space-like simultaneities, whether it be the retrospective 'single flash' time-collapse of Bigelow's near-death experiences, or Mozart's

---

[15] In Herman Weyl's formulation of Einstein's theory of relativity: 'The objective world simply is, it does not happen. Only to the gaze of my consciousness, crawling upward along the life line of my body, does a section of this world come to life as a fleeting image in space which continuously changes in time' (Weyl, 1963, p. 116).

prospective time-collapse, cited by James in the *Principles* (James, 1890, p. 255), of how he composes a sonata, bits and pieces coming together in his mind until

> ...at last it gets almost finished in my head, even when it is a long piece, so that I can see the whole of it at a single glance in my mind, as if it were a beautiful painting or a handsome human being; in which way I do not hear it in my imagination at all as a succession — the way it must come later — but all at once, as it were. It is a rare feast! All the inventing and making goes on in me as in a beautiful strong dream. But the best of all is the *hearing of it all at once*. (James, 1890)

The active process of this uncovering, whether retrospective or prospective, is less like James's caricature of an iron block universe,[16] and more like the Tantric Yoga dance of Shiva and Shakti: with 'Shiva... described as the unchangeable static aspect of great consciousness, while Shakti represents the dynamic, active side of the same consciousness' (Hinze, 1979, p. 36). James's greatest protégé, Santayana, wrote what could be taken as a gloss on this dynamism inherent in James's mystical suggestion: Even if 'the realm of truth is indeed eternal and static', there must be something akin to an 'exploring spirit... that may traverse [or uncover] it by one or another narrow path in a thousand directions without adding, removing, or changing a single feature of that indestructible labyrinth' (Santayana, 1930, p. 75). 'Flux', writes Santayana, is not 'abolished' by this 'hypothesis',

> ...but only transferred from the panorama of facts to the living spirit which, in gradually discovering them, would be really passing through a succession of different states. (*ibid.*)

Since James's 'panorama of facts' pre-exists any *given* 'passing through... succession', its uncovering in any moment can run the gamut from all-at-once-inclusiveness, like an omniscient centrepoint of a sphere accessing all its radial endpoints,[17] to a linear temporal landscape, kept in line by an 'I' defining what comes before and after *its* centrepoint, a point between past and future. The first is the

---

[16] 'The future has no ambiguous possibilities hidden in its womb: the part we call the present is compatible with only one totality. Any other future complement than the one fixed from eternity is impossible. The whole is in each and every part, and welds it with the rest into an absolute unity, an iron block, in which there can be no equivocation or shadow of turning' (James, 1897, p. 570).

[17] Although James the pluralist insisted that 'there is nowhere extant a *complete* gathering up of the universe in *one* focus... *Something* escapes, even from God' (Skrupskelis and Berkeley, 2004, p. 407), the year before he published 'A Suggestion About Mysticism' James pondered whether '[e]very bit of us at every moment is part and parcel of... some more really central self in things which is co-conscious with the whole of us?' and 'quivers along various radii like the wind-rose on a compass' (James, 1909b, p. 762).

perspective of what James's beloved friend and foremost adversary, Royce, called the eternal Absolute; the second, the perspective of everyday experience that Royce called the 'perfectly arbitrary limitation of our own special type of consciousness' (Royce, 1920, p. 142). James's mystical paroxysms fell somewhere in between these two perspectives, with 'certain special directions only... in the field of reality getting "suddenly uncovered"' (James, 1910a, p. 1275), rather than either the unilinear direction of commonsense, or the 'whole of reality uncovered... at once' of 'classical mystical experiences' (*ibid.*). This in-between state was especially evident in his fourth experience, which came to him as he was awakening from dreams:

> I awoke suddenly from my first sleep, which appeared to have been very heavy, in the middle of a dream, in thinking of which I became suddenly confused by the contents of two other dreams that shuffled themselves abruptly in between the parts of the first dream, and of which I couldn't grasp the origin. Whence come *these dreams?* I asked. They were close to *me*, and fresh, as if I had just dreamed them; and yet they were far away from the first dream. The contents of the three had absolutely no connection. One had a cockney atmosphere, it had happened to someone in London. The other two were American. One involved the trying on of a coat (was this the dream I seemed to wake from?) the other was a sort of nightmare and had to do with soldiers. (James, 1910a, p. 1276)

Because each dream had a 'wholly distinct emotional atmosphere', with a 'discontinuous' 'individuality', that 'repelled' each other, the different dream scenarios were not experienced as a surreal assemblage in one dream, or successive dreams within dreams,[18] but rather each was experienced as its own 'dream-system' (*ibid.*). 'Alternately telescoped into and out of each other' (*ibid.*), the three dream-systems did not connect to each other or to James's waking life. He felt himself to be their 'common dreamer' and yet 'quite as distinctly', he felt them '*not to have been dreamed in succession, in that one sleep*' (*ibid.*, emphasis added).

James considered 'the distressing confusion of mind' in his experience to be 'the exact opposite of mystical illumination' (*ibid.*, p. 1278) and thought of several alternative explanations, indeed, diagnoses — 'am I getting into other people's dreams? Is this a "telepathic" experience? Or an invasion of double (or treble) personality? Or is it a thrombus in a cortical artery? and the beginning of a general mental "confusion" and disorientation which is going on to develop who knows how far?' (*ibid.*, pp. 1276–1277) — before accepting that he

---

[18] See Krippner (2002, pp. 77–82).

might well have just received the profoundest mystical insight of his life:

> ...the exaltation of the sense of relation was mystical (the perplexity all revolved around the fact that the three dreams *both did and did not belong in the most intimate way together*), and the sense that *reality was being uncovered* was mystical in the highest degree. To this day I feel that those extra dreams were dreamed in reality, but when, where, and by whom, I cannot guess. (*ibid.*, p. 1279)

James's sense of such sequence confusion, with its radical 'de-localizing'[19] and de-selfing, a mystical-in-the-highest-degree 'reality being *un*covered', is consistent with his belief, as we said, that reality as ordinarily experienced is covered by, '*wears the form of*', time (James, 1904b, p. 1169). 'All felt times', James wrote, 'co-exist and overlap or compenetrate each other... vaguely'. By 'the *artifice* of plotting them on a... conceptual time-scale' 'cut into numbered instants', 'aboriginal confusion' is replaced by the '*notion* of one objective and "evenly flowing" time' (James, 1909, p. 734, emphasis added). In these dreams of 'aboriginal confusion' that artifice failed.

James's young contemporary Einstein, already in James's lifetime on the verge of becoming the world's foremost revelationist of veridical reality, shared his view that 'evenly flowing' linear time was just an artifice, however 'natural' such artifice appears (Einstein, 1961, p. 150). Beyond our common-sense notion of reality — what he termed the '*evolution* of a three-dimensional existence' — Einstein championed the 'more natural', pre-existing reality of space-time (*ibid.*). As one of his ablest disciples, de Broglie, put it:

> In Space-time everything which for each of us constitutes the past, the present and the future is given in block, and the entire collection of events, successive for each one of us, which form the existence of a material particle... each observer, as his time passes, discovers, so to speak, new slices of Space-time which appear to him as successive aspects of the material world, though in reality the ensemble of events constituting Space-time exist prior to his knowledge of them. (de Broglie, cited in Schlipp, 1959, p. 114)

Like precognition,[20] James's mystical dreams, 'the most intensely peculiar experience of my whole life' (James, 1910a, p. 1275), seemed to have tapped into (or 'uncovered') the more encompassing existence

---

[19] In Mrs. Willett's word.

[20] James did not interchange mystical and psychical. While he allowed that mystical states were states in which 'the mind ascend[s] to a more enveloping point of view' (James, 1902, pp. 385ff), he held that their hallmark was 'ineffability' (*ibid.*, p. 343 and ff.). Along with the 'distressing confusion of mind' (James, 1910a, p. 1278), he thought the

of pre-existing space-time reality. In those dreams, an 'immense spreading of the margin of the field [of consciousness]' (*ibid.*, p. 1270), James lost his 'hold' on his sense of 'self', a 'sinking, giddying anxiety that one may have when, in the woods, one discovers that one is really "lost"' (*ibid.*, p. 1277). Although he felt himself to be the common dreamer of the 'extra' dreams, those dreams did not, as he put it, '*attach*' to his sense of 'when', 'where' and 'by whom' (*ibid.*, pp. 1277–1279). James had lost, in other words, what Einstein called the 'reference body' (Einstein, 1961, p. 26) around which successive, linear perspective is constructed. The deeper, or 'veridical', reality of a universe where consciousness was already there waiting to be uncovered was not accessible to the relative centre that is self, but only when 'all was diffusion from [that]… center, and foothold swept away, the brace itself disintegrating' (James, 1910a, pp. 1277, 1280). Beyond the narrow field of consciousness-arrayed-around-a-reference-body-self was a 'transmarginal panorama' where 'vast tracts usually covered are… revealed to view' (*ibid.*, pp. 1272–1274). In so far as James was perplexed and disturbed by his dreams, he was as if caught between two worlds: one, the ordinarily-experienced world of a fixed self in a 'gradually changing present'; the other, a 'suddenly revealed' world beyond the boundary of self, a world of 'tremendous *muchness*', revealing what 'always stood there to be known' (*ibid.*, p. 1274).

3. A Suggestion From the Anaesthetic Revelation

> Your thought is obscure — lightning flashes, darting gleams — but that's the way truth is… Life and mysticism exceed the articulable, and if there is a *One*, (and surely men will never be weaned from the idea of it) it must remain mystically expressed. (James, in a letter to Benjamin Paul Blood; Skrupskelis and Berkeley, 2000, p. 263)

To fortify his mystical suggestion of consciousness already there waiting to be uncovered, James introduced the ether experience of one of his correspondents, Frederic Hall (James, 1910a, p. 1279). Ether, we now know, rising up naturally through a fault in the earth, was the secret of Delphi, the agency of the Oracle's trance, in which the future appeared to be accessed.[21] James himself held that the 'artificial mys-

---

'definiteness of what was perceived' in his own 'mystical paroxysm' as 'unmystical'. But his overall sense of the experience was mystical, as well as his subsequent suggestion of its source.

[21] See Fontenrose (1978) for a critique of the authenticity of reported Delphic visions of the future, and Broad (2006) for the compelling case to be made for some of them.

tic state of mind' induced by nitrous oxide and ether[22] had 'metaphysical significance' (James, 1902, p. 350). In the *Principles*, he relates two of his own such metaphysically significant experiences.[23] In the first, as he came-to, he felt himself awakening to a sense of his own existence as 'something additional to what had previously been there' (James, 1890, p. 264), an experience that formed part of his foundational challenge to the commonly held notion that thought, in knowing, must 'discriminate between its object and itself' (*ibid.*, p. 265). In the second, as he went into anaesthesia, it was his relationship with objects that was transformed, with all the objects in the room receding, shrinking away into the distance (*ibid.*, p. 785). James believed that these and other commonly experienced transpersonal effects of anaesthetic drugs 'forbid a premature closing of our accounts with reality' (James, 1902, p. 349). By invoking Hall's mystical ether experience, James was forbidding a premature closing of his mystical paroxysm as some form of psychosis, and linking it with what had remained for him an unshakable truth of the anaesthetic revelation (*ibid.*, p. 349):

> Our normal waking consciousness, rational consciousness, is but one special type of consciousness, while all about it, parted from it by the filmiest of screens, there are potential forms of consciousness entirely different. (*ibid.*)

Doctors surrounding the etherized Hall, talking amongst themselves, believed that they were generating their own thoughts in the ongoing present. But Hall, observing from what he experienced as a privileged and far more comprehensive view, a view beyond linear time, believed otherwise:

> The knowledge of how little [the doctors] actually did see, coupled with their evident feeling that they saw all there was, was funny to the last degree... [They] knew as little of the real causes as does the child who, viewing a passing train and noting its revolving wheels, supposes that they, turning of themselves, give to coaches and locomotive their momentum. Or imagine a man seated in a boat, surrounded by dense fog, and out of the fog seeing a flat stone leap from the crest of one wave to another. *If he had always sat thus*, his explanations must be very crude as compared with those of a man whose eyes could pierce fog, and who saw upon the shore the boy skipping stones. In some such way the remarks of the two physicians seemed to me like the last two 'skips' of a

---

[22] Due to its asphyxial properties, nitrous oxide was not considered safe until it was mixed with oxygen. But once mixed, its effects appeared to be the same as ether, both in its 'initial sensations' and in the 'main features' of deep anaesthetics (Hewitt, 1901, p. 71).

[23] Both were 'chloriformisations', an anaesthetic frequently mixed with ether.

stone thrown from my side. All that was essential in the remark *I knew before it was made*. Thus to discover convincingly and for myself, that the things which are unseen are those of real importance, this was sufficiently stimulating. (James, 1910a, p. 1279, second emphasis added)

Hall's 'ether-mysticism', said James, 'agrees with my formula [of consciousness and/or reality being uncovered] very well' (*ibid.*). It also agreed with the 'tremendously exciting sense of an intense metaphysical illumination' that James claimed as the 'keynote' experience for himself and others experimenting with ether and nitrous oxide (James, 1897, p. 676), the uncovering of a pre-existing relatedness behind the apparent many:

> Truth lies open to the view in depth beneath depth of almost blinding evidence. The mind sees all logical relations of being with an apparent subtlety and instantaneity to which its normal consciousness offers no parallel; only as sobriety returns, the feeling of insight fades, and one is left staring vacantly at a few disjointed words and phrases, as one stares at a cadaverous-looking snowpeak from which sunset glow has just fled, or at a black cinder left by an extinguished brand. (*ibid.*)

Likewise, there was the ether experience of Nobel chemist Sir William Ramsay, published in the *Proceedings of the Society for Psychical Research*, and cited in a letter to James by Benjamin Paul Blood (Skrupskelis and Berkeley, 2004, p. 104). Blood first introduced James to the metaphysical significance of nitrous oxide and became a kind of mystical coach to him, a debt James repaid in his last published essay (James, 1909b), devoted exclusively to Blood's writings. In the article that Blood brought to James's attention, Ramsay echoed James's instantaneous seeing of 'all logical relations of being' by claiming 'one little piece of enormous coherence' for his experience, a coherence in which everything was revealed as 'having been always there' (Ramsay, 1894, p. 240).

In proposing his own having-been-always-there eternalism in 'A Suggestion About Mysticism', the antepenultimate essay published in his lifetime, James was accessing what he had once characterized as 'the password primeval' to a 'mystical region' that 'finds its support in a "hear, hear!" or an "amen," which floats up from that mysteriously deeper level', passwords 'we recognize' but 'cannot use ourselves' (James, 1902, p. 381). But in his last published essay, 'A Pluralistic Mystic', James returned from 'that mysteriously deeper level', bringing, or attempting to bring, his mystical coach up with him. Early in his career, James had read Blood's drug-induced passwords to the mystical region, which, he said, 'fascinated me... so "weirdly" that I am conscious of its having been one of the stepping-stones of my thinking ever since' (James, 1909b, p. 1295). But however much he came to believe that the 'metaphysical revelation' of drug-induced trances from nitrous oxide was 'genuine' (James, 1902, p. 349), James always tried to set limits to this revelation, from his first youthful public response to Blood's writing, to his near-deathbed tribute ('A Pluralistic Mystic').

In his first comment, a book review of Blood's *The Anaesthetic Revelation* published in the *Atlantic Monthly* in 1874, less than five years after his conversion to free will, James proselytized:

> What blunts the mind and weakens the will is no full channel for truth, even if it assist us to a view of a certain aspect of it... the faith that comes of willing, the intoxication of moral volition, has a million times better credentials. (James, 1987, p. 287)

Blood's response to that salvo was not to appear until after his own death, in a posthumous work titled *Pluriverse*, published in 1920, deliberately evoking James's essay title, but repudiating 'the conceit of originality' that James had ascribed to pluralism (Blood, 1920, p. 241). To James's 'ear' Blood's later writings had 'a radically pluralistic sound' (James, 1910b, p. 1295), suggesting to him that '[m]onism can no longer claim to be the only beneficiary of whatever right mysticism may possess to lend prestige' (*ibid.*). But however pluralistic it may have sounded to James, Blood's pluralism was a celebration of the 'wild-game-flavored' Many (Blood, quoted by James, 1910b, p. 1312), not an overthrow of the One. 'The One remains, the many change and pass', wrote Blood, quoting Shelley,[24] and then added: 'and every one of us is the One that remains' (Blood, quoted by James, 1910b, p. 1303). *Pluriverse* does deny that the universe can be known as 'an independent Whole and one, a totality within its own comprehension' (Blood, 1920, p. 82), but it also denies the ultimate condition for pluralism in James's sense of the word — novelty.[25] Not only does *Pluriverse* deny originality and novelty to its parts, it denies the novelty that James cared about most — free will. Blood had no problem accommodating 'the thoroughgoing causal integration' that James himself had associated with ether revelation (James, 1910a, p. 1279).

---

[24] From Shelley's poem *Adonais*, the last two lines of which James quoted in support of his timemask proposal (James, 1898, p. 1110). The whole stanza is as follows:
The One remains, the Many change and pass;
Heaven's light for ever shines, Earth's shadows fly;
Life, like a dome of many-colored glass,
Stains the white radiance of Eternity.

[25] 'Towards the... reality or unreality of novelty... the pragmatic difference between monism and pluralism seems to converge' (James, 1911, p. 1055).

Indeed, *Pluriverse* contains one of the strongest attacks on free will in Western literature (Blood, 1920, pp. 182–203).[26]

While James read much into Blood's disparagement of 'ultimate purpose' (James, 1910b, p. 1304) and his concordant belief that '[t]hought evolves no longer a centered whole, a One, but rather a numberless many, adjust it how we will' (*ibid.*), and saw in Blood a fellow crusader against the excesses of monism, 'a sort of "left-wing" voice of defiance' (*ibid.*, p. 1295), Blood was hardly the 'man converted from one faith to its opposite' that James suggested (*ibid.*, p. 1304), or the 'pluralistic mystic' in the sense that James understood pluralism. Blood's anaesthetic revelation was, above all else, a revelation of timeless *being*, not becoming.[27] Like Parmenides, a central figure in *Pluriverse*, Blood concluded '*it is everything to be*' (Blood, 1920, p. 244). Confirming Parmenides' revelation that generation or destruction is no part of that being which is 'everything', Blood had found (and had told James that he had found) 'much confirmation' in Ramsay's ether experience of timeless being (Skrupskelis and Berkeley, 2004, p. 104). Highlighting this experience in *Pluriverse*, Blood quotes Ramsay: 'Everything... the table, mantel, etc., having been *always* there' (Blood, 1920, p. 220). And just as the Zen monk Han Shan found verification of enlightenment in a briefly experienced transformation of becoming into being, losing 'the perception of anything in motion' (Lu, 1971, p. 77), so, too, Blood, in describing the essence of the Anaesthetic Revelation to James, told him: '*I always get a hint of the mystery when the clock stops of itself*' (Perry, 1935, p. 227).

Just after James died, Blood published a memorial essay claiming that the 'insight of the anaesthetic revelation' was, for James, 'the secret of the world' (Blood, 1910). And although James worried that Blood's anaesthetic dialectic between the one (that remains) and the many (that change and pass) might be 'too pure for me to catch' (James, 1909b, p.1304), his veridical revelation had caught it exactly.

---

[26] Concluding with this quote from Meister Eckhart: 'All error and depravity come from God's creatures presuming to be or do something on their own account' (Blood, 1920, p. 203). Blood's first book was entitled *Optimism: The Lesson of the Ages. A Compendium of Democratic Theology, Designed To Illustrate Necessities Whereby All Things Are As They Are, And To Reconcile The Discontents Of Men With The Perfect Love and Power of Ever-Present God* (See Blood, 1860).

[27] In James's first draft, he correctly identified Blood's Parmenidean manifesto — 'There is no reason for what is not; but for what there is reason, that *is* and ever was' (Blood, quoted by James, 1910b, p. 1301) — as 'timeless' (Burkhardt *et al.*, 1978, p. 308); but apparently James could not tolerate the dissonance with what he admitted to be his *pro domo mea* ('for my house') version of Blood (James, 1910b, p. 1296), and changed 'timeless' to 'vibrant' (Burkhardt *et al.*, 1978, p. 308).

'Consciousness already there waiting to be uncovered' is but a restatement of what James had quoted as the anaesthetic revelation's 'real secret':

> ...the formula by which the 'now' keeps exfoliating out of itself, yet never escapes... The truth is that we travel on a journey that was accomplished before we set out. (Xenos Clark,[28] quoted by James, 1902, p. 350)

4. Psychical Research

...the present condition of opinion regarding [psychical research] is scandalous, there being a mass of testimony, or apparent testimony, about such things, at which the only men capable of a critical judgment — men of scientific education — will not even look. (James, 1886 letter to the philosopher Carl Stumpf, James, 1920, p. 248)

Given that James — the would-be catatonic — was 'primarily concerned' to promote a 'world... still in the process of making', rather than 'an "eternal" edition of it ready-made and complete' (James, 1909a, p. 940), it is little wonder that he would not connect the dots between the 'most intensely peculiar experience of [his] whole life' and his intensely peculiar psychical research. But just the year before, in much the same language as 'A Suggestion About Mysticism', James proclaimed that psychical research had also pointed to a 'continuum of cosmic consciousness' in which all minds are merged or 'plunged' (James, 1909c, p. 1264). And clearly 'always stood there to be known' accounts for the most baffling phenomena investigated by James and his colleagues in psychical research:[29] precognition, and its 'partial mirror image' retrocognition (Barrington *et al.*, 2005, p.131), the seeing of a *past* event in eerily accurate, vivid detail, that cannot be explained either as one's own recovered memory or telepathic access to the memory of another.[30]

James was impressed by such 'records of "supernormal seership"' that the *Society of Psychical Research* had amassed 'of various types and grades' (James, 1907a, p. 243), and found the scientific community's outright rejection of them 'absurd' (*ibid.*). He wrote the intro-

---

[28] Blood's co-anaesthetic-revelationist.

[29] James was an active member of the British *Society for Psychical Research* and a founder and President of its American offspring, still active today.

[30] For the ancient Greeks, as E.R. Dodds has pointed out, divination (*mantike*), referred to both precognition *and* retrocognition, the 'typical diviner' being Homer's Kalchas, 'who knew things past, present, and to come' (Dodds, 1973, p. 160). Indeed, says Dodds, the most celebrated seers would 'sometimes exhibit supernormal knowledge of past events as evidence that their vision of the future will prove true. The implied assumption is that retrocognition and precognition are manifestations of the same power'(*ibid.*).

duction for Myers' magnus opus, *Human Personality and its Survival of Bodily Death*, which included compelling accounts of precognition such as the following by John George Haggard, a nineteenth-century British Consul in Trieste, Austria, that was investigated by the *Society for Psychical Research*:

> A few months ago I had an extraordinarily vivid dream, and waking up repeated it to my wife at once. All I dreamt actually occurred about six weeks afterwards, the details of my dream falling out exactly. There seems to have been no purpose whatsoever in the dream; and one cannot help thinking, what was the good of it? I dreamt that I was asked to dinner by the German Consul-General, and accepting, was ushered into a large room with trophies of East African arms on shields against the walls. (N.B. — I have myself been a great deal in East Africa.) After dinner I went to inspect the arms, and amongst them saw a beautifully gold-mounted sword which I pointed out to the French Vice-Consul — who at that moment joined me — as having probably been a present from the Sultan of Zanzibar to my host the German Consul-General. At that moment the Russian Consul came up too. He pointed out how small was the hilt of the sword and how impossible in consequence it would be for a European to use the weapon, and whilst talking he waved his arm in an excited manner over his head as if he was wielding the sword, and to illustrate what he was saying. At that moment I woke up and marveled so at the vividness of the dream that I woke my wife up too and told it to her. About six weeks afterwards my wife and myself were asked to dine with the German Consul-General; but the dream had long been forgotten by us both. We were shown into a large withdrawing room which I have never been in before, but which somehow seemed familiar to me. Against the walls were some beautiful trophies of East African arms, amongst which was a gold-hilted sword, a gift to my host from the Sultan of Zanzibar. To make a long story short, everything happened exactly as I had dreamt — but I never remembered the dream until the Russian Consul began to wave his arm over his head, when it came back to me like a flash. Without saying a word to the Russian Consul and French Vice-Consul (whom I left standing before the trophy), I walked quickly across to my wife, who was standing at the entrance of a boudoir opening out of the withdrawing room, and said to her: 'Do you remember my dream about the Zanzibar arms?' She remembered everything perfectly, and was a witness to its realization. On the spot we informed all the persons concerned of the dream, which naturally much interested them. (F. Myers, 1903a, pp. 408–409)

James also contributed to Myers' book a precognitive incident that had been sent to him and that he, Myers, and the dogged sceptical researcher Richard Hodgson had investigated: a highly detailed scene dreamed by a mother of her son's death (F. Myers, 1903a, pp. 401–406). And James's most thoroughly investigated psychical incident (James, 1907a, pp. 231–245) was a retrocognitive vision by a woman, Mrs. Titus, who, in a trance, so re-inhabited the wintry scene of a woman falling backwards off a bridge into a deep lake below that she shivered with cold, and was later able to point to the exact spot and the exact position of the body at the bottom of the murky waters where a professional diver had already searched. The diver later told the investigators that he was 'stunned' and 'frightened', not by the body, but 'by the woman on the bridge' (*ibid.*, p. 240):

> She located the place where I was to go down; also told me that the body was lying, head in, in a deep hole, with one foot sticking up, with a new rubber. I was down in about 18 feet of water. It was so dark, nobody could see anything down there. (*ibid.*)

Along with his team of researchers, James concluded that the alternative 'naturalistic explanations' did not have 'the least plausibility' (*ibid.*, p. 243). And given that Titus, a New England homemaker who in no way profited from, or even encouraged, the ensuing notoriety, and that, moreover, incidents such as this were painful experiences for her, trickery or fraud was also not plausible. After his investigation (including cross examinations) of the various people involved, James concluded that Titus's apparent witnessing, in precise detail, of a past event that she had not been present for, was a 'supernormal faculty of seership' (*ibid.*).

Precise witnessing of a past event not attended by the witnesser was also the hallmark of the psychic who most impressed James — Leonora Piper, a Boston housewife and mother, who never set up shop to peddle her prowess.[31] On James's first visit, Piper told him specific details of events that had occurred in his house including, earlier that day, 'my killing of a grey-and-white cat, with ether', describing how it had 'spun round and round before dying' (James, 1996, p. 88). Although Piper accessed her information in a trance and apparently as a medium, she never affirmed that her remote information was channelled through spirits (Sage, 1904, pp. 128–130). And as with Titus and other entranced people James had studied, it was Piper's completely unexplainable access to remote facts about people she had

---

[31] For an excellent account of Piper see Blum (2006). This well-researched book serves as a rebuttal of Martin Gardner's highly speculative essay 'How Mrs. Piper Bamboozled William James' (Gardner, 2003, p. 252–262). For a detailed account of Gardner's own bamboozling in his essay, see Prescott (2008). Piper is one of LeShan's 'serious clairvoyants'.

never seen or heard of before that he found most significant,[32] stating it 'deliberately, having practically no doubt whatever of its truth', and 'well aware of all the liabilities to which this statement exposes me' (James, 1983, p. 268).

Whatever Piper's actual source, her own integrity was vouched for by Richard Hodgson, whose 15-year systematic study of her was so encroaching it was tantamount to a house arrest.[33] As impressed as he was baffled, James labelled Piper his 'white crow':

> If you wish to upset the law that all crows are black, you must not seek to show that no crows are; it is enough if you prove one single crow to be white. My own white crow is Mrs. Piper. In the trances of this medium, I cannot resist the conviction that knowledge appears which she has never gained by the ordinary waking use of her eyes and ears and wits. What the source of this knowledge may be I know not, and have not the glimmer of an explanatory suggestion to make; but from admitting the fact of such knowledge I can see no escape. (James, 1897, p. 694)

But a glimmer did come, years later, in his suggestion of 'consciousness already there waiting to be uncovered'.

Master Inference

Right after James declared that 'we shall not understand these alterations of consciousness either in this generation or the next' (James, 1910a, p. 1280), he concluded his essay with a prescription to aid that understanding:

> ...we know so little of the noetic value of abnormal mental states of any kind that in my own opinion we had better keep an open mind and collect facts sympathetically for a long time to come. (*ibid.*)

Absent James's morbid fear of determinism, James's psychical research colleagues, Frederic Myers and Sir Oliver Lodge, were able to derive a more emphatic 'noetic' conclusion than James from the 'abnormal mental states' they researched. Myers, a co-founder of the *Society for Psychical Research*, who urged his colleagues to 'make no terms with any hollow mysticism' (Hamilton, 2009, p. 246), believed that the evidence for precognition made time itself hollow:

---

[32] As opposed to the French school of neurologists investigating trances, led by Janet, who, according to Taylor, ignored the metaphysical implications of accessing this remote transmarginal realm (See Taylor, 1996, p. 46).

[33] Debra Blum, in her recent G*host Hunters: William James and the Search for Scientific Proof of Life After Death* (2006), gives an excellent account of Hodgson's work with Mrs. Piper.

> Few... have pondered long on these problems of Past and Future without wondering whether Past or Future be in very truth more than a name — whether we may not be apprehending as a stream of sequence that which is an ocean of co-existence, and slicing our subjective years and centuries from timeless and absolute things. The precognitions dealt with here, indeed, hardly overpass the life of the individual percipient. Let us keep to that small span, and let us imagine that a whole earth-life is in reality an absolutely instantaneous although an infinitely complex phenomenon. Let us suppose that my transcendental self discerns with equal directness and immediacy every element of this phenomenon; but that my empirical self receives each element immediately and through media involving different rates of retardation; just as I receive the lightning more quickly than the thunder. May not then seventy years intervene between my perceptions of birth and death as easily as seven seconds between my perceptions of the flash and peal? And may not some inter-communication of consciousness enable the wider self to call to the narrower, the more central to the more external, 'At such an hour this shock will reach you! Listen for the nearing roar!' (F. Myers, 1903b, p. 273)

Lodge, a distinguished inventor and physicist, and one of the pioneers of wireless radio, quoted this passage in his own book defending precognition (Lodge, 1900, pp. 163–164), or what he termed 'prevision' (*ibid.*, p. 155). He also had rigorously tested James's 'white crow', Leonora Piper, in his home in England, and was astounded at her ability to access precise, minute details of his uncles' distant past, known only to his uncles living far away and who later corroborated them.[34] Soon after those tests, he became the first scientist to propose the absolute relativity of time — the same absolute relativity that Einstein's beloved colleague Gödel (among others) would propose as the logical interpretation of Einstein's theory (see Yourgrau, 2006), and that Einstein himself espoused late in life as an article of faith consistent with his theory: 'For us believing physicists, the separation between past, present, and future is only an illusion, even if a stubborn one' (Hoffmann, 1973, p. 254). In 1891, the year that the 12-year-old Einstein was given his first geometry book, Lodge became the first such 'believing physicist':

> A luminous and helpful idea is that time is but a relative mode of regarding things; we progress through phenomena at a certain definitive pace, and this subjective advance we interpret in an objective manner, as if events moved necessarily in this order and at this precise rate. But that may be only our mode of regarding them. The events may be in some sense in existence always, both past and future, and it may be we who are arriving at them, not they which are happening. The analogy of a

---

[34] For an excellent account of Lodge's psychical research, see Blum (2006).

> traveler in a railway train is useful; if he could never leave the train nor alter its pace, he would probably consider the landscapes as necessarily successive and be unable to conceive their coexistence.
>
> The analogy of a solid cut into sections is closer. We recognize the universe in sections, and each section we call the present. It is like the string of slices cut by a microtome; it is our way of studying the whole. But we may err in supposing that the body only exists in the slices which pass before our microscope in regular order and succession.
>
> We perceive, therefore, a possible fourth dimensional aspect about time, the inexorableness of whose flow may be a natural part of our present limitations... (Lodge, 1891, p. 554)

This 'luminous and helpful idea' is not so much a theory as a master inference, the same inference as Royce's Absolute or 'Eternal Consciousness':

> ...the events of the temporal order... are divided, with reference to the point of view of any finite Self, into what *now* is, and what *no longer* is, and what *is to be*, but is *not yet*. These same events, however, in so far as they are viewed at once by the Absolute, are for such view, all equally present. (Royce, 1920, p. 141)

James perpetually tried to 'overthrow' this Absolute — 'the centre of my gaze, the pole of my mental magnet' (Skrupskelis and Berkeley, 2001, p. 320) and, as a tentative response to his most profound mystical experience, his own.

5. 'The Witness'

In India, a civilization that has for millennia kept an open mind about all aspects of consciousness, including 'abnormal mental states', the inference of consciousness being uncovered as in a field that stood there always to be known can be found in the seminal Advaita Vedanta concept *saksin*: a word which means both witness and field.[35] Many Indian sages, such as Jnaneshwar Maharaj, have affirmed this 'single most important postulate... of revelation... in experience' (Singh, 1997, p. 1379), the witness/consciousness/field, as the only reality, consciousness uncovering itself:

> The appearance is seen, to be sure;
> But the appearance is in fact
> Nothing but the seer.
> How can something else
> That does not exist be seen. (Jnaneshwar, 1979, p. 57)

---

[35] In his essay 'The Concept of Saksin in Advaita Vedanta', Andrew Fort 'differentiates two conceptions of saksin: saksin as witness, an eternal, passive observer, and saksin as field, the context or "space" for all contents or form' (Fort, 1984).

James handwrote 'the Witness' next to the word 'sciousness', his word for consciousness without consciousness of self, in his own copy of *The Principles of Psychology* (Burkhardt, 1981, p. 1149). He had learned of the prime reality of 'the Witness' from a western metaphysician (E.D. Fawcett) deeply influenced by Vedantic thought (*ibid.*). Like *saksin*, not knowable because it is 'the element of awareness in all knowing' (Singh, 1997, p. 1379), sciousness is the prime reality of a knowing and witnessing, prior to the distinction of a knowable subject and object (Bricklin, 2003). Speculatively in the *Principles*, but decisively in his essays on radical empiricism (Bricklin, 2007), James saw 'prime reality' not as an objectified world appearing to a subject self, but as a 'monism' of 'pure experiences', a stream of sciousness, 'thinking objects of some of which it makes what it calls a "Me", and only aware of its "pure" Self in an abstract, hypothetic or conceptual way' (James, 1890, p. 291). These pure experiences 'exist and succeed one another', 'enter into infinitely varied relations' (James, 1905, p. 62), and 'throw the question of *who the knower really is* wide open...' (James, 1892, p. 467).

Famously declaiming that the 'the passing Thought[36] itself is the only *verifiable* thinker' (James, 1890, p. 328) and dismissing the notion of 'the closed individuality of each personal consciousness', of 'being-an-individual in some inaccessible metaphysical way' (*ibid.*, p. 331), James deconstructed the self (see Bricklin, 2003), claiming, in part, that the 'word "I" is *primarily* a 'noun of position, just like "this" and "here"' (James, 1909b, p. 803n). In *The Principles*,[37] he recorded a friend's 'hasheesh-delirium' that revealed just how 'infinitely varied' a monism of 'pure experiences' could be, freed from the ordinary constraints of a subject 'here' experiencing objects 'there':

> Any animal or thing that I thought of could be made the being which held my mind. I thought of a fox, and instantly I was transformed into that animal. I could distinctly feel myself a fox, could see my long ears and bushy tail, and by a sort of introvision felt that my complete anatomy was that of a fox. Suddenly the point of vision changed. My eyes seemed to be located at the back of my mouth; I looked out between the parted lips, saw the two rows of pointed teeth, and, closing my mouth with a snap, saw — nothing. I was next transformed into a bombshell, felt my size, weight, and thickness, and experienced the sensation of being shot up out of a giant mortar, looking down upon the earth, bursting and falling back in a shower of iron fragments.
>
> Into countless other objects was I transformed, many of them so

---

[36] Capitalized by James to mean 'the present mental state'.

[37] Before he had elaborated the monism of pure experience.

absurd that I am unable to conceive what suggested them. For example, I was a little china doll, deep down in a bottle of olive oil, next moment a stick of twisted candy, then a skeleton inclosed in a whirling coffin, and so on ad infinitum. (James, 1890, p. 765)

That consciousness can transcend the 'this' and 'here' *positioning* body/self 'I' (flesh or astral) was made clear to Krishnamurti, as well, in *his* mystical paroxysm:

> On the first day, while I was in that state [of great physical pain] and more conscious of the things around me, I had the... most extraordinary experience. There was a man mending the road; that man was myself; the pickaxe he held was myself; the very stone which he was breaking up was a part of me; the tender blade of grass was my very being, and the tree beside the man was myself. I almost could feel and think like the roadmender, and I could feel the wind passing through the tree, and the little ant on the blade of grass I could feel. The birds, the dust, and the very noise were a part of me. Just then there was a car passing by at some distance; I was the driver, the engine, and the tires; as the car went further away from me, I was going away from myself. I was in everything, or rather everything was in me, inanimate and animate, the mountain, the worm, and all breathing things. (Krishnamurti, in Luytens, 2003, p. 42)

The dispersal of 'I' into a succession of myriad objects, animate and inanimate alike, is less a migration than a dissolution of individuated, body-dependent (flesh or astral) 'I's' into a free-ranging consciousness.[38] Such dissolution is consistent with James's deconstruction of both terms 'soul' and 'I' in *The Principles*,[39] later emphasized in his radical empiricism, and brought to a crescendo in his mystical suggestion, where the prime reality of non-dual witnessing became identified, like *saksin*, with a field, consistent with what he had, in his 'timemask' essay, suggested consciousness might ultimately be: '...not... generated *de novo* [anew] in a vast number of places. It exists already, behind the scenes, coeval with the world' (James, 1898, p.1113).

Cosmic Picture Gallery

We see evidence of change everywhere, but as anyone who has passed back and forth in front of a holographic photo can attest, evidence of

---

[38] Stanislav Grof — another MD, like James, who followed the trail of psychology to the transpersonal — researched and help induce (first with LSD and later with deep breathing exercises) many such states which he called 'holotropic' — that is, 'oriented toward wholeness' and 'transcend[ing] the narrow boundaries of the body ego' (Grof, 2000, p. 2).

[39] James quotes with approval Shadworth Hodgson's maxim about the soul: 'Whatever you are totally ignorant of, assert to be the explanation of everything else' (James, 1890, p. 329).

change is not evidence of generation and destruction. It may be evidence only of a change in perspective. If James's mystical suggestion is indeed a veridical revelation of ultimate reality, and the content of the universe in some sense pre-exists any given manifestation, then the universe may well be some sort of hologram, or what Myers called 'a cosmic picture gallery' (Myers, 1903a, p. 142).[40]

Despite his championing of agency and novelty, James, too, knew that generation, destruction, and becoming are not ultimately verifiable events. The only verifiable 'events', the only events that truly 'happen', are 'transitions and arrivals (or terminations)' (James, 1904b, p. 1170). And his mystical suggestion went further: beyond the illusion of becoming, of generation and destruction, it may well be that consciousness merely uncovers what is, pre-existing, 'ready-made'.

Our everyday concept of generation and destruction requires material objects. Mere ideas, mere perceptions, mere phenomena, even though they flash in and out of view, exist in a timeless realm of non-change since they can recur intact indefinitely. Only material objects, as 'something behind physical phenomena', can be said to be subject to the process of generation and destruction; not only are material objects subject to apparent ravages of time, they are what make the conventional sense of time, as a force to be reckoned with, gotten under control, or submitted to, possible. Indeed, for Einstein the very 'concept of the material object must precede our concept... of time' (Einstein, 1954, p. 141). But what if, as James proposed, in a long tradition stretching from the fifth century[41] through Berkeley's, Hegel's and Bradley's denial of the thing-in-itself, there are no material objects 'behind' phenomena (James, 1890, p. 291)? What *if* the more emphatic proposal James derived from his psychical research, and others, today, continue to derive from their research, is true: 'human experiences, on its material as well as its mental side', are 'only an extract from the larger psycho-physical world' (James, 1896, p. 1264).

Parmenides, who dismissed the reality of conventional time, also dismissed the concept of the material objects that support it. In words echoed by the Eastern traditions of meditation from which he

---

[40] However 'dimly decipherable' (as Lodge put it) this gallery might be (Lodge, 1900, p. 155).

[41] Phyrro: 'We see that a man moves, and that he perishes; how it happens we do not know. We merely object to accepting the unknown substance behind phenomena' (Hicks, 1970, p. 514).

sprang,[42] he declared: 'the same thing exists for both thinking and for being' (Tarán, 1965, p. 44). Like Parmenides, James, too, denied the independence of material objects that is conventional time's essential prop:

> Things and thoughts are not at all fundamentally heterogeneous; they are made of one and the same stuff, stuff which cannot be defined as such but only experienced; and which one can call, if one wishes, the stuff of experience in general. (James, 1905, p. 64)

'Subjects' knowing, 'things' known, are 'roles' played, says James, not 'ontological' facts (*ibid.*). 'Consciousness as it is ordinarily understood does not exist, any more than does Matter' (*ibid.*, p. 63). Consciousness and matter as they are ordinarily understood are created, destroyed, or transformed in time. *Genuine* consciousness, which includes that aspect of consciousness experienced as matter, cannot be created, destroyed, or transformed. The most that it can be is 'uncovered'.

Conclusion

Although most James scholars have ignored his mystical suggestion as if it were a detour into senility,[43] 'consciousness already there waiting to be uncovered' is consistent with his previously expressed views on the relation between consciousness and reality. While a younger James would have viewed this mystical suggestion as a most unattractive, radical idealism, akin to what he dubbed Hegel's 'absolute block whose parts have no loose play' (James, 1897, p. 674), he had also declared that 'new discriminations or discoveries' might well bring him around (*ibid.*, p. 673). Ultimately left still doubting by his own discriminations and discoveries, what might James have made of those by contemporary physicists such as Gerardus 't Hooft, Leonard Susskind,[44] and Craig Hogan[45] (in support of a holographic universe), as well as Julian Barbour (1999) and Carlo Rovelli (Gefter, 2008) (in support of a timeless universe), all as if on schedule to affirm his mystical suggestion as a veridical revelation?

---

[42] See Kingsley (2003).

[43] One notable exception is Eugene Taylor's highly perceptive account in an interview by the French philosopher Thibaud Trochu (Trochu, 2008, p. 11).

[44] 'Getting our collective head around the Holographic Principle is probably the biggest challenge that we physicists have had since the discovery of Quantum Mechanics' (Susskind, 2008, p. 305).

[45] '[Fermilab's head of the Center for Particle Astrophysics, Craig] Hogan realised that the holographic principle changes everything. If space-time is a grainy hologram, then you can think of the universe as a sphere whose outer surface is papered in Planck length-sized squares, each containing one bit of information' (Chowan, 2009).

References

Allen, G.W. (1967) *William James: A Biography*, New York: Viking.
Barbour, J. (1999) *The End of Time: The Next Revolution in Physics*, Oxford: Oxford University Press.
Barnard, G.W. (1997) *Exploring Unseen Worlds: William James and the Philosophy of Mysticism*, Albany, NY: SUNY Press.
Barrington, M., Stevenson, I. & Weaver, Z. (2005) *A World in a Grain of Sand: The Clairvoyance of Stefan Ossowiecki*, Jefferson, NC: McFarland.
Bigelow, W.S. (1908) *Buddhism and Immortality*, Boston, MA: Houghton, Mifflin & Co.
Bjork, D. (1983) *The Compromised Scientist*, New York: Columbia University Press.
Blood, B.P. (1860/2009) *Optimism*, Guilford, CT: Eirini Press.
Blood, B.P. (1910) The secret of William James and anesthetic revelation, *Springfield Sunday Republican*, 16 October.
Blood, B.P. (1920) *Pluriverse*, Boston, MA: Marshall Jones Company.
Blum, D. (2006) *Ghost Hunters: William James and the Search for Scientific Proof of Life After Death*, New York: The Penguin Press.
Bricklin, J. (1999) A variety of religious experience: William James and the non-reality of free will, in Libet, B., Freeman, A. & Sutherland, K. (eds.) *The Volitional Brain: Towards a Neuroscience of Free Will*, Exeter: Imprint Academic.
Bricklin, J. (2003) Sciousness and *con*sciousness: William James and the prime reality of non-dual experience, *Journal of Transpersonal Psychology*, **35** (2), pp. 85–110.
Bricklin, J. (2007) *Sciousness*, Guilford, CT: Eirini Press.
Broad, W.J. (2006) *The Oracle: The Lost Secrets and Hidden Messages of Ancient Delphi*, New York: The Penguin Press.
Burkhardt, F. (1981) *The Works of William James: The Principles of Psychology*, Vol. III, Cambridge, MA: Harvard University Press.
Burkhardt, F., Bowers, F. & Skrupskelis, I. (1978) *Essays in Philosophy (The Works of William James)*, Cambridge, MA: Harvard University Press.
Chowan, M. (2009) Our world may be a giant hologram, *New Scientist*, **2691** (January).
Dodds, E.R. (1973) *The Ancient Concept of Progress and Other Essays on Greek Literature and Belief*, New York: Oxford University Press.
Einstein, A. (1954) *Ideas and Opinions*, New York: Crown Publishers.
Einstein, A. (1961) *Relativity*, New York: Random House.
Fontenrose, J. (1978) *The Delphic Oracle, Its Responses and Operations, with a Catalogue of Responses*, Berkeley, CA: University of California Press.
Fort, A. (1984) The concept of Saksin in Advaita Vedanta, *Journal of Indian Philosophy*, **12**, pp. 277–290.
Gale, R. (1999) *The Divided Self of William James*, Cambridge: Cambridge University Press.
Gardner, M. (2003) *Are Universes Thicker Than Blackberries*, New York: W.W. Norton.
Gefter, A. (2008), Is time an illusion?, *New Scientist*, **2639** (January).
Gribbin, J. (2002) *The Scientists: A History of Science Told Through the Lives of Its Greatest Inventors*, New York: Random House.
Grof, S. (2000) *Psychology of the Future: Lessons from Modern Consciousness Research*, Albany, NY: SUNY Press.

Hamilton, T. (2009) *Immortal Longings: F.W.H. Myers and the Victorian Search for Life After Death*, Exeter: Imprint Academic.
Hewitt, F.W. (1901) *Anaesthetics and their Administration*, New York: Macmillan.
Hicks, R.D. (1970) *Diogenes Laertius, Lives of Eminent Philosophers*, Cambridge, MA: Harvard University Press.
Hinze, O.M. (1979) *Tantra Vidya*, Delhi: Motilal Banarsidass Publishers.
Hoffmann, B. (1973) *A. Einstein: Creator and Rebel*, New York: The Penguin Press.
James, W. (1890/1983) *The Principles of Psychology*, Cambridge, MA: Harvard University Press.
James, W. (1892/1992) Psychology: Briefer Course, in *William James: Writings: 1878–1899*, New York: Library of America.
James, W. (1896/1986) Address of the President before the *Society for Psychical Research*, in *The Works of William James: Essays in Psychical Research*, Cambridge, MA: Harvard University Press.
James, W. (1897/1992) The dilemma of determinism, in *The Will to Believe and Other Essays in Popular Philosophy*, in *William James: Writings: 1878–1899*, New York: Library of America.
James, W. (1898/1992) Human immortality, in *William James: Writings: 1878–1899*, New York: Library of America.
James, W. (1902/1987) The Varieties of Religious Experience, in *William James: Writings 1902–1910*, New York: Library of America.
James, W. (1903/1986) *The Works of William James: Essays in Psychical Research*, Cambridge, MA: Harvard University Press.
James, W. (1904a/1987) Does 'consciousness' exist?, in *William James: Writings 1902–1910*, New York: Library of America.
James, W. (1904b/1987) A world of pure experience, in *William James: Writings 1902–1910*, New York: Library of America.
James, W. (1905/2005) The notion of consciousness, a translation by J. Bricklin of La notion de conscience, *Journal of Consciousness Studies*, **12** (7), pp. 55–64.
James, W. (1907a/1986) A case of clairvoyance, in *The Works of William James: Essays in Psychical Research*, Cambridge, MA: Harvard University Press.
James, W. (1907b/1987) Pragmatism: A New Name for Some Old Ways of Thinking, in *William James: Writings 1902–1910*, New York: Library of America.
James, W. (1909/1978) *The Works of William James: A Pluralistic Universe*, Burkhardt, F. & Bowers, H. (eds.), Cambridge, MA: Harvard University Press.
James, W. (1909a/1987) The Meaning of Truth: A Sequel to Pragmatism, in *William James: Writings 1902–1910*, New York: Library of America.
James, W. (1909b/1987) A Pluralistic Universe, in *William James: Writings 1902–1910*, New York: Library of America.
James, W. (1909c/1987) The confidences of a psychical researcher, in *William James: Writings 1902–1910*, New York: Library of America.
James, W. (1910a/1987) A suggestion about mysticism, in *William James: Writings 1902–1910*, New York: Library of America.
James, W. (1910b/1987) A pluralistic mystic, in *William James: Writings 1902–1910*, New York: Library of America.
James, W. (1911/1987) Some Problems of Philosophy: A Beginning of an Introduction to Philosophy, in *William James: Writings 1902–1910*, New York: Library of America.
James, W. (1920) *The Letters of William James*, Vols. I–II, Boston MA: The Atlantic Monthly Press.

James, W. (1983) *The Works of William James: Essays in Psychology*, Burkhardt, F., Bowers, F. & Skrupskelis, I. (eds.), Cambridge, MA: Harvard University Press.
James, W. (1987) *The Works of William James: Essays, Comments, and Reviews*, Burkhardt, F.H. & Bowers, F. (eds.), Cambridge, MA: Harvard University Press.
James, W. (1996) *Essays in Psychical Research*, Cambridge, MA: Harvard University Press.
Jnaneshwar, M. (13th Century/1979) *Amritanubhav*, New York: SYDA Foundation.
Kingsley, P. (2003) *Reality*, Inverness: Golden Sufi Press.
Krippner, S. (2002) *Extraordinary Dreams and How to Work with Them*, Albany, NY: SUNY Press.
Krishnamurti, J. (1954) *The First and Last Freedom*, New York: Harper and Row.
LeShan, L. (1974) *The Medium, The Mystic, and The Physicist*, New York: Arkana/Penguin.
Lodge, O. (1891/1892) *Report of the Sixty-First Meeting of the British Association for the Advancement of Science, Held at Cardiff in August 1891*, London: Spottewodde and Co.
Lodge, O. (1900) *The Survival of Man: A Study in Unrecognized Human Faculty*, New York: George H. Doran Company.
Lu, K.Y. (1971), *Practical Buddhism*, London: Rider.
Luytens, M. (2003) *The Life and Death of Krishnamurti*, Bramdean: Krishnamurti Foundation Trust.
Mazur, J. (2007) *The Motion Paradox: The 2,500-Year Old Puzzle Behind All the Mysteries of Time and Space*, New York: Dutton.
Myers, F.W.H. (1903a) *Human Personality and its Survival of Bodily Death*, Vol. I, London: Longmans, Green, and Co.
Myers, F.W.H. (1903b) *Human Personality and its Survival of Bodily Death*, Vol. II, London: Longmans, Green, and Co.
Myers, G. (1986) *William James: His Life and Thought*, New Haven, CT: Yale University Press.
Newton, I. (1687/2002) *Principia*, Philadelphia, PA: Running Press.
Perry, R.B. (1935) *The Thought and Character of William James*, Vol. II, Boston, MA: Little, Brown and Company.
Prescott, M. (2008) *How Martin Gardner Bamboozled His Readers*, [Online], http://michaelprescott.typepad.com/michael_prescotts_blog/2007/08/how-martin-gard.html [Spring 2010].
Ramsay, W. (1894) Partial anesthesia, in *Proceedings of the Society for Psychical Research*, **9** (January).
Ray, R.A. (2001) *Secret of the Vajra World: The Tantric Buddhism of Tibet*, Boston, MA: Shambhala.
Royce, J. (1920) *The World and the Individual*, London: Macmillan.
Sacks, O. (2004) In the river of consciousness, *New York Review of Books*, [Online], http://www.nybooks.com/articles/17030 [January 2010].
Sage, M. (1904) *Mrs. Piper & The Society for Psychical Research*, trans. and abridged from French by N. Robertson, New York: Scott-Thaw.
Santayana, G. (1930) *The Realm of Matter: Book Second of Realms of Being*, London: Constable and Co.
Schlipp, P.A. (1959) *A. Einstein, Philosopher-Scientist*, New York: Harper.
Singh, N.K. (1997) *Encyclopaedia of Hinduism*, New Dehli: Anmol Publication.
Skrupskelis, I. & Berkeley, E. (eds.) (1997) *The Correspondence of William James*, Vol. 5, Charlottesville, VA: University of Virginia.

Skrupskelis, I. & Berkeley, E. (eds.) (2000) *The Correspondence of William James*, Vol. 8, Charlottesville, VA: University of Virginia.
Skrupskelis, I. & Berkeley, E. (eds.) (2001) *The Correspondence of William James*, Vol. 9, Charlottesville, VA: University of Virginia.
Skrupskelis, I. & Berkeley, E. (eds.) (2002) *The Correspondence of William James*, Vol. 10, Charlottesville, VA: University of Virginia.
Skrupskelis, I. & Berkeley, E. (eds.) (2003) *The Correspondence of William James*, Vol. 11, Charlottesville, VA: University of Virginia.
Skrupskelis, I. & Berkeley, E. (eds.) (2004) *The Correspondence of William James*, Vol. 12, Charlottesville, VA: University of Virginia.
Smith, H. (no date) *Imitations of Immortality: Three Case Studies*, [Online], http://www.theisticscience.org/spirituality/Ingersoll3.htm [Oct 2010].
Susskind, L. (2008) *The Black Hole War: My Battle with Stephen Hawking to Make the World Safe for Quantum Mechanics*, New York: Little, Brown, and Co.
Tarán, L. (1965) *Parmenides: A Text with Translation, Commentary and Critical Essays*, Princeton, NJ: Princeton University Press.
Taylor, E. (1996) *William James on Consciousness Beyond the Margin*, Princeton, NJ: Princeton University Press.
Trochu, T. (2008) Investigations into the William James collection at Harvard: An interview with Eugene Taylor, *Streams of William James*, **3** (1).
Weyl, H. (1963) *Philosophy and Mathematics and Natural Science*, New York: Atheneum.
Yourgrau, P. (2006) *A World Without Time: The Forgotten Legacy of Gödel and Einstein*, New York: Basic Books.

Paper received August 2010.

Allan Combs

Neurology and the Mind at the Turn of the Century

Abstract: *Trends in thought about consciousness, the mind, and the brain at the turn of the century were surprisingly similar to major trends in thinking about these topics today. For instance, some psychiatrists as well as physiologists considered all actions of the human mind, as well as all behaviours, entirely the product of the electrochemical actions of nerve cells, while others emphasized the importance of consciousness, free will, and even the soul. The action of nerve cells, and thus the brain itself, was understood largely in terms of electrical activity, energy, and resistances, all leading to views of mental health and pathology based on energy and the loss of energy. Modern metaphors for understanding the brain, and along with them mental health and illness, emphasize information processing and neurochemistry. Such differences are reflected in the differences between typical treatments at the turn of the century and today.*

Key words: consciousness, brain, nerve cells, neurons, metaphors, health, illness, neurasthenia, turn of the century, Charles Darwin, William James, John Hughlings Jackson, Henri Bergson, Paul Broca, Carl Wernicke, Max Nordau, degeneration

It is a point of interest that most turn of the twentieth century theorists of consciousness were originally trained as physicians, after which their careers led them into psychology, psychiatry, or philosophy. William James, for example, received his degree in medicine in 1869, and after a period of poor health and depression accepted an offer by the president of Harvard to teach an undergraduate course in comparative physiology. In 1873 he accepted an appointment to teach anatomy and physiology, but immediately postponed it for a year of travel in Europe, and in 1874 began teaching psychology. Many of his colleagues in New England and in Europe were medically trained psychiatrists. Notable exceptions were F.W.H. Myers, an essayist and poet, and Henri Bergson, discussed in William Barnard's article in this issue, who was broadly trained in science and mathematics but began his career in the humanities, publishing an essay on Lucretius.

This all means that a significant amount of the speculation about the nature of consciousness and mind from that period might well be termed 'turn of the century cognitive neuroscience'. Indeed, James's first major work, *The Principles of Psychology*, published in 1890, was a mixture of neurology, psychology, and philosophy. Interestingly, the trends in thought about consciousness, the mind, and the brain were then, for their own time, surprisingly similar to major trends in thinking about these topics today. For instance, there were psychiatrists as well as physiologists who considered all actions of the human mind, and all behaviours controlled by the brain, entirely the product of the electrochemical actions of nerve cells. One is reminded of Francis Crick's (1995) recent book, *The Astonishing Hypothesis*. Perhaps the most reductionistic of these was the mid-century Russian physiologist Ivan Sechenov, who worked with Helmholtz early in his career. But even the latter could not go along with his extreme view that all brain activity amounts to mechanically driven reflexes. His student, Ivan Pavlov, also relied heavily on the notion of reflexes, influencing Russian psychology right through much of the twentieth century, and by way of J.B. Watson's translation of his ideas from physiology into Watson's new behaviourist psychology, also becoming a major influence on American psychology. In this vein it is worth mentioning that the first major publication by the great turn of the century British physiologist, Sir Charles Sherrington, *The Integrative Action of the Nervous System* (1906), relied heavily on reflex action, but stressed the idea that such reflexes are goal-directive and purposive.

Meanwhile the problem of 'specificity of function' in the brain was a major issue in those days, as in more sophisticated clothing it is today. Phrenology was still a popular trend at the turn of the century, though not one supported by most academic physiologists. A century earlier, Jean Pierre Flourens had been asked by no less than Napoleon Bonaparte himself to look into the matter, and after considerable experimentation, some of which was done on birds, Flourens concluded that while different areas of the brain such as the neocortex and the cerebellum regulate different functions, he was not able to validate the claims made by phrenologists.

In 1861 the French neurologist Paul Broca had presented to the Anthropological Society of Paris his soon-to-be famous findings concerning the brain of a patient known as Tan. His claims were initially rejected by the Society, but he returned the next day with the brain in a bottle for all to see! By 1874 Carl Wernicke had published a more detailed model of where word meanings are processed in the brain, and where speech is generated. Curiously, Wernicke's drawing (Figure 1) shows these areas to be on the *right* side of the brain, though he knew that language was usually located on the left side. And for some inexplicable reason he seems to have used an ape brain as his model!

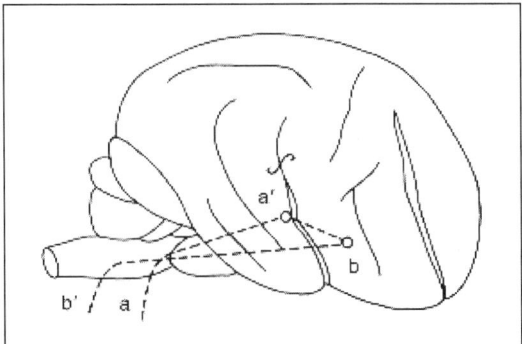

Figure 1: Wernicke's drawing of where word meanings are processed in the brain and where speech is generated.

Wernicke's model of language processing areas in the brain was updated during the 1970's by the prominent American neurologist Norman Geschwind to create the Wernicke-Geschwind model that was very useful for understanding different types of aphasia. Contemporary issues concerning localization of brain function often involve questions concerning the extent and validity of brain modularity and the importance of local and distributed neuronal networks of various types.

One of the most important issues to play out during the eighteenth, nineteenth, and early years of the twentieth centuries concerns nerve action itself. During the late 1700s Luigi Galvani had discovered an intimate relationship between electricity and nerve as well as muscle action, but the nature of electricity itself was not well understood so the enigma of the relationship between electricity and neuromuscular action was a puzzle with both major elements conceptualized only in a preliminary way. Some observers, for example, tended to associate electricity with vitality and health. Already in 1818 Mary Shelley described her Frankenstein, 'The Modern Prometheus', as coming to life through the injection of large amounts of electricity drawn down in a lightning storm. As late as the early twentieth century, American physicians regularly prescribed 'electrotherapy' that amounted to nothing more than forcing currents of electricity through the human body. James himself was treated this way for his heart condition.

Through the latter years of the nineteenth century there was much discussion of ideas such as nerve or nervous energy and the related notions such as nerve force.

In 1872, for example, Charles Darwin had written, 'Why the irritation of nerve-cells should generate or liberate nerve force is not known; but that this is the case seems to be the conclusion arrived at by all the greatest physiologists such as Müller, Virchow and Bernard, and so on' (1872, p. 70). At about the same time, Herbert Spencer (1863, p. 109) observed that it is 'an unquestionable truth that, at any moment, the existing quantity of liberated nerve-force, which in an inscrutable way produces in us the state we call feeling, must expand itself in some direction' leading to motivated behaviours of one kind or another. John Hughlings Jackson, 'father of British neurology', seems to have taken a physicist's view of electricity in the action of the nervous system when in 1884 he wrote, 'A normal discharge starting in some elements of the highest centres [of the brain] overcomes the resistance of some of the middle, next the resistance of some of the lowest centres is overcome, and the muscles are ... moved... *RESISTANCES* will be considered later' (1884/1958, p. 42–44). Here we have gone from the vague notion of 'nerve force' to the very concrete idea of electrical resistance, neither of which play any significant role in modern discussions of the brain (except the latter in technical treatments of the bio-physics of the cell membranes). Ideas such as these seem a far cry from today's notions of the electrical currents that play a part in the chemistry, or perhaps we should say *electro-chemistry*, of nerve action.

It is not difficult to see how notions such as nerve force or nervous energy could and did bleed over into the public eye in terms of health issues. Indeed, it was commonly supposed by lay and professional persons alike that a failure of sufficient nerve force could drain a person, leaving them with too little energy to effectively organize their own faculties, ultimately leading to depression or even insanity. A supposedly common version of this malady was commonly known at the turn of the century as *neurasthenia*, generally attributed to the stress of living in the modern age of that time. This condition, which could include depression, poor health, and disorganization, including clinical dissociation states, was purportedly so common in the United States that James (Schultz and Schultz, 2004; pp. 178–179) is said to have dubbed it *americanitis*. Diagnoses of neurasthenia were common well into the 1920s, and devices ranging from electrical belt buckles to 'nerve and brain tablets' and 'Bile Beans' were available to help one regain one's natural vigour.

Here we see the importance of the metaphors we choose for understanding the nervous system. Ideas such as 'nerve energy' and 'vital force' suggest the threat of running down like an old flashlight battery, and they offer cures in the form of redeemed energy, both literally and figuratively. We might contrast this approach to modern *cognitive therapy* techniques, designed to re-program the individual's thought and behaviour much like one might re-program the information flow in a computer (e.g. Butler, Chapman, Forman and Beck, 2006). James himself was so caught up in this energetic metaphor that, despite his sophistication as a physiologist, he spent much time and effort worrying over the threat posed by the loss of his vital energy. Oddly enough, he also took this metaphor of energy in the opposite direction when he published a now-obscure but highly optimistic tract on human potentialities titled *The Energies of Man* (1907), an essay that caused some reviewers to accuse him of being completely out of touch with reality. Today's dominant metaphors are about cognitive information processing and neurochemical processes in the brain. These offer their own lines of approach to understanding human nature, and treating the dysfunctions that haunt it, lines such as cognitive therapy and treatment with neuro-pharmaceuticals.

Before completing this short tour of the neurology of the turn of the century, I would be remiss if I did not mention the social contexts in which all this occurred. This was only a few decades after Darwin's publication in 1859 of the *Origin of Species*, and the impact of evolutionary thought was still being sorted out, as it is still being sorted out today. But one theme apparent in intellectual circles of that day was an optimistic notion that evolution had carried the human species forward into an enlightened age of science and reason, and might well continue carrying the evolutionary cutting edge of human nature on into new and greater forms of expression in the future. Such an optimistic view is apparent in Henri Bergson's visions of humanity's place in the cosmos, and is reflected again in the thought of his spiritual descendant, Teilhard de Chardin. Many turn of the century thinkers embraced this optimistic view, but paradoxically the *fin de siècle* also harboured a widely held social and literary theme that civilization and its values were in a state of degeneration.

In 1892 the social critic, Max Nordau, published the book, *Degeneration*, widely read and celebrated at the time. In it he argued for the degeneration of values in art, religion, and society in general. At roughly the same time a number of popular novels seemed to herald this motif, including Robert Louis Stevenson's *The Strange Case of Dr Jekyll and Mr Hyde* in 1886, Oscar Wilde's *The Picture of Dorian Gray* in 1890, H.G. Wells' *The Island of Doctor Moreau* in 1896, and Bram Stoker's *Dracula* in 1897; all within a period of eleven years. Wells' futuristic novel, *The Time Machine*, published in 1895, literally divided the humanity of the future into two factions, simplistic but lovable *eloi* and intelligent but animal-like *morlocks*.

The idea implicit in all of this seems to have been that we civilized people may be harbouring an inner beast, which given the proper circumstances might spring out and show its leering face. Early depth psychologists, particularly those of the Freudian persuasion, did little to discourage this notion, and indeed made considerable hay with it.

References

Butler, A.C., Chapman, J.E., Forman, E.M. & Beck, A.T. (2006) The empirical status of cognitive-behavioral therapy: A review of meta-analyses, *Clinical Psychology Review*, **26** (1), pp. 17–31.

Crick, F. (1995) *The Astonishing Hypothesis: The Scientific Search for the Soul*, New York: Scribner.

Darwin, C. (1859) *On the Origin of Species by Means of Natural Selection*, London: Murray.

Darwin, C. (1872) *The Expression of Emotion in Man and Animals*, London: Murray.

Jackson, J.H. (1884/1958) Evolution and dissolution of the nervous system: Lecture III, in Taylor, J. (ed.) *Selected Writings*, New York: Basic Books.

James, W. (1890) *The Principles of Psychology*, Cambridge, MA: Harvard University Press.

James, W. (1907) The energies of man, *Science*, **25** (635), pp. 321–332.

Nordau, M. (1892) *Degeneration*, New York, D. Appleton & Co.

Schultz, D.P. & Schultz, E.S. (2004) *A History of Modern Psychology*, Belmont, CA: Thomson Wadsworth.

Shelley, M. (1818) *Frankenstein*, London, Penguin.

Sherrington, C. (1906) *Integrative Action of the Nervous System*, New Haven, CT: Yale University Press.

Spencer, H. (1863) *Essays: Moral, Political, and Aesthetic*, New York: Appelton-Century-Crofts.

Stevenson, R.L. (1886) *The Strange Case of Dr Jekyll and Mr Hyde and Other Tales*, London: Longmans, Green, & Co.

Stoker, B. (1897) *Dracula*, London: Archibald Constable and Company.

Wells, H.G. (1895) *The Time Machine*, London: William Heinemann.

Wells, H.G. (1896) *The Island of Doctor Moreau*, London: Heinemann, Stone, and Kimball.
Wilde, O. (1890) *The Picture of Dorian Gray*, Philadelphia: Lippincott's Monthly Magazine.

Paper received August 2010.

Allan Combs, Stanley Krippner
& Eugene Taylor

Is there Awareness Outside Attention?

A Psychological Perspective

> *The parasitism [of psychoneurosis] is well brought out in the attitude of the patient towards these morbid mental states. He regards the whole system-complex as foreign to his personality... These states do not belong to the patient's normal associative life, but appear to the patient himself as opposed to his usual normal life-activities.*
>
> Boris Sidis, 1910, pp. 321–322

Abstract: *This paper approaches the question of awareness outside of attention through a broader psychological examination of human consciousness. Questions regarding the boundaries of conscious awareness, as well as the possibility of 'subconscious' or 'unconscious' mental processes, were widely discussed 100 years and more ago when they played a central role in the thinking of turn-of-the-century theorists such as William James, F.W.H. Myers, Jean-Martin Charcot, and Pierre Janet, all of whom were interested in dissociative phenomena suggestive of consciousness, or awareness, beyond the margins of attention. Such phenomena included hypnosis, hysteria, trance states, and motor automatisms, and, for many scholars, also sleep related conditions such as dreaming and hypnogogic states.*

Keywords: Consciousness, unconscious, self, dissociation, disaggregation, William James, chaos theory, sciences of complexity, strange attractor, basin

Correspondence:
Allan Combs, California Institute of Integral Studies Email: Acombs@ciis.edu
Stanley Krippner, Saybrook University Email: SKrippner@saybrook.edu
Eugene Taylor, Saybrook University Email: Etaylor@saybrook.edu

Introduction

To begin, it is useful to make a distinction between notions of the 'unconscious' mind, familiar in psychoanalysis and Jung's 'complex psychology', and the idea of multiple states of consciousness to varying degrees aware or unaware of each other (Baruss, 2003; Krippner and Powers, 1997; Taylor, 1984; Prince, 1906; Myers, 1903).[1] The former can be traced to the tradition of Schopenhauer and von Hartmann in Germany, and nineteenth century British writers such as Maudsley, Carpenter, and Lewes. The latter was especially well developed in what one of the present authors has termed the *French-Swiss-English-and-American therapeutic axis*, which in Paris included Charcot and his foremost student Janet, and in Nancy, Charcot's rival, Hippolyte Bernheim, in England F.W.H. Myers, in Switzerland Theodore Flournoy, and in Boston William James, among others (Taylor, 1996) — see Figure 1.

---

[1] While the designation may at first appear arbitrary, there is evidence to suggest that the difference was ethnic. The Germans used the term 'unconscious', while the French employed the word 'subconscious', referring to two entirely different underlying epistemologies. The unconscious was defined in the context of German idealism, based on the introspective analysis of consciousness, which presumed there was a fixed hierarchy to reality, which only the Germans had fully worked out, and that waking rational consciousness was the *summum bonum* from which all other states should be understood. The British psychiatrists such as Maudsley, Lewes, and Carpenter developed a literature around the concept of unconscious cerebration, relying mainly on physiological explanations, while the British founders of the Society for Psychical Research, particularly F.W.H. Myers, fielded another approach (Myers, 1976). Myers developed a model of consciousness around the idea of 'subliminal' states that focused on the hyper-suggestibility of the hypnotic stratum and incorporated psychic phenomena as part of the spiritual evolution of the psyche, as well as his own idiosyncratic views on life after death. In the US, William James was a principal interpreter of mainly the French but also the German literature, even introducing Breuer and Freud's work for the first time to the American psychological public. He was more enamoured with the French and the Swiss, but cleaved to Myers' view, developed it further, only touching upon the issue of life after death, and referred in the professional literature to Myers' observations along the lines of a fully fledged subliminal psychology. The true roots of James's model of consciousness, however, can be found in the Swedenborgian and Transcendentalist legacy defined as a spiritual psychology of self-realization (Taylor, 2000). Meanwhile, Morton Prince, at first under the influence of William James, Pierre Janet, and the so-called French Experimental Psychology of the Subconscious (Binet, 1890), used the term subconscious, following Pierre Janet, in his writings on multiple personality in the early part of his career (Prince, 1906), but later turned to the term unconscious once he had fused his earlier views with the work of John Hughlings Jackson and Ivan Pavlov (Prince, 1914).

Boston School of Psychopathology:
William James, James Jackson Putnam, Henry Pickering Bowditch,
Josiah Royce, Morton Prince, Richard Hodgson, Richard Cabot,
Joseph Pratt, Elwood Worcester, Edward Cowles, A. Meyer,
B. Sidis, L. Eugene Emerson, Wm. McDougall

The Society for Psychical Research (British) and other
Hypnotic Researchers:
F.W.H. Myers, Edmund Gurney, H. Sidgwick, S. Hodgson
Milne Bramwell, C. Loyd Tuckey

Experimental Psychology in Switzerland:
Flournoy, Claparède, Piaget, Forel,
Bleuler, Jung, DuBois

The French Experimental
Psychology of the Subconscious:
Charcot, Ribot, Richet, Richer,
Janet, Binet, Tissié, Babinski
Ochorowicz [Poland]

©Taylor, 2000

Figure 1: Charcot's Axis — A loose-knit consortium of French, Swiss, English and American psychotherapeutic investigators (1882–1920).

The investigators within Charcot's Axis were guided largely by the dissociation model, where all psychological phenomena from remembering what you had to eat five days ago, to the development of hysteria into a full-blown multiple personality, were understood in terms of the reigning theory of dissociation. Dissociation was the explanatory mechanism for understanding human experience. This model, interpreted by some like F.W.H. Myers, posited that it was possible for consciousness to split, and two halves could share the field of waking consciousness; consciousness could be considered a domain of multiple states of consciousness ranging from the psychopathic to the transcendent, with waking rational consciousness somewhere in between. Meanwhile, surrounding the waking state, there could be other states of both an evolutive as well as a dissolutive nature. That is, some less developed than the self in waking consciousness, and some more well developed, in fact, higher in intelligence than rationality in the waking state — both dissolutive and evolutive systems having a simultaneous influence on what is perceived at the centre of attention in the waking state. The reason why both the psychopathic and the transcendent are often confused with each other, however, is that they come to waking consciousness through the self-same channels, presenting a constant stream of moral decisions the individual is called upon to make. This was James's injunction in *The Will to Believe* (1897), namely that states of consciousness within us lay *in potentia*. This is expressed through our choices — we have both a right and duty to continually choose the good, knowing that choosing the bad or even opting for indifference allows the bad, or at least the lowest common denominator, to come into existence.

From a strictly psychological standpoint, Ernest Hilgard's (1977) *neodissociation theory* is a modern continuation of this tradition. Though the German notion of the unconscious gives some small consideration to consciousness on the margins of attention, for example with the idea of the 'pre-preconscious' mind and Freud's late recognition of the importance of the peripheral attention in the therapist, or the concepts of consciousness coming from the early existential and phenomenological theorists such as Binswanger, the theoretical ideas of the members of the French-Swiss-English-and-American axis seem remarkably well-matched to contemporary views of mind and consciousness developed in the sciences of complexity (Combs, 2002; Combs and Krippner, 1999; 2003). The present paper is a step toward connecting these traditions, separated by a century.

The mind as a chaotic attractor

Here we introduce the idea of the mind as a dynamical process that can be characterized as a chaotic attractor.

Consciousness as a total event is, as William James (1890) pointed out in *The Principles of Psychology*, a constantly changing process, clearly not static or even following a fixed cycle, but nevertheless one that has an identifiable global character, at least for each individual. Memories come and go, thoughts pass through the mind only to disappear and return again later, moods are continually changing, alertness and energy levels vary from hour to hour. These are the elements of a kind of mental weather, with the equivalent to the latter's constantly fluctuating temperature, humidity, wind, barometric pressure, and so on. It is not surprising that weather is chaotic. Indeed, the elements that comprise it oscillate in roughly identifiable cycles from hour to hour and day to day, but cannot be predicted with precision. What is more, it is unlikely, for example, that temperature fluctuations ever follow exactly the same course on any two days.

Now, much the same can be said about mental weather.[2] It is comprised of the interactions of elements such as moods, thoughts, memories, and so on. For some of these, such as moods, there is already empirical evidence that they are indeed chaotic (e.g. Combs, Winkler and Daley, 1994; Sacks, 1973/1990; Winkler and Combs, 1993), while virtually all seem consistent with the general characteristics of chaotic processes (Combs, 1996). As a group, their interactions, like the interactions of the elements of the weather, yield an exquisitely complex process fabric that we know as the stream of experience. This fabric is far too complex to describe in detail, but efforts have been made to mathematically conceptualize it as a grand chaotic attractor. Chaos mathematician Ben Goertzel (1994), for instance, developed the broadly conceived mathematical expression that he calls the *cognitive equation*, that represents the entire process structure of an individual's experiential life. He imagines this structure as operating on two levels, that of the mind and that of the brain, observing that 'the brain, like other extremely complex systems, is unpredictable on the level of detail but roughly predictable on the level of structure. This means that the dynamics of its physical variables display a strange attractor with a complex structure of "wings" or "compartments"' (Goertzel, 1994, p. 157). These wings or compartments are in effect small attractors that reside in the larger attractor of the overall neurological activity of the brain. They might, for example, be associated with individual states of consciousness. Goertzel views mental activity as running on top of the brain process, creating the second level of the system. The mental level is somewhat less finely detailed, however, and more generalized than the neurological level of activity: 'If physical level attractors are drawn in ball-point pen, process [mental] level attractors are in magic marker' (*ibid.*, p. 158). Nevertheless, the same overall process structure is apparent at both levels.

---

[2] See Chauncey E. Wright on 'Cosmic weather'. Wright coined the metaphor 'cosmic weather', a most apt term, to reveal the continual presence of irregularities as a product of the causal complexity, mixture of law and accident, in the continual production of natural and physical causes unhinged from a teleological framework and continually prone to what he called '*counter-movements*' — or the action and counter-action and cycles of convertible and reversible mechanical energy. For Wright, 'the physical laws of nature are... the only real type of the general order in the universe... showing at every turn the ultimate play of action and counter-action in the balanced forces from which they spring' (*Letters* 177; The Internet Encyclopedia of Philosophy, http://www.iep.utm.edu/wright/).

This metaphor was evidently first suggested by Helmholtz in his 1867 *Handbuch der Physiologischen Optik, Vol. III*, but is entirely consistent with James's view.

Conceptualizing the natural flow of experience in the mind or the events of the brain as chaotic attractors takes us a good way down the road toward understanding something about their internal dynamics. For one thing, many complex chaotic systems are self-organizing. For example, a living cell is composed of a rich and complex matrix of chemical cycles which self-organize in such a way as to regulate the overall activity of the cell. In 1974 biologists Maturana, Varela, and Uribe carried this notion further, suggesting that the net ongoing product of this matrix of activity is no less than the living cell itself. In other words the principle activity of a living cell, when all its complex metabolic activities are summed up, is the continuing creation of itself. The authors termed this process *autopoiesis*, or self-creation. Living cells are autopoietic systems. So are ecologies, as it turns out, as are many other complex systems such as the international economy and even human societies (Laszlo, Csányi, Combs and Artigiani, 1996).

As implied above, we believe that the mind, undergirded by brain processes, is also an autopoietic event (Combs, 2002; Combs and Krippner, 2003). Like a living cell, it is made up of complex processes that interact in such a fashion as to create a stable mental regimen, or personality, as its net result. Indeed, it seems that self-regulating, essentially autopoietic activity, is seen at all levels of the system. For instance, beliefs rush to support each other even if they have to be invented on the spot, and even if they fail to form a logically coherent cloth (e.g. Festinger, Riecken and Schacter, 1956). Reasoning processes are built up out of a self-supporting scaffolding of logical operations that mutually reinforce and sustain each other (Combs, 2002; Flavell, 1963), and emotional states tend to become self-reinforcing, supporting themselves by selective memory (Bower, 1981) and behaviours. All of this gives a coherence to our own individual experience, and a day to day stability to who we are.

The coherence of the self

This general approach to understanding the stream of consciousness offers an insight into how the natural flow of experience forms a continuous and coherent event. And it sheds light on what holds all the parts of the experiential moment together in something like a single self-resonant Gestalt. The question of how such unity of experience is brought about is most important for psychology. James (1890) makes it his first topic in *The Principles*. On the first page he outlines two broad approaches to its solution. According to the first of these:

> The most natural and consequently the earliest way of unifying the [mental] material was, first, to classify it as well as might be, and secondly, to affiliate the diverse modes thus found upon a simple entity, the personal Soul, of which they are taken to be so may facultative manifestations. (James, 1890, Vol. 1, p. 1)

The second is somewhat more complex:

> Another and less obvious way of unifying the chaos is to seek common elements *in* the divers mental facts rather than a common agent behind them, and to explain them constructively by the various forms of arrangement of these elements, as one explains houses by stones and bricks. (*ibid.*, p. 1)

James referred to the first of these as the *spiritualist* and the second as the *associationist* approach. Years later in *The Varieties of Religious Experience* he noted that 'Buddhists or humanists can perfectly well describe the facts [of mental life] in the phenomenal terms which are their favorites. For them the soul is only a succession of fields of consciousness...' (1902/1929, p. 182). Nevertheless, throughout his career he seemed to have held both of these broad views in tension, sometimes appearing to favour one and sometimes the other. Here we note that the affinity of the second, associationist view, with the modern dynamical systems approach described above can hardly be missed. Lest there be any question about this, on the third page of *The Principles* James goes on to write that the multitude of our mental events weave 'an endless carpet of themselves, like dominoes in ceaseless change, or bits of a glass kaleidoscope' (James, 1890, p. 3).

When we conceptualize the flow of mental events in terms of chaotic attractors, we are led to the possibility of multiple states within the same individual, each representing a separate 'basin' on a common dynamical landscape. Two ordinary examples are normal waking consciousness and dream sleep, though the latter may represent more than one possible state of consciousness (Combs and Krippner, 1998). As we have said, theorists of the French-Swiss-English-and-American axis were keenly interested in alternative states of consciousness such as trances and hypnotic states, pathological conditions such as hysteria, and dissociative phenomena including motor automatisms like automatic writing. In *The Principles* James notes that Janet (1889) postulated the existence of 'secondary' or 'subliminal' selves, suggesting that hysterical symptoms are owned by such selves outside the purview of ordinary consciousness. In his chapter on the stream of thought, James recounts a report by Janet of the creation of such as secondary personality in a patient named Lucie. The latter exhibited a hysterically anaesthetic hand that could produce automatic writing.

While engaging Lucie's attention in a conversation with a third party, Janet whispered in her ear, receiving replies through such writing:

> 'Do you hear me?' he asked. '*No,*' was the unconsciously written reply. 'But to answer you must hear.' '*Yes, quite so.*' 'Then how do you manage?' '*I don't know.*' 'There must be someone who hears me.' '*Yes.*' 'Who?' '*Someone other than Lucie.*' 'Ah! Another person. Shall we give her a name?' '*No.*' 'Yes, it will be more convenient.' '*Well Adrienne then*'. (James, 1890, Vol. 1, p. 222)

Janet observed that after being thus 'baptized' this secondary personality became more definite, displaying characteristics of its own.

This example is of special interest because it offers an insight into the process by which a dissociated subliminal personality might be created: that it does not start off full-blown, but seems to grow from a dim embryonic proto-personality.[3] At least this was the case with Lucie. It is worth taking a moment to consider how such an event might occur from the complex systems perspective.

Considering an individual's self or personality in terms of the autopoietic psychological processes that create the ongoing structure of his or her inner life, the appearance of a dissociated 'secondary self' represents a significant change in the organizational structure of the system as a whole. In dynamical terms, the original self system might be said to undergo a *bifurcation* to a new structure. Though bifurcations can sometimes occur abruptly as is the case with 'catastrophic' bifurcations, they are often initiated by small local changes in patterns of organization, 'seed perturbations', that spread into all or significantly large portions of the whole system (Goerner, 1999). Many instances of this kind are seen in complex chemical, biological, and social systems. Strictly speaking, in Lucie's case the personality system, viewed as a whole, has not actually given birth to a new and completely independent secondary self, as would appear from casual observation, but has reorganized itself to include two attractor basins instead of one. An action graph of Lucie's personality structure would show a small

---

[3] This idea was referred to back in the nineteenth century as 'the reality of the buried idea'. The origin of the traumatic neuroses was believed to begin when experiences the person were unable to fully integrate into their normal worldview, such as the effects of a horrendous train wreck or some sexual trauma in a girl at a very young age, become split off fragments of the waking state and deposited in the subconscious where they begin to operate according to laws of their own. As the years go by and the experiences remain unintegrated, they attract like-experiences, growing in energetic power until at some moment of developmental weakness they burst into the field of waking consciousness as a physical or mental symptom. In certain cases of extreme trauma, where the waking state becomes dissociated in a major way, such subconscious complexes can burst forth as a full-blown alternate personality, sometimes even taking over the entire field (Taylor, 1984).

secondary, or dissociated, centre of activity growing beside the primary centre, connected to it by a thin pathway or 'trajectory'. Were there no such connection, Lucie would have no means to move between these centres. Interestingly, she already had developed a hysterically anaesthetic hand, which may have been the sufficient seed perturbation around which the secondary self coalesced. In other words, the already dissociated aspect of the mind which controlled the anaesthetic hand may have served as a ready vehicle for the evolution of the secondary self.

An interesting feature of cases such as that of Lucie is that the different selves may not have equal access to all of the system's memories, suggesting that some of the trajectories are in fact one-way streets. James (1895) followed the tradition of Locke in suggesting that our sense of self-identity is based in memory. Janet and James both tell us that the creation of a secondary self outside of the attention of the primary personality results in the creation of a second, dissociated, thread of memories (Taylor, 1984; 1996). As this secondary self is given more time to become its own person it will develop its own trove of recollections, leading toward a full-fledged sense of independence. Thus we see the beginnings of a multiple personality within the complex psychological structure of the person.

In a sense, the *dissociation identity disorder* is the most extreme of the entire spectrum of dissociative syndromes. In the late nineteenth century and the first decade of the twentieth century, psychology was intensely interested in all types of dissociation. Today, a century later, psychology is again seeing dissociation syndromes in large numbers and the topic has once more come under active discussion (Baruss, 2003; Krippner and Powers, 1997). Interestingly, in the French-Swiss-English-and-American therapeutic axis it was well known even before Freud that the roots of pathological dissociation were often to be found in childhood traumas. In line with the dynamical approach proposed here, the 1910 quotation by Boris Sidis, seen at the beginning of the this article, notes the independence of certain episodes of pathological behaviour which seem to have a life of their own. Here Sidis even refers to such events in terms of 'a whole system-complex' foreign to the individual's ordinary personality — a secondary personality or perhaps a fragment of one, it would seem. Along these lines, James (1890) refers not only to secondary selves outside of awareness, and thus 'sub-conscious', but also to fragmented mental elements such as thoughts, emotions, and memories, that have not yet attached themselves to either the primary or to secondary selves.

Disaggregation and depletion of neural energy

The idea of the loss of coherence of the self was at the centre of much theorizing about psychopathology at the end of the nineteenth century. The basic notion was that the continuity of one's mental life, and thus the self, relies on the association of ideas — meaning thoughts, feelings, memories and the like. The actual processes that undergirds such associations was a matter for discussion, but in *The Principles* James attributes them to habits of experience supported by nerve action. For a person with insufficient strength or energy to maintain a coherent flow of associations there was a risk of dissociation, or *disaggregation* as it was sometimes called, leading to a variety of types of hysteria ranging from simple effects such as the anaesthetic hand in Lucie's case, to full-fledged dissociative identity disorders.

Janet spoke of these conditions in terms of psychological weakness, while G.M. Beard used the phrase *neurasthenic exhaustion*, putting the emphasis on the underlying neurological events (Taylor, 1984; 1996). This was in line with James's emphasis on neurological processes as the basis for the habits that largely determine associations. In all this it is apparent that speculation about the nature of neurological events in the brain cannot be separated from ideas at the psychological level. Here it is helpful to note that during the nineteenth century much theorizing about the nervous system was carried out in terms of the vague concept of electrical 'nerve force'. In 1780 the Italian physicist Luigi Galvani had discovered that a static discharge to the nerve of a frog's leg caused the leg muscle to contract. By 1791 he had constructed the world's first 'wet cell' battery by placing this muscle in series with two metals. Sometime later an electrical 'current of injury' was found to flow from bare muscle tissue exposed in wounds received on the battle field. From such observations it became apparent that muscles and nerves alike operated by electricity, or at least involved electricity in some essential way (Freeman, 1995).

Just how to understand the role of electricity in the nervous system was far from clear. As late as 1872, for example, Charles Darwin pondered, 'Why the irritation of nerve-cells should generate or liberate nerve force is not known; but that this is the case seems to be the conclusion arrived at by all the greatest physiologists such as Müller, Virchow and Bernard, and so on' (Darwin, 1872, p. 70). At about the same time, Herbert Spencer (1863, p. 109), Darwin's spokesman for evolution, observed that it is 'an unquestionable truth that, at any moment, the existing quantity of liberated nerve-force, which in an inscrutable way produces in us the state we call feeling, must expand itself in some direction...' leading to motivated behaviours of one kind or another. Ideas such as these seem a far cry from today's notions of electro-chemistry which play an essential role in nerve action. Indeed, J. Hughlings Jackson, 'father of British neurology', seems to have taken a physicist's view of electricity in the action of the nervous system. In 1884 he wrote, 'A normal discharge starting in some elements of the highest centres [of the brain] overcomes the resistance of some of the middle, next the resistance of some of the lowest centres, and the muscles are ... moved... *Resistances* will be considered later' (Jackson, 1884, p. 42–44). Here we have gone from the vague notion of 'nerve force' to the very concrete idea of electrical resistance, neither of which play any significant role in modern discussions of the brain except in highly technical treatments of the bio-physics of the cell membranes. As a young neurologist Freud did not miss the potential implications for thinking of the brain in terms of nerve force, especially in the core structures of the forebrain. And it was natural at that time to suspect that hysterics, suffering from dissociations, were victims of weak, energy deficient, constitutions. It was only a short step further to formulate these ideas in psychological terms such as character weakness, or an insufficiency of psychological energy. James's interest in such matters was especially apparent in *The Energies of Man*, published in 1907.

Such ideas seem strange to us today because our metaphors for understanding the brain have changed. Now we speak of the 'computational brain' and 'neural networks'. The first of these emphasizes the idea of the brain as a computer that operates in terms of information processing. The second emphasizes the idea that the brain is a fluid dynamical system. Both metaphors commonly lead to theoretical representations in terms of algorithms rather than energy. They consider the electrical aspect of brain function as secondary, as is the electrical operation of a computer secondary to its program. Nevertheless, in either computational or network dynamical terms it is still not difficult to imagine that the self-organizing aspects of the brain might lead to the appearance of more than one attractor basin in the same person. Like our predecessors a century ago, we also look for the source of such dissociations in early traumatic experiences. But we view the situation in terms of the kinds of information received and processed by the individual's mind or brain.

Awareness and the spotlight of attention

Another way to approach the topic of disaggregation is through an understanding of attention. Consider the metaphor of attention as a spotlight coloured and given meaning by the mental processes that surround it just out of view in the penumbra. This is the region of *consciousness beyond the margin* (Taylor, 1996), which fades into the sub-conscious realm of thoughts, feelings, and memories (as contrasted with the psychoanalytic notion of the *unconscious*). James expressed this notion in *The Principles* by calling up an image of the stream of consciousness as a river in which containers of various sizes and shapes representing attention can be placed:

> Every definite image in the mind is steeped and dyed in the water that flows around it. With it goes the sense of its relations, near and remote, the dying echo of whence it came to us, the dawning sense of whither it is to lead. The significance, the value, the image is all in this halo or penumbra that surrounds and escorts it, — or rather that is fused into one with it, and has become bone of its bone and flesh of its flesh; leaving it, it is true, an image of the same *thing* it was before, but making it an image of that thing newly taken and freshly understood. (James, 1890, Vol.1, p. 255)

Continuing with this metaphor, it is easy to imagine that a person who is too mentally or neurologically weak to effectively regulate their own attention process might lose focus, drifting beyond the container of ordinary consciousness through vague and dissociated states in a condition Janet termed *somnambulism* (Taylor, 1984), perhaps even leading under certain conditions to the inception of two or more dissociated selves. In dynamical systems terms, the first might be described as a broad and poorly defined attractor basin representing an equally indefinite self, while the second as a distributed but more discrete system with multiple basins. Here we note that James, Janet, and Myers all entertained ideas of multiple simultaneous states of consciousness, or selves, beyond the margin of attention. It is to these secondary selves that hysterical symptoms, often launched by traumatic experiences in childhood and tapped through hypnotism, dreams, and automatic writing, were attributed (Taylor, 1996, p. 67).

Is there awareness outside attention?

With all the above in the balance, we now ask whether it makes sense to speak of awareness outside of attention. Since *awareness* and *consciousness* have overlapping meanings, we choose to reframe this question in terms of the present discussion as, 'Is there *consciousness* outside of attention?' Like the term *attention*, the word *consciousness* also has multiple meanings. Here we list of few of these, as proposed by philosopher Ned Block (2002):

1. *Phenomenal consciousness*: Subjectivity, e.g. 'what it is like' to be a bat (Nagel, 1974). In this regard, consciousness is often said to be *intentional* or 'about something'.

2. *Self-consciousness*: To have a concept of self and to use it. Most animals and infants may not have this.

3. *Monitoring consciousness*: Any form of internal scanning. This does not necessarily require phenomenal consciousness. E.g. desk top computers and car engines can do it. Higher order thought *can* be involved, e.g. one can be conscious of one's state of mind.

4. *Access consciousness*: Access to information, e.g. in long term memory, sub-conscious material accessed through hypnosis, etc.

Now, let us turn to the problem of multiple selves in the same person, as in Janet's case of Lucie's primary and secondary selves, or the instance of full-fledged dissociative identity disorders. We might ask, *is it like something to be one of these multiple selves?* Well, we presume it is; otherwise we would be dealing with automata. Next, we might ask, *are they self-conscious?* Again, apparently they are. Even at Adrienne's nascent stage of development she accepted a name, and we can assume from other cases that she had begun to acquire memories of her own.

Access consciousness and monitoring consciousness, however, are more troublesome. Many cases of hysteria seem to involve a failure of both monitoring consciousness and access consciousness, at least on the part of certain selves. The presence of Lucie's anaesthetic hand is an example of this, at least from the point of view of her primary self. As suggested above, cases of dissociative disorders, especially of the dissociative identity type, may involve multiple selves with complex asymmetric relationships regarding memory access and the monitoring of each other's activities (Baruss, 2003; Krippner and Powers, 1997). This is one of the most perplexing aspects of such disorders from a complex systems point of view. Of course, such asymmetry is common in hierarchically organized artificial intelligence systems such as computers, where subsystems are monitored by higher-order executive systems. In his neo-dissociation theory, Hilgard (1977) proposes something very much like this in the human psychological control system, with an executive self ordinarily at the top. In cases of dissociation identity disorder, it is as if the executive self has lost, or perhaps never gained, control over the other systems, and indeed the entire hierarchical regimen has failed, while privileged access remains in the hands of some subsystems but not others. It would seem that the task of the therapist is to rebuild this set of subsystems into something like a working hierarchy. In any case, it is apparent that the question of where access and monitor consciousness lie is complex and must be answered differently for each dissociative disorder.

Perhaps an even more enigmatic question concerns the possibility of truly simultaneous streams of consciousness, perhaps associated with different selves within the same person. Strangely, Myers (1903) seems to have considered this a normal situation, even in healthy persons, let alone those with dissociative disorders. And Janet as well as James seem to have been persuaded in this direction as well. Rare cases such as that of Lucie and Adrienne seem to support this possibility, and there have been reports of one self dreaming while another is awake (Barrett, 1996)! There is nothing in dynamical systems theory to prohibit the possibility of two or even more centres active at once, though they would be considered two basins within a single larger attractor. Such cases, however, would be unlikely if monitoring consciousness were available to either self during their simultaneous activation; otherwise it seems they would not report entirely separate phenomenal conscious experiences.

It would appear from all of the above that the human brain and mind are capable of many complex and sometimes enigmatic processes, sometimes to the consternation of those who experience them. They certainly still constitute an enigma for those who continue to study them.

References

Barrett, D. (1996) Dreams in multiple personality disorder, in Barrett, D. (ed.) *Trauma and Dreams*, Cambridge, MA: Harvard University Press.

Baruss, I. (2003) *Alterations of Consciousness: An Empirical Analysis for Social Scientists*, Washington, DC: American Psychological Association.

Binet, A. (1890) *On Double Consciousness*, Chicago, IL: Open Court.

Block, N. (2002) Concepts of consciousness, in Chalmers, D. (ed.) *Philosophy of Mind: Classical and Contemporary Readings*, New York: Oxford University Press.

Bower, G.H. (1981) Mood and memory, *American Psychologist*, **36**, pp. 129–148.

Combs, A. (1996) Consciousness: Chaotic and strangely attractive, in Sulis, W. & Combs, A. (eds.) *Nonlinear Dynamics in Human Behavior*, London and Singapore: World Scientific.

Combs, A. (2002) *The Radiance of Being: Understanding the Grand Integral Vision; Living the Integral Life*, St Paul, MN: Paragon House.
Combs, A. & Krippner, S. (1998) Dream sleep and waking reality: A dynamical view of two states of consciousness, in Hameroff, S., Kaszniak, A.W. & Scott, A.C. (eds.) *Toward a Science of Consciousness: The Second Tucson Discussions and Debates*, Cambridge, MA: MIT Press.
Combs, A. & Krippner, S. (2003) Process, structure, and form: An evolutionary transpersonal psychology of consciousness, *The International Journal of Transpersonal Studies*, **22**, pp. 47–60.
Combs, A., Winkler, M. & Daley, C. (1994) A chaotic systems analysis of circadian rhythms in feeling states, *The Psychological Record*, **44**, pp. 359–368.
Darwin, C. (1872) *The Expression of Emotion in Man and Animals*, London: Murray.
Festinger, L., Riecken, H.W., Jr. & Schacter, S. (1956) *When Prophecy Fails*, Minneapolis, MN: University of Minnesota Press.
Flavell, J.H. (1963) *The Developmental Psychology of Jean Piaget*, New York: Van Nostrand.
Freeman, W.J. (1995) *Societies of Brains: A Study in the Neuroscience of Love and Hate*, Hillsdale, NJ: Erlbaum.
Goerner, S. (1999) *After the Clockwork Universe: The Emerging Science and Culture of Integral Society*, Edinburgh: Floris Publishers.
Goertzel, B. (1994) *Chaotic Logic*, New York: Plenum.
Helmholtz, G. von. (1867) Handbuch der physiologischen optik, vol. III, in Karsten, G. (ed.) *Allgemeine Encyklopädie der Physik*, Leipzig: Leopold Voss.
Hilgard, E.R. (1977) *Divided Consciousness: Multiple Controls in Human Thought and Action*, New York: Wiley.
Jackson, J.H. (1884/1958) Evolution and dissolution of the nervous system: Lecture III, in Taylor, J. (ed.), *Selected Writings*, New York: Basic Books.
James, W. (1890) *The Principles of Psychology*, Cambridge, MA: Harvard University Press.
James, W. (1895) Person and personality, in Adams, C.K. (ed.) *Johnson's Universal Cyclopedia*, **6**, pp. 538–540.
James, W. (1902/1929) *The Varieties of Religious Experience: A Study in Human Nature*, New York: Modern Library.
James, W. (1907) The energies of man, *Science*, **25** (635), pp. 321–332.
Janet, P. (1889) *L'Automatism Psychologique*, Paris: Ancienne Librairie Germer Billiere et c^{ie}.
Krippner, S. & Powers, S.M. (eds.) (1997) *Broken Images, Broken Selves: Dissociative Narratives in Clinical Practice*, Washington, DC: Brunner/Mazel.
Laszlo, E., Csányi, V., Combs, A.L. & Artigiani, R. (1996) *The Evolution Of Cognitive Maps: New Paradigms for the 21st Century*, London: Adamantine Press.
Maturana, H.R., Varela, F.J. & Uribe, R. (1974) Autopoiesis: The organization of living systems, its characterization and model, *Biosystems*, **5**, pp. 187–196.
Myers, F.W.H. (1903) *Human Personality and its Survival of Bodily Death*, New York: Longmans, Green.
Myers, F.W.H. (1976) *Subliminal Consciousness*, New York: Arno Press.
Nagel, T. (1974) What is it like to be a bat?, *The Philosophical Review*, **83**, pp. 435–450.
Prince, M. (1906) *Dissociation of a Personality: A Biographical Study in Abnormal Psychology*, New York: Longmans, Green, and Co.
Prince, M. (1914) *The Unconscious: The Fundamentals of Human Personality, Normal and Abnormal*, New York: Macmillan.
Sacks, O. (1973/1990) *Awakenings*, New York: Harper.

Sidis, B. (1910) Fundamental states in psychoneurosis, *Journal of Abnormal Psychology*, **5**, pp. 321–327.

Spencer, H. (1863) *Essays: Moral, Political, and Aesthetic*, New York: Appleton-Century-Crofts.

Taylor, E. (1984) *William James on Exceptional Mental States: The 1896 Lowell Lectures*, Amherst, MA: University of Massachusetts Press.

Taylor, E. (1996) *William James on Consciousness Beyond the Margin*, Princeton, NJ: Princeton University Press.

Taylor, E. (2000) Introduction, in James, W. *The Varieties Of Religious Experience* [Centennial Edition], New York and London: Routledge, Taylor & Francis.

Winkler, M. & Combs, A. (1993) A chaotic systems analysis of individual differences in affect, *The 24th Interamerican Congress of Psychology*, Santiago, Chile.

Wright, C.E. (no date) Letters 177, *The Internet Encyclopedia of Philosophy*, [Online], http://www.iep.utm.edu/wright/

Paper received August 2010.

Arthur Hastings

William James, Conversion and Rapid, Radical Transformation

Abstract: *This essay briefly considers the psychology of radical psychological transformations, sometimes termed 'quantum change', such as religious conversions. Such transformations are the focus of two of William James's chapters in The Varieties of Religious Experience. They can occur abruptly, resulting in a restructuring of the entire personality, sometimes in the direction of greater health, or recovery from drug addiction. The author summarizes seven reported aspects of quantum change such as positive shifts of values or attitudes, widening of perspectives, and increases in self discipline.*

Keywords: William James, quantum change, rapid psychological transformation, personal transformation, conversion, religious experience

In *The Varieties of Religious Experience*, William James (1929) devotes two chapters to religious conversion, which he describes as a situation in which there is a sudden transformation from an unhappy or conflicted self, to a unified, happy person, with a different centre of personal energy (p. 186), in this case, a religious centre or what might now be called spiritual. Of course the book was written in the days of religious evangelism and tent revivals, with their call to be saved through the grace of God. James includes ample first person reports of these experiences. The conversion, he says, can also be gradual over time, step by step, but his focus is on the more rapid, transformative

Correspondence:
Arthur Hastings, Institute of Transpersonal Psychology, 1069 E. Meadow Cir., Palo Alto, CA 94303   Phone: (650) 493-4430   *Email: ahastings@itp.edu*

experience, and this is the subject of this paper. James notes that we do not need to believe whether it is divine intervention or not, in order to study the process.

The Transformative Process

These dramatic changes still occur today and there is renewed interest in them as transformative, non-linear processes, not necessarily limited to a religion, but as an experience in everyday life in which the person is suddenly swept up, even taken over, by strong changes of feelings, thoughts, and perceptions, such as love, altruism, insight, happiness, understanding, clarity, beauty, existential meaning, and values which result in a dramatic change in the self. W.R. Miller and J. C'de Baca (1994; 2001; Miller, 2004) have characterized these events as Quantum Changes, because there is no apparent gradual transition but more of a jump from one self to a radically different one. Currently these have been studied initially in cases where persons have given up alcohol, smoking, heroin, and other addictions as a result of the experience. A well known example is that of the founder of Alcoholics Anonymous, Bill W., who had a single mystical experience that ended his alcoholism. In addition Miller and others (e.g. Loder, 1981; Wood, 2009) have reported and discussed a variety of transformative accounts of major personality shifts, insights leading to personal integration, and spiritual epiphanies. This continues as a topic in the psychology of religion, such as studying the triggers of conversion and the aftereffects (Rambo, 1995; Hood, Hill and Spilka, 2009). However, comparatively little is known in psychology, religion, and neuroscience about the dynamics underlying these changes.

How Does This Work?

Although there is scant mention of this topic in human development and in neuroscience, it poses questions that could stimulate research and theory in both fields. For example, how does this dramatic and often long-lasting change happen? James's explanation for this process is that everyone has various groups of related thoughts, feelings, and behaviours connected together in sets of internal systems. A system is a 'center of energy' (James, 1929, pp. 192–193) for a particular role, purpose or aim. Different systems may be in charge for different contexts or purposes. James uses an example about the president of the United States putting aside his presidential behaviour and habits (a group system) to become a 'man of nature', or outdoorsman, chopping wood, trekking through jungles, etc. (a different group system) and becomes so-to-speak a different person (*ibid.*, p. 190–193). James's dry humour comes to the surface when he says that if the president did not allow politics to gain dominion over him and he did not come back from his 'nature' role, he would be a permanently transformed being. I hasten to note that he was referring to the then president Theodore Roosevelt. These systems of energy described by James have been variously referred to in some psychologies and psychotherapies as complexes, sub-personalities, and systems of condensed experience.

Our ordinary alterations of character through these systems are usually transient and reversible, James says. But, some systems pervade the whole person. He calls such a system the person's 'habitual center of his personal energy' (*ibid.*, p. 193). If one overall system becomes dominant and stable and expels its rivals, says James, we speak of it as a transformation. It may happen suddenly, influence the whole character, and be radically different from the previous self organization, values, and behaviour. The core organizing centre has changed (*ibid.*, p. 206). Perhaps drawing on F.W.H. Myers, James suggests that there are subconscious or subliminal forces 'behind the scenes which in their way work towards rearrangement' (*ibid.*, p. 202; and see pp. 203–206, p. 226).

Andrew Newberg (2006) comments on the difficulties of applying neuroscience to such rapid, radical, spiritual transformations. He notes that for a such a dramatic alteration of physiology and psyche, the neural connections have to be rewired. How can the nerve cells make the experiential changes in such a short time? He speculates that connections in some way may be activated, suppressed, or excluded to allow new primary systems of consciousness to be activated. There may be some clues, Newberg indicates, in the neuroscience findings on meditation states, because some meditation practices create extensive changes in cerebral structures, and sometimes lead to these shifts of the core centre.

Can Transformation be Facilitated?

While it may happen spontaneously, it appears that transformation can also be facilitated, though not forced. Here are examples of some supportive environments or precursors:

- Spiritual practices, e.g. meditation, Zen Buddhism's *satori*; non-dual awareness; prayer, ritual and ceremony.

- 12 Step programmes.
- Psychedelic and psycholytic therapy, e.g. Roland Griffiths and his colleagues at Johns Hopkins and their work with psilocybin; current clinical trials for MDMA and LSD for depression and trauma; Stanislav Grof's psychiatric work.
- Spontaneous mystical and transcendent awareness, e.g. peak experiences.
- Near-death experiences (but, note that some are negative).
- Crises in life, e.g. depression, loss. (Not recommended, but these are common triggers.)
- Deep self reflection, e.g. therapy, introspection, existential exploration.

Some of the Changes That May Occur

These rapid, radical transformations are usually found to have positive effects on the person's life. Here are some of the changes reported in the research:

- A positive shift of values and attitudes.
- Ceasing harmful habits.
- Widening of perspectives.
- A change of core assumptions.
- Increase in self discipline.
- Changes in purpose.
- Existential shifts.

In conclusion, these experiences of transformation link with contemporary themes and are worth further investigation because (1) they occur as an atypical, non-linear process in human development; (2) they are much more common than recognized; (3) they may involve conscious and out-of-consciousness elements; (4) they are usually healthy and integrative; (5) and James thought they are interesting (reason enough!)

References

Hood, R.W., Hill, P.C. & Spilka, B. (2009) *The Psychology of Religion: An Empirical Approach*, New York: Guilford Press.

James, W. (1929) *Varieties of Religious Experience*, New York: Modern Library. Original publication 1902; page numbers in this paper are for 1929 edition.

Loder, J.M. (1981) *The Transforming Moment: Understanding Convictional Experiences*, New York: Harper & Row.

Miller, W.R. (2004) The phenomenon of quantum change, *Journal of Clinical Psychology*, **60** (5), pp. 453–460.

Miller, W.R. & C'de Baca, J. (1994) Quantum change: Toward a psychology of transformation, in Heatherton, T.F. & Weinberger, J.L. (eds.) *Can Personality Change?*, Washington, DC: American Psychological Association.

Miller, W.R. & C'de Baca, J. (2001) *Quantum Change: When Epiphanies And Sudden Insights Transform Ordinary Lives*, New York: Guilford Press.

Newberg, A. (2006) The neurobiology of spiritual transformation, in Koss-Chioino, J. & Hefner, P. (eds.) *Spiritual Transformation and Healing: Anthropological, Theological, Neuroscientific, and Clinical Perspectives*, Lanham, MD: Rowman & Littlefield.

Rambo, L.R. (1995) *Understanding Religious Conversion*, New Haven, CT: Yale University Press.

Wood, D. (2009) *Eucatastrophe: Rapid Recovery From Depression Precipitated By Transformational Subjective Experience*, Palo Alto, CA: unpublished PhD dissertation, Institute of Transpersonal Psychology.

Paper received August 2010.

Gary E. Schwartz

William James and the Search for Scientific Evidence of Life After Death

Past, Present, and Possible Future

Abstract: William James's historic fascination with psychic phenomena, including the possibility of life after death, has become more widely known with the publication of recent books and articles on this controversial aspect of his scientific legacy. However, little is known about the emerging evidence suggesting the possibility that James's scientific interest in these topics has not waned since he died. This paper reviews preliminary observations, including two exploratory double-blinded mediumship investigations, which are consistent with the hypothesis that James (with others) may be continuing his lifelong quest to address the question of the survival of consciousness after physical death 'from the other side'. These proof-of-concept investigations illustrate how future systematic laboratory research is possible. The limitations of current neuroscience methods are explicated in terms of investigating the hypothesis of the brain as a possible antenna-receiver for consciousness. If James's tentative conclusions about the nature of the relationship between consciousness and the brain turn out to be accurate, then it is logically plausible (if not essential) to posit the possibility that his efforts have persisted in the recent past and present, and may even continue in the future. Scientific integrity plus the pursuit of verity require our being open to this important theoretical and empirical possibility.

Correspondence:
Gary E. Schwartz, Laboratory for Advances in Consciousness and Health, Department of Psychology, The University of Arizona, Box 210068, Tucson, AZ 85721-0068, USA. Email: gschwart@u.arizona.edu

Keywords: William James, consciousness, survival of consciousness, mediums, life after death, double-blinded experiments, mind–brain relationship, spirituality, beliefs, materialism

> *Either I or the scientist is of course a fool with our opposite views of probability here.... I may be dooming myself to the pit in the eyes of better-judging posterity; I may be raising myself to honor; I am willing to take the risk, for what I shall write is my truth, as I now see it.*
>
> — William James
>
> *These are the kind of data I wouldn't believe, even if they were true.*
>
> — Statement allegedly made by a sceptic to Margaret Mead
>
> *Do not bite my finger, look where I am pointing.*
>
> — Warren McCulloch

Introduction

As reviewed by Alvardo and Krippner (2010) in this issue, William James had a distinguished (and controversial) history of conducting research investigating the potential legitimacy of certain mediums and psychics of his day. Trained in both philosophy and medicine, and raised in an intellectual home where his family admired the spiritual writings of Emmanuel Swedenborg — one of Sweden's most renowned scientists and mystics — it is perhaps not surprising that James would endeavour to employ his substantial intellect, curiosity, and creativity toward integrating his overarching scientific and spiritual interests.

Blum (2006) has provided a comprehensive review of the history of this work. Blum's book is thoroughly researched with substantial notes and annotations. She chronicles the challenging and volatile nature of psychic research in this era — including the uncovering of fraud in certain purported mediums and psychics, as well as the recounting of frequent vicious attacks on the credibility and sanity of James and other psychic researchers by mainstream staunch sceptics of the time.

The reader interested in James's investigations of Mrs. Piper and other mediums will find Blum's (2006) book particularly useful. The purpose of the present paper is not to review this available history, but rather to present some little known exploratory investigations — including two double-blinded proof-of-concept experiments — concerning the possible continued presence of James since his passing. These controversial observations are reported here with the intent that they not only honour James's history of research on the possibility of life after death, but more importantly that they honour James's deep commitment to verity and pragmatism.

If survival of consciousness after physical death is real — emphasizing the word *'if'* — the question arises: Is it possible that James has continued his devotion to exploring these areas 'from the other side', despite the limited 'resources' available to him at the present time (i.e. the minimal availability of present day scientists remotely open to such a possibility)?

Before describing in some detail two proof-of-concept double-blinded investigations that speak to this empirical possibility, the author shares some of the unanticipated and challenging academic history that ultimately inspired him to design and implement these investigations. Some of this information is provided in more detail in Schwartz (2010a,b). This personal and historical information is shared in the spirit of the opening three quotes of present article — describing the events as they factually occurred, and carefully considering their alternative interpretations.

A challenging question posed by an anonymous reviewer of this paper naturally presents itself: quoting the reviewer, 'was [Schwartz] "chosen" by James (or some other power) to be the researcher with which James worked from "the other side"'? This question will be addressed below.

Hopefully the reader will examine the preliminary observations presented in this paper with an open mind and consider their alternative interpretations in light of the totality of the empirical findings. Readers will differ widely in assessing the probability — recalling James's quote which begins this paper — of whether James was correct in his assessment of the possibility of life after death (ranging from delusion to reality).

The truth is that the current scientific probability estimates are based on individual scientists' beliefs, personal histories, and preferences for specific theories and world views, and not on empirical evidence. The intent of the present paper is to provide some initial observations and rationale to encourage the possibility of conducting future research. As the neuroscientist Warren McCulloch playfully suggested, 'Do not bite my finger; look where I am pointing.'

To assist the reader in evaluating this information, critical questions raised during the review process are included in the paper. Addressing these important questions in a forthright fashion can potentially help to reduce the inherent propensity of the controversial premise of this paper to engender unfounded hostile criticism.

We begin with a challenging thought experiment.

Brief Historical Background:
From William James Hall to 'The Book of James'

Albert Einstein was well known for conducting imaginary 'what if' thought experiments in his head. Let us conduct a 'what if' thought experiment and imagine for the moment (1) that James's essence — his consciousness and personality — did survive his physical death, and (2) that James wanted to have this important fact known to the scientific community.

Two questions immediately present themselves: How would James accomplish this goal, and who would James find to assist him in doing so?

A moment's reflection reveals the obvious fact that the hypothesized surviving James would have exceedingly few opportunities and choices at his disposal. James would be seriously challenged in finding a living scientist:

(1) who was open to the possibility of survival of consciousness in general, and the survival of James's consciousness in particular,

(2) who was conducting laboratory research on the possibility of life after death,

(3) who had the human (e.g. medium) and financial resources to potentially verify whatever findings could occur, and

(4) who ideally had some professional appreciation of James's history and life goals.

The author of this paper suspects that if he was 'chosen' by James (the reviewer's question), it was primarily because the pool of possible scientist candidates who fit these unique requirements was extraordinarily small.

It is also worth pondering the possibility that (1) if James's consciousness did survive, and (2) if James was as thorough in the after life as he was in his physical life — remembering that we are conducting a 'what if' thought experiment — it would be reasonable to hypothesize that the surviving James would probably have performed due diligence and he would have learned key details of the author's professional history and abilities.

When the author was a graduate student in the clinical psychology program in the Department of Social Relations at Harvard in the late

1960s, the debate between behaviourism and cognitive psychology was still heated, and the word 'consciousness' was considered taboo in many academic quarters. The author's early exposure to the writings of William James was limited, despite having completed his PhD in William James Hall (and subsequently having served as an Assistant Professor in the newly formed Department of Psychology and Social Relations; the words Social Relations were subsequently dropped from the name of the department). His early co-edited book series on *Consciousness and Self-Regulation* (e.g. Schwartz and Shapiro, 1976), was initially received with overt hostility from a minority of the Harvard faculty.

In those days the author's theoretical leanings were toward systems thinking and emergent properties in the tradition of Nobel Prize winner Roger W. Sperry (e.g. Sperry, 1970). From this perspective, cognition, including consciousness, was presumed to be an emergent property of neural network and feedback processes, and Schwartz accepted this hypothesis. During the period of time that the author was a professor of psychology and psychiatry at Yale University (1976–1988), when both his parents died, his personal response to their passing was consistent with his reform Jewish as well as scientific upbringing — ashes to ashes, dust to dust, case closed.

It is potentially significant that the author had been approached by a major textbook publisher to write a contemporary introductory text following in the tradition of James (if for no other reason that this stimulated the author to re-examine James's work in more depth). Though the time commitment was too great for him to attempt writing such a text, the author gave it careful consideration and spent dedicated time becoming more familiar with James's writings in psychology.

Contemporary Physics, Systems Theory, and the Persistence of Information

As described in detail in his book integrating systems theory and quantum physics (Schwartz and Russek, 1999), while at Yale he also became open to the possibility that not only did information carried by photons persist in the 'vacuum of space' (a core assumption of quantum physics and astrophysics — without this assumption, there would be no justification for the development and application of precision optical as well as radio telescopes), but that this information retained its systemic / feedback structure, and therefore could continue to function as a dynamical 'info-energy' system. Feedback memory theory theoretically applied to all systems at all levels which contained dynamical feedback loops.

In other words, just as the light from distant stars continues long after the star has 'died' — i.e. the photonic information of the history of the star continues in space (a fact which makes the science of astrophysics possible) — patterns of photonic information and energy comprising biological systems could conceivably continue in space after the organism had died (despite the low intensity of the energy — in quantum physics, intensity is defined as the number of photons per unit period of time).

This led to the novel prediction that learning and memory processes which required the existence of networks of feedback loops could conceivably continue in space (since their informational structure would persist in the vacuum as well). Simply stated, the integration of systems theory with contemporary quantum physics revealed a possible theoretical framework for predicting and explaining a variety of seeming anomalous experiences and phenomena, including the continuity of cognitive processes after physical death. Moreover, since animal brains contained billions of neurons with potentially a hundred or more feedback loop connections (on the average) *per neuron,* this raised the possibility that memories and consciousness associated with all living systems with functional nervous systems could, in principle, continue in some form after physical death.

However, because the systemic / feedback memory hypothesis was so controversial, and because it addressed so many seemingly anomalous phenomena, the author purposely did not attempt to have it published when it was first formulated.

It is one thing to become open to a controversial theoretical possibility (and even consider publishing a theoretical paper); it is another to conduct empirical research based on the theory. As described in two books (Schwartz and Russek, 1999; Schwartz, 2002), the author began research on the possibility of life after death reluctantly (and initially secretly) as a result of meeting a practising clinical psychologist (Dr. L. Russek) from Boca Raton, Florida. She was grieving the death of her distinguished scientist and cardiologist father (Dr. H. Russek). It was she who first inspired the author to use the quantum feedback / systemic memory theory he had formulated at Yale and experimentally apply it to the survival of consciousness hypothesis. At this point in time the author had yet to meet and investigate any purported mediums.

From Physics and Systems Science to Mediums and the Alleged Spirit of William James

It was as a result of subsequently meeting Susy Smith in Tucson, Arizona, and learning of her controversial claims, that the author was faced with a deep scientific challenge related to James. He had became aware of Smith through an article published in a local newspaper in the mid 1990s about her personal 'afterlife codes' experiment (the article was brought to his attention by Dr. Richard Lane, a professor of psychiatry and psychology at the University of Arizona).

Smith was already the well known author of two academic books (e.g. she produced an edited volume of F.W.H. Myers classic *Human Personality and Its Survival of Bodily Death*, with a Foreword by Aldous Huxley; Myers, 1961), followed by more than two dozen books for the general public on psychic phenomena including life after death.

The newspaper article stated not only that Smith, formerly a sceptical journalist herself, had subsequently become psychic after the death of her mother (she preferred not to use the term medium because she was purportedly only able to communicate with a small group of deceased people), but that one of Smith's primary 'guides' (besides her deceased mother) was the renowned Harvard Professor William James.

The author learned that Smith had published two books supposedly in collaboration with James since he had passed (Smith, 1974; 2000). The author discovered that Smith had created a small non-profit foundation (the Survival Research Foundation) to foster research. However, after meeting with Smith, the author learned that she was not only convinced that James was still in communication with her, but that he was claiming to be interested in participating in research!

The author was well aware of the obvious concerns: (1) was Smith a fraud, and / or (2) was she self-deceptive (if not deranged) about James (the same question posed by the reviewer about the author)? From a simple probability point of view, one might predict a 'yes' to one or both of these questions.

Would it be unproductive, if not foolish, to consider the possibility of investigating her claims about James empirically?

For the sake of historical accuracy, the author did wonder, what was the conditional probability of these five James-related events:

(1) that his early academic career would begin in William James Hall,

(2) that he would be recruited to write a textbook in the tradition of William James (a request he seriously considered),

(3) that he would seemingly accidentally develop an integrative quantum systems theory that predicted the continuity of consciousness after death which was curiously consistent with James's receiver theory about the relationship between mind and brain,

(4) that he would eventually meet a formerly well known author, lay scientist, and psychic in his current location who not only claimed to be in communication with James (and have written two books with him), but

(5) that she claimed that James was eager to participate in contemporary afterlife research?

Was this collection of five events simply coincidental, or could it reflect something more, possibly a synchronicity (Combs and Holland, 2000)?

However, it was a sixth event — his unanticipated meeting with a second purported psychic medium (Laurie Campbell) who curiously also claimed to be in communication with distinguished deceased scientists (e.g. Sir James Clerk Maxwell), and following his unanticipated 'reading' with her — which ultimately inspired him and his colleagues to design and conduct two double-blinded proof-of-concept experiments purportedly involving James.

The reader may be wondering (as did a reviewer) whether the author was at this point being like a 'naïve sitter at a reading making past events *fit* with the story being outlined by the psychic' (*fit* italicized by the reviewer)?

The answer in this instance is a definitive 'no'.

First, the author is not a naïve sitter, nor is he a naïve scientist. Quite the contrary, he is a well trained and experienced experimental and clinical psychologist who is knowledgeable and mindful of possible cognitive distortions, perceptual priming, self-deception, and illusory correlates. In fact, he and his colleagues have conducted extensive personality and psychophysiological research on self-deception funded in part by grants from the National Science Foundation and the National Institutes of Mental Health.

Second, the author has read secret books and manuals about how to be a fake medium (sometimes termed a mental magician), and he has even taken a formal course in how to be a fake medium (parenthetically he is quite adept at it).

And third, he collaborates with a group of senior researchers who continually raise such important critical questions. For example, as discussed in Schwartz (2002), the author consistently involves a group of sceptical scientists (sometimes referred to as his 'Friendly Devil's Advocates' or FDAs) to carefully critique the work and its alternative interpretations.

The factual historical professional information about the author is included in this paper not only because (1) it is conceivable, at least in theory, that it might have been relevant to James, but also because (2) the conditional probability of the totality of the six events is so low as to be interesting (if not anomalous, e.g. synchronistic).

For the sake of completeness, a brief description of his initial meeting and observations with Campbell is included here. The author will refer to Smith as Medium 1 and Campbell as Medium 2.

A Chance (and 'Trance') Encounter with Professor James?

As described in detail in Schwartz (2002), the author learned about Medium 2 from Dr. Donald Watson, a retired psychiatrist and neuroscientist who at that time was grieving the tragic death of his son. Watson had become aware of the author's budding interest in this area through reading a then just published paper about Smith and her afterlife codes research (Schwartz and Russek, 1997). Watson claimed that although Medium 2 was a housewife in California, with little more than a high school education, she was interested in science.

When the author was introduced to Medium 2, and without any provocation, she claimed to begin receiving information from both the author's deceased mother and father. For the record, the author had not requested a personal reading (his intent was to witness what Medium 2 did with Dr. Watson), and he attempted to discourage her from conducting one (but with minimal success). The information Medium 2 provided regarding his parents' physical appearances, causes of death, and personality traits was surprisingly specific and accurate.

As mentioned above, the author was well aware of cold reading techniques used by psychic entertainers; hence, he was not a naïve sitter. For example, he was careful not to offer any verbal information which the medium could then claim to interpret.

A reviewer asked the question, 'How can he be sure that no information was offered to the psychic?' Lacking video recordings of the author's verbal and non-verbal behaviour during the session, the reader is justified in being sceptical.

However, as future experiments reported below established, *this medium was equally successful when both she and the experimenters were blind to the information — hence, no unintentional cuing on the part of the experimenter was possible. Moreover, this medium (and others) participated in research where visual and auditory cues were physically eliminated, yet her (and their) performance remained high.* Hence, the most parsimonious interpretation of the totality of the data is that the medium did *not* get her accurate information simply via cold reading techniques.

Though this personal family information was not widely known (and the internet was then in its infancy), the facts which Medium 2 provided could have been obtained through fraudulent means. In addition, the author was well aware of alternative possible parapsychological explanations; for example, in theory Medium 2 could have been reading his mind telepathically. Hence, he remained intentionally sceptical during the meeting.

The author decided to ask Medium 2 if she could obtain any information concerning a person named Dr. Henry Russek; the information she provided proved to be accurate as well.

What was compelling about this portion of the unanticipated reading was the extreme level of intensity of the emotion with which the deceased person purportedly described his love for his daughter (which happened to fit the author's knowledge of their unusually close father-daughter relationship). It is true, as a reviewer noted, that experienced cold readers often assume that a father-daughter relationship is close (an assumption which is not always valid in specific cases). However, the extreme nature of the medium's communication was so dramatic as to appear melodramatic (and it appeared comparable to the unusually close personal and professional relationship involving Dr. Russek and his oldest daughter). *More importantly, Medium 2 obtained specific information known only to the Russek family and select medical professionals* (presented in Schwartz, 2002).

Though also not planned, the author decided to ask if Medium 2 could receive any information from someone named William James. For example, he wondered, would the medium spontaneously confirm Medium 1's claims about James allegedly being interested in research?

Though Medium 1 claimed not to know Medium 2, and the author never mentioned Medium 1 to Medium 2, he was aware that it was possible that both of them could have been lying. Also, it was conceivable that Dr. Watson could have mentioned the Schwartz and Russek

(1997) article to Medium 2. Hence, the author remained appropriately sceptical.

What transpired was completely unanticipated. First, Medium 2 looked obviously perplexed and asked who William James was. Was she feigning ignorance? The author responded with a purposely vague answer: 'He's a friend of a friend' (an informal rephrasing of Smith's purported relationship with James).

The medium went on to describe a man who lived at the turn of the 20th century, was dressed in a long dark robe, wore a beard, and was surrounded by books.

Then, the medium visibly changed her countenance and appeared to go into a 'trance'. She began speaking in a lower, more deliberate and educated voice. For the next ten minutes or so, s/he began pacing and giving a lecture on the nature of consciousness; and in the process the purported spirit allegedly voiced his strong enthusiasm for continuing research.

Having never witnessed a medium before, the author was frankly shocked. He later learned that rarely did this medium (or most mediums) spontaneously fall into a trance where alleged spirits 'speak through' them (most present day mental mediums resist losing conscious control in this fashion, especially when in public).

He wondered, was it possible that Medium 2 was being genuine? Could James have literally 'come through' Medium 2 and forcefully indicated his continued commitment to the work?

Was Medium 1 actually correct in her description of James's desire to participate in research?

Was James (with others) choosing to serve in the role of what the author and his colleagues at the time playfully described as being 'departed hypothesized co-investigators' (DHCIs)?

There was only one way to find out, and that was to design controlled research which tested the mediums' claims empirically. Given the clearly questionable (as well as controversial) nature of these claims, the author was not about to initiate formal IRB approved research protocols without first performing some initial proof-of-concept feasibility investigations. The two proof-of-concept exploratory investigations described herein illustrate the potential promise of conducting systematic research testing such claims.

It is noteworthy that in each instance, the designs of the specific investigations were based upon novel (and experimentally testable) claims made by Mediums 1 and 2.

Medium 1 to Spirit to Medium 2 Communication?

Medium 1 made the following three claims:

Claim 1:
> She was able to communicate with four deceased people who wished to participate in controlled laboratory investigations: the four were (1) her mother, (2) James, (3) Russek, and (4) the author's father.

Claim 2:
> She could ask these individuals questions, and she could receive their answers.

Claim 3:
> Being a skilled painter, she could draw a picture of an image which they provided.

Medium 2 made the following three claims:

Claim 1:
> She was able to communicate with these same four deceased people, and that they wanted to participate in research.

Claim 2:
> She could ask these individuals questions, and she could receive their answers.

Claim 3:
> Though she was not a painter *per se*, she claimed to have good visualization skills and could verbally describe what they were showing her. [This claim was important because Medium 2 was expressly informed that this experiment involved her potentially seeing images purportedly provided by the deceased. Medium 2 claimed to have 'second sight' similar to the child in *The Sixth Sense* who uttered the famous words, 'I see dead people.']

Based on these six claims, the following experiment was designed:

Phase I: In the privacy of her home, Medium 1 was requested to contact the four hypothesized deceased persons and ask each of them to give her a specific image for her to paint or draw. Medium 1 was to place each painting or drawing in a separate, sealed envelope. As a control for the possibility of remote viewing, Medium 1 was requested to select a personal image to paint or draw and place in a sealed envelope. The investigators (Watson, L. Russek, and the author) as

SCIENTIFIC EVIDENCE OF LIFE AFTER DEATH 133

well as Medium 2 would be kept blind to all information concerning the five images and drawings.

Phase II: Medium 2 was invited to Tucson and participated in two separate communication sessions. In both sessions she was asked to contact each of the four DHCIs and request details about the specific images they had allegedly asked Medium 1 to paint or draw. Also in both sessions, Medium 2 was asked to attempt to get information about the image Medium 1 had painted or drawn for her self (i.e. the control image). The author took careful notes concerning the details purportedly ascribed to the images as reported by Medium 2. The investigators as well as Medium 2 remained blind to the specific images painted or drawn by Medium 1.

Phase III: Medium 1 and Medium 2 were introduced (supposedly for the first time). Medium 1 then opened the sealed envelopes and revealed the images (but not the identification of which images were allegedly proposed by which deceased persons). The three investigators, as well as Medium 2, independently rated each of the five images. The images were rated twice:

(1) to determine if the raters' prior knowledge and impressions were sufficient to guess which DHCI was associated with a given image, and

(2) to determine if the information obtained via the medium was required to determine which DHCI was associated with a given image.

The first set of five ratings was made using whatever prior (and idiosyncratic) knowledge and intuitions happened to be available to the investigators and medium. The second set of five ratings was made using the specific set of information that had been provided by Medium 2, and summarized by the author. Each of the four raters made their judgments independently.

Theoretically, if pure guessing was involved, the average accuracy would be 20% (1 out of 5 correct guesses per rater).

After the two sets of independent ratings were completed — and before the ratings were compared and tabulated — Medium 1 shared the alleged identification of each of the five images. The tabulated results were striking.

For the first set of ratings — based only on prior knowledge and rater impressions — the average accuracy turned out to be 20% (4 out of 20 correct; individual ratings of 2, 0, 1, and 1).

However, for the second set of ratings — using the specific information provided by Medium 2 — the average accuracy increased to 100% (20 out of 20 correct). A Fisher's exact test, one tailed, was $p < .00001$.

When these *quantitative* findings are combined with the *qualitative* data presented below, the results further suggest that something more than chance guessing was occurring with the inclusion of Medium 2's information (i.e. the second set of ratings). Moreover, the richness of the qualitative data suggest that mechanisms of receiving information other than (1) simple telepathy with the living, or (2) remote viewing, were involved in the totality of the evidence. The justification for reaching the challenging conclusions that simple telepathy and remote viewing were insufficient to explain the complete set of observations will become clear as the qualitative data are examined.

The complete set of qualitative analyses were published in Schwartz *et al.* (1999); a few exemplars are included here.

Surprisingly, when Medium 2 was requested to receive information about Medium 1's control image, *she claimed to have no difficulty in doing so*. She described the layout of Medium 1's apartment with sufficient detail and accuracy to imply that she was at least able to do remote viewing (presuming that fraud was not involved).

Moreover, when asked specifically about the control picture, she claimed to have no difficulty in doing so. She said she saw:

- a purple vase
- greens
- yellows
- many shapes
- a 'rainbow of colours'

There was only one image (out of the five) which fit the complex description of a purple vase with greens, yellows, many shapes, and a 'rainbow of colours'. The summary 100% percent accuracy scores do not convey the richness of these qualitative details. It turned out to be the image which Medium 1 had painted for her self (see Figure 1).

In light of this detailed qualitative information, the question arose, *what kind of evidence could suggest that anything other than remote viewing (again, presuming that fraud was not involved) was taking place in this proof-of-concept investigation?* In other words, what kind of evidence might suggest survival of consciousness above and beyond possible psychic abilities on the part of the medium?

SCIENTIFIC EVIDENCE OF LIFE AFTER DEATH 135

Figure 1 (Colour version at back of book)

A surprising answer turned out to suggest itself in the process of *more closely examining Medium 2's reports when she was purportedly communicating with the deceased.*

For example, when she was asked to contact Russek, she again reported the profound love he had for his daughter and family. (As mentioned above, cold readers often speak about loving father-daughter relationships, but rarely to the degree emphasized by this medium for this specific father-daugher relationship.) Of course, since Medium 2 was no longer blind to the identity of the deceased, such information was obviously meaningless from a scientific point of view. What would be required was new information not readily known or accessible.

As it so happened, in the first session Medium 2 claimed that Russek was upset because his wife was secretly crying at night, in their bedroom, with the curtains drawn, and he beseeched his daughter to discuss this with her mother. After the session, L. Russek contacted her mother and discovered that she had indeed been closing the curtains to the bedroom at night and crying by herself. The mother claimed to have kept this secret so as not to disturb her daughters.

This specific information was not known to any of the investigators (nor to members of the deceased's family). Since the investigators were blind to this information, Medium 2 could not have received it telepathically from the minds of the investigators.

A reviewer made the comment 'Of course a recently widowed spouse is likely to close the curtains at night and cry quietly — this is exactly the sort of information given by a psychic when they are cold reading.' However, despite this reviewer's definitive assertion about cold reading, it is a fact that none of the books on cold reading studied by the author recommended that a fake medium make such a specific statement. Moreover, this specific ploy was not mentioned in the formal course on cold reading which he took. Finally, in the many hundreds of research readings conducted by this author, on only one occasion did an alleged medium make such a statement — the reading discussed here. The reviewer's comments are included here to illustrate that scientists sometimes make unjustified assumptions about what cold readers allegedly do. Responsible researchers working in this area are not naïve about the techniques of cold readers.

More importantly, and surprisingly, was that Medium 2 reported *significant difficulty in getting information about the image from the deceased (whereas as mentioned previously she had no trouble getting information about Medium 1's personal image).* Medium 2 claimed that she was distracted by other more personal and emotional information coming from the deceased. In fact, the author had to press Medium 2 repeatedly to try and focus on receiving the requested image.

For Russek's image she reported:

- red
- pink
- vibrant
- 'heart in hands' (she saw the deceased holding the flower in his hands)
- a single 'rose long stem?' (Medium 2 was not sure about the type of flower)

There was only one image out of five that turned out to be mostly red and pink, vibrant, of a single long stem flower, which might be associated with a 'heart in hands', and it was the image supposedly drawn for Russek. The painting is shown below (Figure 2).

This painting of a single-stemmed red flower was not of a rose; it was of a poinsettia. Curiously, according to Medium 1, Russek had actually asked her to draw a rose (the image Medium 2 thought she saw). Medium 1 claimed not to be skilled at painting roses, and purportedly asked Russek if it was acceptable to him for her to paint a

SCIENTIFIC EVIDENCE OF LIFE AFTER DEATH 137

Figure 2 (Colour version at back of book)

poinsettia. Depending upon one's theoretical leanings and estimates of probabilities, one can consider various possible interpretations of this statement ranging from simple lying to genuine medium-to-spirit communication.

It is noteworthy that Medium 2 repeatedly claimed it was difficult for her to get information about the specific images from the deceased. She claimed that the reason was that personal thoughts and feelings of the deceased were stronger than their alleged transmission of the details in the image. A telling example involves the image purportedly suggested by James.

When requested to contact James, Medium 2 continued with her claims about his continued devotion to this area of research. Again, since she was no longer blind to the identity of James, such information was now scientifically meaningless.

When asked about the picture, she again expressed her difficulty and offered the following details:

- black pencil
- stencil
- maybe a 'picture of himself?' (Medium 2 was not sure of the face; she also made the editorial comment, 'Boy, is he arrogant!')

There was only one picture out of five that was not coloured, drawn with a black pencil, a stencil; however, it was clearly not a picture of a human. It was of a dog; more precisely, a puppy which had been purchased for Medium 1 named Sammy. At the request of the author, Medium 1 subsequently signed the drawing on the front of the image (Figure 3).

Figure 3

Since the author found it difficult to imagine why the alleged James would have requested that Medium 1 draw an image of this puppy, he gently asked Medium 1 if this was James's actual selection. Medium 1 confessed that James had allegedly requested that she draw a picture of her deceased dachshund Junior. Upon reflection, this request was potentially plausible.

According to Medium 1, at the time she was writing 'The Book of James' allegedly with James, Junior would spend time sleeping on her lap. After Junior died, he supposedly spent some of his time with James 'on the other side', and some of his time visiting with Medium 1. Medium 1 explained that she did not have a photo available of Junior, but she did have one of her new puppy. She claimed that she asked James if she could draw Sammy instead, and he supposedly agreed.

One reviewer wrote, 'You say that you "gently" questioned the medium about this, but surely the whole business deserved a more robust interrogation? Can't the woman remember what her loved deceased dog looked like?'

The author agrees that more thorough discussion with Medium 1 would have been valuable. However, given her age and relative frailty (she was in the mid 80s when this experiment was conducted), the author was careful to be gentle so as to not to make her defensive about her ability to paint, nor to 'interrogate' her regarding what her standards were for painting a beloved living creature from memory.

This reviewer also wondered, 'And if the whole purpose of the exercise is to convey the deceased's psychic attachment to the dog at the time, why is the image not conveyed psychically,' and 'This raises a question about the value of the drawing and painting exercise altogether. What exactly is it meant to achieve?' Hopefully it is clear that the 'whole purpose of the exercise' was not to convey Medium's 1 attachment to her dog *per se*, but to explore the experimental feasibility of investigating whether visual information could be conveyed from one medium to another via the mediation of allegedly creative, motivated and collaborating spirits. The use of images and visual imagery provided a novel possibility of exploring both quantitative and qualitative descriptions which could be compared with known information (i.e. actual drawings).

A reviewer made the following comment: 'the author seems to be claiming that animals have a soul and pass to the "other-side" to be with humans. This is an exceptionally controversial claim that will undoubtedly be met with great hostility by many readers. The author should make an attempt to clarify this point'. Another reviewer commented that the assumption that animal consciousness survives physical death is a contentious one 'because researchers can barely agree that animals actually are conscious in a similar way to humans in the first place, let alone capable of retaining a dog-shaped psyche on the "other side"'.

The reviewer was correct in that Medium 1 was making this claim. Moreover, every research medium the author has worked with has claimed that animal consciousness is no different from human consciousness in its essence; i.e. it continues to survive after physical death. Space does not permit providing the theoretical or empirical justification for the hypothesis that consciousness, *regardless of its level or complexity,* continues in some form after physical death (e.g. see Schwartz and Russek, 1999, mentioned above). Hence, a reader's response of 'great hostility' would be more indicative of an emotional reaction to — rather than an informed conceptual analysis of — this hypothesis.

Obviously it was not possible to verify the accuracy of such information; it was reported here because it happened. Various questions arise: (1) was Medium 1 lying, (2) did she have a creative imagination, or (3) was this an accurate account of her alleged communication with James?

A reviewer raised an interesting question: 'Why would a deceased person, who is actively trying to assist with research, project information to a psychic about something they were going to ask to be painted, but change their mind to something else? Why wouldn't they just project the image that was actually painted? It doesn't make sense....' To make sense of such seeming oddities, the reviewer suggested that 'It points toward telepathy (if you are looking for parapsychological explanation) or fraud rather than communication with the dead.'

The author appreciates the fact that some of the observations made do not make obvious sense (though potentially plausible explanations can be formulated — see below), and that telepathy or fraud might be preferred explanations to communication with the dead.

One of the more interesting and important questions for future research is to better understand the nature of the kinds of errors that skilled psychics and mediums make. For example, though the quantitative data indicate that blinded judges had no difficulty picking the image associated with James — since it was the only black and white penciled sketch — it was obvious that the qualitative content was not accurate. One reviewer wondered why the James image was 'the least well described.' There are various possible explanations for Medium 2's difficulty in seeing the image of the picture, including:

1. Her personal experience and image of James himself was in shades of black and white, and James's grey scale image might have conflicted with the soft penciled picture drawn by Medium 1.

2. The medium experienced James as 'arrogant' and she might have been distracted by her emotional reactions to her perceptions of James.

3. The other images were drawn in colour, and colour adds brightness and clarity to description.

These explanations could equally apply to causing errors in telepathy and remote viewing as they would to causing errors in getting details related to survival of consciousness. Hence, the presence of this error of perception on the part of Medium 2 does not justify therefore choosing more preferred explanations such as telepathy or fraud.

Just because a few observations cannot be readily accounted for by a given hypothesis (e.g. survival of consciousness) this does not justify resorting to less controversial explanations (e.g. telepathy or fraud) which turn out to account for even less of the findings (including findings for which no clear explanation is currently available). The fact remains that the totality of the evidence does not support either (1) simple telepathy or (2) fraud as viable explanations.

As Blum (2006) points out in her book about James and the early history of mediumship research, in some cases (1) specific mediums occasionally resorted to fraud, (2) these same mediums also showed genuine psychic abilities from time to time which could be explained as telepathy, *and* (3) they also provided certain kinds of compelling evidence which pointed strongly to the conclusion that they were somehow communicating with the deceased.

Though it is relatively easy to rule out fraud in controlled scientific experiments, as mentioned previously, the deep theoretical challenge is to discern whether parapsychological explanations are sufficient to account for all the observations, or whether actual communication with the deceased is occurring.

It is important to appreciate that the author and his colleagues conducted a large number of subsequent experiments with Medium 2 (as well as other mediums; this research is summarized in Schwartz, 2002; 2005). The totality of this evidence in the context of the various experimental designs convincingly rules out fraud and cold reading as being plausible explanations of the findings. In sum, Medium 2 demonstrated striking evidence of being psychic replicated over multiple experiments.

The question arises, do the findings from (1) this original 'medium-to-spirit-to-medium' *double*-blind experiment (which happened to have been conducted before some more naturalistic, *single*-blinded experiments were performed in the late 1990s), combined with (2) the most recent *triple*-blinded experiments (e.g. Beischel and Schwartz, 2007), provide convincing evidence for life after death? The answer is clearly no; the experiments do not rule out more speculative, 'super-psi' explanations (Braude, 2003; Fontana, 2005).

However, the totality of the evidence suggests that mechanisms other than (1) simple telepathy with the physically living, or (2) remote viewing, are involved. Moreover, *the precise manner in which the information is received appears to have qualities that closely resemble the 'look and feel' of consciousness*. This possibility will be returned to at the conclusion of this paper.

Can the Deceased Choose to Show Up (or Not) in an Experiment?

A fundamental assumption of the above proof-of-concept double-blind investigation was that the deceased could 'choose' to participate in research, and therefore by extension, could choose to 'show up' (or not) for a given session. When Medium 2, for example, was requested to attempt to receive information from a given deceased person, did this mean that she would automatically be able to do so? Is it possible that mediums are not simply 'retrieving' information but are 'receiving' (i.e. being given) it?

Using a current communication metaphor, the question arises, can alleged spirits, so to speak, intentionally 'screen their calls?' The following proof-of-concept investigation was designed to explore this theoretical possibility.

Medium 1 made the following two claims:

Claim 1:
> The set of four deceased persons who allegedly participated in the previous proof-of-concept experiment wished to continue to participate in research. This included James.

Claim 2:
> They could choose to 'show up' in California and be read by Medium 2, or not.

Medium 2 made the following two claims:

Claim 1:
> She could contact each of the four individuals and receive information from them without having to come to Tucson to do so.

Claim 2:
> She believed that the nature of the information she received would vary depending upon whether the deceased chose to be present (or not).

Based on these four claims, the following exploratory double-blind investigation was designed:

Phase I: Medium 1 contacted each of the four deceased persons, she explained the purpose and proposed design of the experiment, and asked if they were interested in participating. According to Medium 1, their answers were allegedly (and enthusiastically) affirmative.

Phase II: The author prepared six sealed envelopes, each containing an index card indicating the names of two DHCI's who would be requested in a given session to 'show up' for a reading with Medium 2; the other two DHCI's would be requested for that session to 'be somewhere else' (or at least *not* communicate with Medium 2). Six envelopes were required to cover all six possible combinations of the two present and two absent. The six envelopes were shuffled; consequently the author became blind to the order of their subsequent opening. In addition, Medium 1 was requested to shuffle them as well.

Phase III: On a designated night (which the author confirmed fit Medium 2's schedule the following morning), Medium 1 (in Tucson) would open a given envelope in the privacy of her home. She would then contact each of the four deceased persons and explain who of the two would be requested to visit with Medium 2 the next morning (and who would not). She recorded the date on the index card for later scoring of the data. The next morning, Medium 2 (in California), in the privacy of her home, would attempt to contact each of the four deceased persons and receive whatever information she could. Following the morning session, and using her notes, she selected who of the two she estimated had been invited the previous night to visit with her. Presumably Medium 2 did the readings and ratings blindly (with no collusion between mediums 1 and 2). The pattern of findings turned out to be consistent with the conclusion that collusion was not involved.

Phase IV: Upon completing the six sessions, and before breaking the code and analysing the data, the author requested that the medium contact each of the deceased people and describe what they were purportedly doing during their respective 'no show' sessions. At this point both Medium 2 and the author were blind to the potential accuracy of her readings and estimates.

Phase V: Medium 2's accuracy scores for estimating the presence (and absence) of each of the four deceased persons were calculated.

The average findings were in the predicted direction; 75% accuracy (50% would be chance). A Fisher's exact test, one tailed, was $p < .07$; a non-significant trend in the expected direction. However, careful examination of the individual scores revealed that for two of the deceased persons, Medium 2's percent accuracy scores happened to be 100% (6 of 6, per deceased person); for the other two deceased persons, the percent accuracy scores were at chance, 50% (3 of 6, per deceased person). As explained below, the justification for reporting these preliminary observations was their surprisingly close relationship to Medium 2's accounts of *what the deceased were allegedly doing when they were not present for a session.*

According to Medium 1, for 'no show' sessions:

- Russek was spending time *away* with his cardiology colleagues
- The author's father was spending time *away* with the author's deceased mother
- James was personally curious about what was happening in the experiment and he was '*watching* what was going on with Medium 2'
- Medium 1's mother was also curious and *watched* Medium 2 as well.

As it so happened, Medium 2's performance turned out to be 100% accurate for both Russek and for the author's father, the two deceased persons who claimed to have been '*away*' doing other things (Fisher's exact test, one tailed, $p < .007$).

Medium 2's performance was 50% (chance) for James and Medium 1's mother, the two deceased people who were purportedly 'curious' and '*watching*' and were supposedly present (but not communicative) at the sessions (Fisher's exact test, $p < .7$ NS).

If fraud was not involved here, and the results are not dismissed as chance, the *pattern* of the findings suggests that mechanisms other than (1) simple telepathy of the living, or (2) remote viewing, were involved. Again, *the totality of the findings appears to have the 'look and feel' of consciousness and intention.*

Why Formal Programmatic Research with James was Not Initiated

Though Medium 1 and 2 were both enthusiastic about conducting future systematic research allegedly with James and his apparent team, untoward circumstances interviewed. On Feb 11, 2001, Smith suffered a fatal heart attack, and the author's research attention shifted from James to Smith.

A reviewer requested more details about why the author 'abandoned the possibility of communicating with a great Victorian scientist, in favour of communicating with a purported ex-psychic?' There were four primary reasons:

First, at that point in the research, the author had not reached any firm conclusions about the source(s) of the accurate information obtained by successful psychics. He was not prepared to conclude that the information received by research mediums reflected actual 'communication' with anyone — be he a great scientist or otherwise.

Second, he was inspired to conduct research related to James significantly because of Smith's claims. When she died, the author's inspiration shifted from verifying Smith's claims about James to verifying Smith's predictions about her own continued consciousness.

Third, Smith was not simply a 'purported ex-psychic'. She was a scholarly lay researcher who critically examined the available scientific literature and made it comprehensible for the general public. Smith was more knowledgeable about the totality of research related to the survival of consciousness hypothesis than the majority of professional scientists in psychology and neuroscience. It is not inconceivable that the hypothesized surviving James may have 'chosen' Smith to work with him because of her journalistic sceptical yet open mind, combined with her devotion to this area of research and her excellent writing skills.

And finally, the author was cognizant of the fact that hostility toward positive findings would likely be less severe if they involved a relatively unknown former psychic compared to a famous scientist like James.

As described in Schwartz (2005), within twenty-four hours of Smith's passing, he initiated blinded readings with multiple mediums; this was the first time he served in the role of a research sitter rather than experimenter. The first reading happened to involve Medium 2; the actual reading was conducted by another experimenter, the author served as a secret sitter who listened as the reading was being conducted long distance over the telephone.

The reading included three pieces of information which were known only to the author (and not the experimenter). Smith had privately told him that she had three wishes upon her death. These three wishes will sound incredulous to those who believe that the probability of survival of consciousness is minimal or nil:

- That she would spend the next year of her life, 'on the other side', dancing with William James. Smith had been confined to a wheel chair for the last twenty years of her life, and she loved to dance.

- That she would raise an infant who had died. Smith had never had children, and she spent the predominance of her life single.

- That she would participate in future laboratory research on life after death, just as James had done before her.

The medium made three observations about the person she was presumably observing in spirit. For the record, at no time during the reading did Medium 2 identify the deceased person as Smith; moreover, it was not yet public knowledge that Smith had died.

- Medium 2 claimed that she saw the deceased person dancing with a distinguished gentleman, and that this would be meaningful and important to the secret sitter (in a later reading with a different medium, she claimed that she saw the deceased woman with someone who looked like William James).
- Medium 2 said that the deceased was showing her holding a young child, and
- Though confused about this, Medium 2 stated that the deceased was claiming that she was going to continue to participate in future research in the laboratory (something no previous deceased person had ever purportedly said regarding the author and the research).

Given the increasingly unanticipated (and controversial) direction which the research was taking, as explained above, the author was reluctant to pursue systematic research concerning highly visible deceased persons (academic or otherwise). However, as described in Schwartz (2010b), aspects of the research were increasingly appearing to take on a 'life of their own'; the emerging spontaneous evidence appeared to be consistent with the thesis that the survival of consciousness hypothesis — including memory, choice, intention, and self-determination — was potentially viable.

James's Question: Does Consciousness Require a Brain?

Let us assume, just for the moment, that the above observations can be replicated in future research. The critical question arises, how could such findings be reconciled with mainstream cognitive neuroscience?

Materialistically-oriented scientists typically view such findings as being confusing if not inconceivable. However, a close examination of the methods of contemporary cognitive neuroscience suggests a compelling (and parsimonious) solution.

As described in Schwartz (2002; 2005; 2010a,b), there are three types of experimental evidence that together 'seem' to point to the conclusion that consciousness is created by the brain. The word 'seem' is emphasized here because careful examination of the totality of evidence, when viewed from the perspective of electronics and electrical engineering, reveals how the evidence is actually *as consistent with the explanation that the mind is separate from brain as it is with the explanation that the mind is created by brain.* Unfortunately it is not widely appreciated by mainstream scientists that the three experimental approaches used to investigate mind–brain relationships do *not*, by themselves, require a materialistic conclusion — and they are wholly consistent with a non-materialistic explanation.

The three kinds of evidence are:

1. **Evidence from Recordings** — Neuroscientists record brain waves (EEGs) using sensitive electronic devices. For example, it is well known that occipital alpha waves decrease when people see visual objects or imagine them.

2. **Evidence from Stimulation** — Various areas of the brain can be stimulated using electrodes placed inside the head or magnetic coils placed outside the head. For example, stimulation of the occipital cortex is typically associated with people experiencing visual sensations and images.

3. **Evidence from Ablation** — Various areas of the brain can be removed with surgical techniques (or areas can be damaged through injury or disease). For example, when areas of the occipital cortex are removed, people and lower animals lose aspects of vision.

The generally accepted — and seemingly common sense — neuroscience interpretation of this set of findings is that visual experience is created by the brain.

However, the critical question is whether this *creation of consciousness* explanation is the *only* possible interpretation of this set of findings? The answer is actually no. The three kinds of evidence are *also consistent with* the brain as being a *receiver of external consciousness information* (Schwartz, 2002; 2005; 2010a,b).

The reasoning is straightforward and is illustrated in electronics and electrical engineering. Though it is rare to discuss an electronics example in the context of a psychology article, it turns out to be productive and prudent to do so here.

Consider the television (be it analogue or digital). It is well known — and generally accepted — that televisions work as *receivers* for processing information carried by *external* electromagnetic fields oscillating in specific frequency bands. Television receivers do *not create* the visual information (i.e. they are *not the source* of the information) — they *detect* the information, *amplify* it, *process* it, and *display* it.

Apparently it is not generally appreciated by neuroscientists that electrical engineers conduct the same three kinds of experiments as they do. The parallel between the investigation of the brain and the television is virtually perfect.

1. **Evidence from Recordings** — Electrical engineers can monitor signals inside the television set using sensitive electronic devices. For example, electrodes can be placed on particular components in circuits that correlate with the visual images seen on the screen.

2. **Evidence from Stimulation** — Electrical engineers can stimulate various components of the television using electrodes placed inside the television set or magnetic coils placed outside the set. For example, particular circuits can be stimulated with specific patterns of information, and replicable patterns can be observed on the TV screen.

3. **Evidence from Ablation** — Electrical engineers can remove various components from the television (or areas can be damaged or wear out). For example, key components can be removed and the visual images on the screen will disappear.

However, do these three kinds of evidence imply that the *source* or *origin* of the TV signals is *inside* the television — i.e. that the television *created* the signals? The answer is obviously no.

It should be clear how the basic logic — as applied to television receivers — can be equally applied to neural network (brain) receivers. The three kinds of evidence (correlation, stimulation, and ablation) only allow us to conclude that television sets — as well as brains — play some sort of *role* in visual experience. The truth is that these three kinds of evidence, by themselves as well as in combination, do not allow us to conclude whether television sets, or brains:

(1) 'self-create' the information internally — the materialist assumption, or

(2) function as complex receivers of external information — which allows for the possible existence of survival of consciousness after death and a larger spiritual reality.

In other words, the three kinds of evidence, by themselves as well as in combination, do not speak to (and do not enable us to determine) whether the signals — i.e. the information fields — are:

(1) coming from *inside* the system (the materialistic interpretation applied to brains), or

(2) coming from *outside* the system (the interpretation routinely applied to televisions).

It follows that *additional kinds of experiments are required to distinguish between the 'self-creation' versus 'receiver' hypotheses.*

Experiments on the survival of consciousness hypothesis with skilled research mediums provide an important fourth kind of evidence that can neither be predicted nor explained by the self-creation (i.e. materialism) hypothesis, but it can be predicted and explained by the receiver hypothesis (Schwartz; 2002; 2005; 2010a,b).

It should be noted that in physics, external electromagnetic fields are not labeled as being 'material' *per se*. They do not have mass (e.g. they do not have weight) and are invisible; they are described by a set of equations which characterize an as yet unexplained property of the 'vacuum' of space.

Conclusions — Looking Toward the Future

There are special moments in the history of science when major conceptual breakthroughs occur. They are sometimes called paradigm shifts or changes (Kuhn, 1996).

Classic examples of paradigm changes include the following shifts in understanding (1) believing that the earth was *flat*, to discovering that the earth was *spherical*, (2) believing that the sun revolved around the earth, to discovering that the earth revolved around the sun, (3) believing that matter was *solid and fixed* (how we conventionally experience it), to discovering that matter was mostly *'empty space'* and *dynamically probabilistic* (quantum physics), and (4) believing that the vacuum was *'empty'*, to discovering that space was *filled with invisible energy and fields of information* (e.g. the zero-point field).

Major advances linking quantum physics (and other more innovative and visionary physics) with consciousness and spirituality is capturing the imagination of contemporary researchers (Radin 2006; Goswami, 2001), and some of the core underpinnings of the materialistic world view is being seriously challenged if not disproved (Tart, 2009; Kelly *et al.*, 2009).

As the author illustrates (Schwartz, 2010b), new advances in technology (including the recording of patterns of cosmic rays as well as individual photons of light) are making it possible to address the presence and effects of a greater spiritual reality. A recent paper documents how a super-sensitive silicon photomultiplier system can be used to monitor the presence of spirit and potentially serve as a communication device (Schwartz, 2010c).

Though the idea of technology advancing to the point of creating a reliable spirit-communication device — what the author has playfully termed the evolution of the cell phone to the 'soul phone' — might sound to some readers like wistful (and misguided) science fiction, the history of science reminds us of countless instances where what was once assumed to be science fiction eventually became science fact.

If there is a greater spiritual reality, and *if* consciousness is the key to it — again, emphasizing *if* — then psychology will need to revise and expand its vision of (1) what is mind, (2) how does mind operate, (3) what are its limitations and potentials.

Just as a television set is required for receiving and converting the external EMF signals into viewable information and energy which can be processed by human beings, a receiving brain may be needed for human beings to function effectively in the physical world.

Interestingly, the hypothesis that the brain might serve as a receiver (as well as a transmitter) of information and energy for consciousness has an illustrious history. The brain-receiver hypothesis was seriously entertained not only by James, but also by Wilder Penfield, the distinguished Canadian neurosurgeon who mapped consciousness and the brain, and Sir John Eccles, the British neurophysiologist who won the Nobel Prize in Medicine for discoveries involving the neuron. These luminaries may have had the correct thesis (Kelly *et al.*, 2009; Van Lommel, 2010).

Will future research reveal that James's view about the relationship between mind and brain was correct?

Moreover, will future research further reveal that James and others like him are continuing to contribute to our understanding of consciousness and the brain?

As James asked the question, was he 'dooming' himself to 'the pit in the eyes of better-judging posterity'?

Or, was he raising himself to future 'honour' in the history of science?

James explicitly stated he was 'willing to take the risk' for what he would write was his 'truth' as he saw it then. Inspired by James's visionary words, and encouraged by the available evidence, the present author is taking the risk as well.

The answer will come with future research.

Acknowledgements

I would like to thank Leslie Combs, Anthony Freeman, and anonymous reviewers of this manuscript for their scientific openness as well as their thoughtful criticalness. The preparation of this paper was supported in part from private foundation funds gifted to the Voyager Program in the Laboratory for Advances in Consciousness and Health at the University of Arizona.

References

Alvardo, C.S. & Krippner. S. (2010) Nineteenth-century pioneers in the study of dissociation: Williams James and psychical research, *Journal of Consciousness Studies*, **17** (11–12), pp. 19–43.

Blum, D. (2006) *Ghost Hunters: William James and the Search for Scientific Proof of Life after Death*, New York: Penguin.

Beischel. J. & Schwartz, G.E. (2007) Anomalous information reception by research mediums demonstrated using a novel triple-blind procedure, *EXPLORE: The Journal of Science and Healing*, **3** (1), pp. 23–26.

Braude, S.E. (2003) *Immortal Remains: The Evidence for Life after Death*, Lanham, MD: Rowman & Littlefield.

Combs H, & Holland M. (2000) *Synchronicity: Through the Eyes of Science, Myth and the Trickster*, Cambridge, MA: Da Capo Press, 3rd edition.

Fontana, D. (2005) *Is There an Afterlife?* Oakland, CA: O Books.

Goswami, A. (2001) *Physics of the Soul: The Quantum Book of Living, Dying, Reincarnation, and Immortality*, Newburyport, MA: Hampton Roads Publishing.

Kelly, E.F., Kelly, E.W., Crabtree, A., Gauld, A., Grosso, M. & Greyson, B. (2009) *Irreducible Minds*, Lanham, MD: Rowman & Littlefield Publishers.

Kuhn, T.S. (1996) *The Structure of Scientific Revolutions*, Chicago, IL: The University of Chicago Press.

Myers, F.W.H. (1961) *Human personality and its survival of bodily death*, ed. Smith, S., New Hyde Park, NY; University Books.

Radin, D. (2006), *Entangled Minds: Extrasensory Experiences in a Quantum Reality*, New York: Paraview Pocket Books / Simon and Schuster.

Schwartz, G.E. (2002) *The Afterlife Experiments: Breakthrough Scientific Evidence for Life after Death*, New York: Atria Books / Simon and Schuster.

Schwartz, G.E. (2005) *The Truth about Medium: Extraordinary Experiments with the real Allison DuBois of NBC's Medium and Other Remarkable Psychics*, Newburyport, MA: Hampton Roads Publishing.

Schwartz, G.E. (2010a in press) Consciousness and Spirituality: An empirical and experiential approach. In L. Miller (Ed). *The Oxford Handbook of Psychology and Spirituality*, Oxford: Oxford University Press.

Schwartz, G.E. (2010b in press) *The Sacred Promise: How Science Is Discovering Spirit's Collaboration With Us In Our Daily Lives*, Hillsboro, OR: Beyond Words Publishing / Atria / Simon & Schuster.

Schwartz, G.E. (2010c) Possible application of silicon photomultiplier technology to detect the presence of spirit and intention: Three proof-of-concept experiments, *EXPLORE: The Journal of Science and Healing*, **6** (3), pp. 166–171.

Schwartz, G.E.R. and Russek, L.G.S. (1997) Testing the survival of consciousness hypothesis: The goal of the codes, *Journal of Scientific Exploration*, **11** (1), pp. 79–88.

Schwartz, G.E. & Russek, L.G. (1999) *The Living Energy Universe: A Fundamental Discovery that Transforms Science and Medicine*, Newburyport, MA: Hampton Roads Publishing.

Schwartz, G.E., Russek, L.G., Watson, D.E., Campbell, L, Smith, S, Smith, E.H., James, W., Russek, H.I. & Schwartz, H.(1999) Potential medium to departed to medium communication of pictorial information: Exploratory evidence consistent with psi and survival of consciousness, *The Noetic Journal*, **2** (3), pp. 283–294.

Schwartz, G.E. & Shapiro, D. (1976) *Consciousness and Self-regulation: Advances in Research and Theory* (*Vol. I*), New York: Plenum Press.

Smith, S. (1974) *The Book of James: Conversations from Beyond*, New York: G.P. Putnam.

Smith, S. (2000) *Ghost Writers in the Sky: More Communication from James*, Tucson, AZ: Vision Press.

Sperry, R.W. (1970) An objective approach to subjective experience: Further explanation of a hypothesis, *Psychological Review*, **77**, pp. 585–590.

Tart, C.T. (2009) *The End of Materialism: How Evidence of the Paranormal Is Bringing Science and Spirit Together*, Oakland, CA: New Harbinger Publications.

Van Lommel, P. (2010) *Consciousness Beyond Life: The Science of the Near-Death Experience*, San Francisco, CA: HarperCollins.

Paper received August 2010.

Eugene Taylor

Who Was Frederic William Henry Myers?[1]

Abstract: The scientific study of consciousness in the late 19th century, which took place in Western countries across disciplines such as neurology, physiology, neuropathology, psychology, psychiatry and philosophy, appears to have striking parallels to current cross-disciplinary developments in the neurosciences. The 19th century period, however, has received little scholarly attention from historians of medicine, psychology, or science. Historians of depth psychology have investigated the area as part of the history of psychiatry, but cleaved most closely to the versions presented by early psychoanalysts-turned-historians, who have consistently portrayed Freud as the only legitimate history of the period, thus marking the territory of the late 19th century as inherently Freudo-centric. More recently a new line of historiography emanating from the work of the late Henri Ellenberger has launched a post-Freudian perspective in which the classical depth psychologies of Freud, Jung, and Adler may now be understood in a wider and deeper historical context defined by the development of a so-called French, Swiss, English, and American psychotherapeutic axis between 1881 and 1918, before the advent of psychoanalysis. Chief among the prime movers of this axis was Frederic William Henry Myers, graduate of Cambridge University, and co-founder of the Society for Psychical Research in England in 1882. Myers' grasp of the literature of the day regarding the scientific study of consciousness was both profound, and highly influential, particularly on such figures as William James. Since the period itself has

Correspondence:
Eugene Taylor, Saybrook University, 747 Front Street, 3rd floor, San Francisco, CA, 94111-1920, USA. *Email: Etaylor@saybrook.edu*

---

[1] Adapted in part from Taylor (1982; 2009).

yet to be fully reconstructed, the identity of Myers and his contribution to the scientific study of consciousness remain obscure, but are also receiving new attention in the area of modern consciousness studies.

Keywords: Frederic William Henry Myers, William James, Edmund Gurney, Richard Maurice Bucke, Jackson Putnam, Boris Sidis, Charles Richet, Pierre Janet, Sigmund Freud, Carl Jung, Society for Psychical Research, American Society for Psychical Research, Edmund Gurney, Frank Podmore, consciousness, hypnosis, automatic writing, automatism, degeneration, dissociation, spiritualism, séance, mediumship, subliminal, hysterical blindness, unconscious, hypnogogic state, secondary personality, crystal gazing, mythopoesis, Lowell Lectures.

Myers the Researcher

Frederic William Henry Myers (1843–1901), classicist, poet, and psychical researcher, was a Fellow and Lecturer at Trinity College, Cambridge, from 1865–69; Inspector of Schools from 1862–1901; and founding member of the Society for Psychical Research in England in 1882. He was the son of an Anglican minister. While his background was in literature and poetry, his knowledge of the sciences was extensive, and he played a crucial role in abstracting advances in dynamic theories of personality from the French and German literature so they might reach a larger English-speaking audience. With Edmund Gurney, Frank Podmore, and others, Myers replicated the hypnotic researches of the French in the hope of not only finding out more about the interior life, but also of producing evidence for life after death. Thus, his own study of séances and mediums was also extensive.

As the French physicians had discovered, all the symptoms of hysteria could be induced under hypnosis. Myers and his colleagues similarly maintained that all the phenomena of mediumship could be reproduced in the hypnotic trance as well. With this he now had a means to open the door to the interior life of the person, and the scope of what he found there astonished him, in what became the reigning era of the hysteric, the multiple, and the medium. He consumed all the known information of the day on these subjects and began to formulate his own theories about the nature of personality and states of consciousness possible for human beings to experience. This work culminated in his posthumously published *Human Personality and Its Survival of Bodily Death* (1903)

The mediumistic séance was the living laboratory of experiments for the psychical researchers. Séances had sprung up everywhere, in which a circle of sensitive and sympathetic individuals joined hands and attempted to call forth a departed spirit. Usually, one would allegedly return but speak through a control or entity, who would make themselves known through someone sitting at the table who was a sensitive or medium. The person who had recently lost a loved one could then speak through the medium to the control, who would transmit messages from the departed. The medium would frequently pass off into a trance, and could also assist others in the group to communicate through the control with additional spirits to learn more details of the afterlife.

While entranced, the medium, if a woman, might speak like a man. Similarly, a man might take on the aura of a woman. Married women, who were usually not permitted to speak in pubic except through their husbands, would here be permitted to address audiences sometimes of thousands, giving communications from beyond the grave while entranced (Braude, 1989). It was also not infrequent for those who discovered they possessed mediumistic powers thereafter to demonstrate other capacities such as clairvoyant visions and telepathic communication. In this regard, mediums held the same status as subjects prone to hysteria and multiple personality. Both mediums and hysterics were considered viable means for investigators to enter what was variously called the unconscious or the subconscious. Myers, however, preferred the term subliminal.

Hypnosis was the main avenue of exploration. Different levels of trance could be demonstrated, suggesting successively deeper strata of personality. Through suggestion, the subject could have parts of his or her body made anaesthetic, or perhaps paralytic, or completely limp. Hysterical blindness could be induced or suggested away. Through post-hypnotic suggestion, the subject could be made to perform acts at a later time. And when entranced during the interval, it was found that at the subconscious level, the patient was counting the days and the hours until the appointed time. But in waking consciousness, the subject denied any knowledge that any suggestion of such a kind had been made. The only exception was that, at the precise moment the act was to be carried out, the waking state of the subject would disappear and the trance state reappear, during which time the suggested act would be performed, without the later memory of the subject for the act. Another post-hypnotic suggestion could also be implanted at this time, so the subject would perform some other unconscious act at some even later date.

Myers had also been experimenting with the technique of automatic writing, which took different forms (Myers, 1885; Shamdasani, 1993). He had long known of writers who could pass off into a lightly distracted state and write continuously, only half-conscious of what they wrote. Automatic writing, however, was a more systematic version of this phenomenon, in which the hypnotized subject could be made to sit at a table with a screen between his head and his hand, which held a pencil over a piece of paper, and to write automatically from deeper and more profound springs of intelligence from within. The hypnotist could speak to the subject, or else speak to the hand, which the subject could not see, and get two different versions of the same story. A subject in a light trance might be asked about some incident involving a plausible explanation, which the hand would then contradict through a written statement when asked about the same incident. The hand behind the screen would remain immobile while the subject talked to the investigator, and when the investigator talked to the hand, the subject's head would fall to the side and his eyes would close, as he seemed to pass into a deeper trance as long as the hand was writing. Thus, different states of consciousness holding different sets of memories emerged as a defining characteristic of personality.

Crystal gazing was yet another means that Myers and the psychical researchers used to tap into interior states of consciousness. The image reminds us of the circus magician looking into the crystal ball, but neurological records at the Massachusetts General Hospital show that the method of crystal gazing was used there as early as the 1880s to induce a dissociated state of consciousness in hysteric patients (Taylor, 1988). Thoreau did this when he sat by Walden Pond meditating on the reflection of the setting sun on the water, after which he would write about insights that resulted from his trance reverie in nature. James Jackson Putnam, MD, would induce the trance state in his patients by getting them to do relaxed breathing while gazing at a source of light reflected off the surface of a common glass of water. Myers called this the subliminal region and soon came to champion, as his colleague William James also did, what he called a subliminal psychology (James, 1902b).

Myers was convinced that not only do we live perpetually ignorant of these interior states of consciousness, but that the majority of who we are can be found there. Others may think we are only whom we appear to be in the external world, but within is a vast interior life which actually determines who we are and how we then shape our outward personality, which may show little of what is actually within. Myers called the layer immediately beyond the waking state the hypnotic stratum and identified it as both highly susceptible to suggestion and also the source of our interior imaginative productions. Normal psychology stops here and declares all that is beyond cognitive thought is mere fantasy, but Myers believed that there were potentially different levels, or strata of the person, each level containing knowledge and memories which may or may not be known to the other levels. The condition most in the dark about these other states was particularly our own daily habitual state of waking awareness.

The deeper we went, the more ideas became images, which then took on a numinous character, sometimes creating visions of mythic proportions. To the insane, such visions come unbidden and are known as unwanted hallucinations. To the physician they are mere fantasy. To the psychic, the medium, and the religious adept, they are welcomed as signs of a higher spiritual state of consciousness beyond the normal everyday waking one. Myers called this visionary capacity mythopoesis, referring not only to the creative capacity of our imagination, but to the manner in which representations from a universal source deep within each of us find expression through the life of the individual personality. This included the mythic, numinous, and energic power of our inner symbolic life, as well as the image laden domain of the person allegedly suffering from mental illness.

Hysteria, Myers maintained, was a disease of the hypnotic stratum, while instances of telepathy, clairvoyance, and telekinesis gave us a clue to the growth oriented dimension of personality.[2] The disintegration of personality he referred to as the dissolutive dimension of the subliminal, while visions of ecstasy, spiritual epiphanies, and psychic occurrences he called evolutive — indications of where mankind as a whole could evolve into in the future.

We are thus an ultimate plurality of selves in Myers' scheme, capable of experiencing states of consciousness that range from the psychopathic to the transcendent. Waking consciousness occurs probably somewhere in the middle — its function being primarily the biological survival of the physical organism, so that we could experience those other states of consciousness beyond waking. According to William James, as yet unknown, each somewhere had their appropriate fields of application and adaptation.

Myers developed these ideas in a series of essays first published both in the *Proceedings* (*PSPR*) and also the *Journal of the Society for Psychical Research* (*JSPR,* both British) beginning in 1884. During this same period, he traveled to Paris and visited Charcot at the

---

[2] The term telepathy was originally coined by Myers.

Salpêtrière and to Nancy, where he met with Bernheim and Liébeault. On his return, he and his brother, A.T. Myers, along with Edmund Gurney and Frank Podmore, attempted to replicate the findings of the French investigators and to report their results in the *JSPR*, copies of which were immediately distributed to British and American audiences.

Of particular importance was his essay 'Human Personality in Light of Hypnotic Suggestion' (1886). There, Myers emphasized the possibility of a supernormal dimension to personality development. Experimental psychology in its strictest sense, Myers said, at least acknowledged normal and abnormal functioning, both mental and physical, of all kinds. Spontaneous states included sleep and dreams, somnambulism, trance, hysteria, automatism, alternating consciousness, epilepsy, insanity, death, and dissolution. Induced states included narcotism, hypnotic catalepsy, hypnotic somnambulism, and the like, which M. Beaunis had called 'psychical vivisection'. These topics are generally disregarded by scientists who focus on the rational ordering of sense data alone as the only acceptable method for conducting empirical science.

Following Reid's common sense philosophy, Myers characterized the normal view of personality as one of personal identity, which:

> implies the continued existence of that indivisible thing which I call myself. Whatever this self may be, it is something which thinks, and deliberates, and resolves, and acts, and suffers. I am not thought, I am not action. I am not feeling: I am something that thinks, and acts, and suffers. My thoughts and actions and feelings change every moment: they have no continued effect, but a successive existence; but that *self* or *I*, to which they belong, is permanent, and has the same relation to all the succeeding thoughts, actions, and feelings which I call mine... (Myers, 1886, p. 3).

A central will, continuous memory, and homogenous character represent, he said, the three key elements of the theory of personality put forth at that time by psychophysical inquiry. Yet hypnotism, when employed as a tool in experimental psychology, can show through post-hypnotic suggestion that the will can be held in abeyance and also preprogrammed from without; that memories are not continuous but state dependent; and that the self may actually exist within us as fragments, each being a part of the greater whole. Personality, in other words, is neither definite, permanent, nor stationary, but is, rather, shifting, illusory, and modifiable.

Myers went on to examine cases where the hypnotic trance could not be considered abnormal, such as its successful use in problems of alcohol and nicotine addiction and recovery from a variety of functional disturbances of the nervous system. He presented in the end, what William James was later to call 'Myers's problem', the fact that waking consciousness confuses the psychopathic and the transcendent, because both ends of the psychic spectrum present themselves to waking rational consciousness through the self-same channels. How to differentiate them is the question, for each one of us ought to want to move, both individually and collectively, from the lower, dissolutive states to the higher evolutive levels.

His major publication in 1886 was Gurney, Myers, and Podmore's *Phantasms of the Living* (1886). The book was ostensibly about telepathy, apparitions, and phantasms of all kinds, meaning not just visual, but auditory, tactile, and even purely ideational and emotional impressions. Essentially, as I read it, this is a contribution to the early scientific study of mental imagery. The cases they collected were purely anecdotal, but soon gave way to the international census on hallucinations, the first truly scientific attempt in experimental psychology to collect data on a single subject of study on a mass scale.[3]

The Influence of Myers on William James

James had known about Myers since 1882, when, waiting in London for news of his dying father in America, he had presented several papers to a loose knit band of philosophers called 'The Scratch Eight'. Croom Robertson, Henry Balfour, Edmund Gurney, Henry Sidgwick were among its members, most of whom had recently participated along with Myers in founding The Society for Psychical Research. Their intent was to employ the methods of science to investigate clairvoyance, telepathy, and other psychic phenomena, and possibly produce proof for life after death.

Two years later, a small band of investigators in the United States, urged on by Sir William Barrett, began plans to found the American Society for Psychical Research, an independent organization from the British group. James was one of its founding Vice Presidents. They founded Committees for Experimental Psychology, Thought Transference, Apparitions and Haunted Houses, and others such as the Committee on Hypnotism, to investigate any and all claims from the

---

[3] Remarking on his year at Harvard in 1892–1893, James Angell wrote: 'I enjoyed a peculiarly intimate contact with James by virtue of his turning over to me for study and digest the great mass of documentary material which had come to him in connection with the effort of the American Society for Psychical Research to secure exhaustive and reliable information regarding abnormal psychic experiences of normal individuals — especially so-called veridical hallucinations' (Murchison, 1930/1961).

spiritualists and mental healers. The Committees were led by Professors from Harvard and MIT and they held their first meetings at the American Academy of Arts and Sciences. Their first President was Simon Newcomb, Director of the Smithsonian Institution. Their collective interest was not in producing evidence for life after death, but they did believe they would discover what they called 'consistent laws of mental action'. Indeed, their study of hypnotism, mental imagery, post hypnotic suggestion, automatic writing, and crystal gazing led to the first use of these techniques to diagnose and treat cases of the ambulatory psychoneuroses that appeared in the walk-in clinics at the Massachusetts General Hospital, the Boston City Hospital, and elsewhere, and contributed to the rise of graduate courses at local universities in the first courses taught in experimental psychopathology (Taylor, 1996).

The earliest correspondence between James and Myers to be catalogued by Ignas Skrupskelis, editor of the James *Letters*, was not until 1885, just when the ASPR was officially declared to have been launched.[4] Myers had sent James a copy of an article he had recently published on automatic writing (Myers, 1885). James reciprocated by describing studies he had been recently performing on the so-called phantom limb phenomena. Employing the questionnaire method, James had sent around some 300 circulars on sensations of lost limbs, collected some data, and was about to send out more.[5]

We have a letter from Myers to James, written from Leckhampton House, Cambridge, England, Dec 14, 1888 (Skrupskelis & Berkeley, 1998, vol.6, p. 458), which opened with a note on Richard Hodgson, then current secretary of the American Society for Psychical Research. Hodgson, originally from Australia, had, as a member of the Society for Psychical Research, investigated the so-called Mahatma Letters, which allegedly exposed Madame Blavatsky as a fraud. There were other factors than Hodgson's investigation, but afterwards Madame Blavatsky was forced to abandon the headquarters of the Theosophical Society in Adyar, India, and move into seclusion in Paris. Having established a name for himself in the psychic world, the SPR sent him to the United States to become the secretary of the American Society, where he immediately took over the study of James's case of Mrs. Leonora Piper.

---

[4] James, W. to F.W.H. Myers, Feb. 25, 1885. From Cambridge, Mass. (Skrupskelis & Berkeley, 1998, vol.6, pp. 13-14).

[5] This data was subsequently published with only a sample of 154 cases in James (1887).

Myers tried to make the case for why Hodgson should stay with the ASPR instead of returning to England. He argued that they had enough workers in England, just not enough people who continued to be interested in the work of the Society. Hence, the work needed to be extended to other locations, such as the US. Myers hinted that the British group would even be willing to pay Hodgson's salary to remain in Boston.

James, meanwhile, had himself hinted that the ASPR might have to close down as an independent society. Many of the most prominent scientists had not renewed their membership, and the increasing costs became the responsibility of a smaller membership. The ASPR indeed did cease as an independent organization, a year later in 1889. Thereafter, they became a branch of the British group but continued to do important work up until Hodgson's death in 1905, when the Society moved to New York and began a new and different era.

Possibly one of the more significant events in the Myers-James connection occurred in August, 1889, when James attended the International Congress of Physiological Psychology in Paris. To assure his coming, Myers appears to have arranged for James's lodgings in Paris. Once he had arrived, James was pressed into service at the event with an opening statement. He also chaired one of the sessions. Freud, who had come to Paris to consult with Bernheim about a patient, evidently attended as well, but he remained an auditor only, lurking in the wings. Janet, on the other hand, was feted for the completion of his dissertation in philosophy on 'Psychological Automatisms'.

The Congress, among other events, had been organized by Charcot's group, but he was too ill to preside. Other members of his *Société de psychologie physiologique* presided instead, although Bernheim's followers evidently dominated the agenda. There were a number of German investigators there, such as Münsterberg, but by and large the Congress was boycotted by most of the Germans who were expected to attend.

The importance of the event lay in the meeting of the emerging Boston school of psychopathologists with the British psychical researchers, and key members of the so-called French Experimental Psychology of the Subconscious. James had come from the United States. His student Boris Sidis was also there, as well as others, such as Morton Prince. Charles Richet, Pierre Janet, and other members of Charcot's circle were there, as were the British psychical researchers. These three streams merged at the conference, as it was the first time that these investigators had actually convened in one place at the same time to discuss their mutual interests in dissociation theory, psychopathology, experimental psychology, and psychical research.[6]

Myers' Review of James's *Principles of Psychology*

By 1890, James had completed his monumental two volume *Principles of Psychology,* a work that launched psychology internationally as an experimental science rather than continuing to identify it as a category of philosophy. James had contracted to write it in 1878, expecting to be finished in two years, but it took him twelve. In the interim, his beloved mother died; his father, Henry James Sr., followed a few months later; then his God Father, Ralph Waldo Emerson, passed away soon thereafter. His first task was to collect and publish his father's literary remains, which appeared in 1885 (James, 1885). Meanwhile, James had become involved with psychical research and also the discoveries of the French psychopathologists, through whom he had been able to renew his interests in the possibility of altered states of consciousness beyond the rational waking state. Nevertheless, in his *Principles* (1890), he decided to stick to his original commitment to reductionist positivism and work only within the confines of the waking rational state. But discussions of the fringe of consciousness and cases of multiple personality kept seeping in nonetheless.

In a letter to James dated January 12, 1890, Myers wrote from England, announcing that he had read volume one in its entirety, but with volume two he had gotten about half-way through (Myers, 1891–1892, pp. 133–135). He believed James had done a good job of laying the contents of the books out, but then dictated in the friendliest way the idea that James should spend the rest of his career working on psychic phenomena rather then anything else, particularly due to his new stature in the world. Myers believed James was the only one of their little band who could carry the search for life after death through to its conclusion. Myers also appended a list of errors he had found for correction in the next revision.

In the review, Myers said he intended to forego a survey of the entire 1400 pages and only confine himself to commenting on those points of contact between what James said about psychology in relation to the field of interest occupied by psychical research. The difficulty was that telepathy, clairvoyance, and the evidence for life after

---

[6] The psychical researchers from England and the French psychopathologists had accidently met up once before in 1885, when, independently, both groups had sent teams of investigators to examine Janet's case of Leonié at Le Havre at the same time.

death, could not be admitted by the experimental psychologists lest it contradict their underlying philosophy of materialism. At the same time, fully committed spiritualists believed that the experimental psychologists were functionally incapable of understanding psychic events beyond the rational ordering of sense data alone.

Myers, however, pointed out that James, to his credit, avoided falling into any one of these camps, though he did opt for the positivistic point of view as a temporary platform to understand mental states. It was no rigid system but 'a map of descriptive details running out into queries which only a metaphysics alive to her task can hope successively to deal with' (Myers, 1891–1892, p. 113).

Myers posits secondary or isolated chains of memory rather than just memory per se of the conscious self. In *The Principles*, James, on the other hand, restricted consciousness to the primary self and to any other states he presumed of which waking consciousness had no knowledge. Myers countered with certain conditions of anaesthesis, recovery from feinting, and even during apparent coma. His key example, of course, was hypnosis. Also, in this regard, both James and Myers were in agreement that experiments with anaesthetics should continue because of what they revealed about consciousnes.

Myers then took up James on the reality of conscious states about which waking consciousness remained unaware. James says yes 'when secondary automatic performances must consist of unconscious perceptions, inferences, and volitions..., a consciousness of these actions exists, but is split off from the rest of the consciousness of the hemispheres'.[7]

Myers noted that James reviewed the conception of the soul and, without committing himself either for or against it, nevertheless examined its implications as if it were true. According to Myers, when James acknowledged in *The Principles* that the person exhibits it as a trance state, it was 'for the first time ... in any accredited manual of psychology' (Myers, 1891–1892, p. 120). Myers finished the review with pages of his own interest in clairvoyance and telepathy and returned to James occasionally in order to remain anchored in James's original subject.

James wrote from Cambridge, Massachusetts May 5, 1891, responding to the review:

> I think the article very masterly from the point of view of composition, and very impressive indeed from the point of view of content — in fact a

---

[7] Myers (1891–1892), p. 117. Universal consciousness, the farther reaches of these unconscious states, Myers called the *anima mundi* (p. 119).

most weighty production. I don't even see how the 'scientist' can help becoming grave at the considerations you present. Each of your successive manifestations gets more solid sounding, and it may be that the crown which comes to recognized leaders of new eras of thought will descend upon your brow sooner than you ever hoped it might. Surely no one has ever discussed these facts as *broadly* as you — it amounts to an entirely new attitude and point of view and if that doesn't mean 'epoch making,' what does? (Skrupskelis & Berkeley, 1998, vol.7, p 157).

The 1896 Lowell Lectures on 'Exceptional Mental States'

It is a basic truism that most psychologists as well as neuroscientists read only James's *Principles of Psychology*(1890), while philosophers confine themselves mainly to James's *Will to Believe* (1897) and his *Pragmatism* (1907), and religious scholars tend to focus on his *Varieties of Religious Experience* (1902a). Little known is that James focused on experimental psychopathology during the mid-1890s and developed a dynamic psychology of subconscious states applicable to both individual and group experiences. Contemplating his entire oeuvre, one is tempted to suggest that his emphasis on a cognitive psychology of consciousness in *The Principles* and the ultimately transforming mystical states of consciousness described in *The Varieties*, was bridged by this dynamic psychology of the subconscious in 1896.

Indeed, the 1896 Lowell Lectures on 'Exceptional Mental States', which James himself never published, did find a significant place in the early chapters of *The Varieties of Religious Experience*, insofar as James's message there was that an exploration of one's own subconscious was the road leading to the experience of ultimately transforming states of mystical consciousness. The 1896 Lowell Lectures also launched the so-called Boston School of Psychopathology, which in turn fueled a major explosion in the field of psychotherapeutics in the US after 1900.

James's lecture titles were Dreams and Hypnotism, Automatism, Hysteria, Multiple Personality, Demoniacal Possession, Witchcraft, Degeneration, and Genius. He opened with the idea that probably the largest problem with understanding psychopathology is our attitude toward it rather than the symptoms themselves. The difference between the normal and the insane is a fuzzy one and cannot always be accurately drawn. At the same time there is no such thing as a perfectly sane person. All of us have morbid traits, some more than others. At any rate, we should remember that 'no one flaw is fatal' (Taylor, 1984/2010).

His first lecture established that, in addition to waking rational consciousness, we have alternate realities within a dynamic subconscious in which numerous states remain active to one degree or another at different times, beyond the awareness of waking rational consciousness. The hypnogogic state, that twilight zone between waking and sleeping at night, was the zone of mental imagery beyond waking consciousness and a portal through which the mind then seems to embrace a confederation of psychic entities.[8] Dreams as well as hypnosis were means of entry into these altered states. He did not subscribe to the method of symbolism, however, which defines the depth psychologies.

James's second lecture defined consciousness as a field with a focus and a margin, but it is the margin that controls meaning. Here, Myers conception of a series of states of consciousness arranged in their order from the dissolutive to the evolutive becomes the basis for James's conception of a dynamic psychology of subconscious states ranging from the psychopathic to the transcendent. He alludes to this spectrum in *The Varieties of Religious Experience* (1902a), where he describes consciousness under nitrous oxide and where he also cites Richard Maurice Bucke, a Canadian psychiatrist, who wrote about cosmic consciousness. According to Bucke, cosmic consciousness is the end goal of the evolutionary process and also the highest state we can possibly experience. Bucke cited the primitive consciousness of the past, present day waking consciousness, and the subsequent evolution of human beings to a higher level of consciousness as the path of our species in the future. F.W.H. Myers was in fundamental agreement with regard to the evolution of human consciousness, believing that the appearance of psychic events — which we would consider today of a paranormal nature — were sign-posts indicating the direction human beings were evolving into in the future.

James, at any rate, took up Myers' model of a spectrum of states from the psychopathic to the transcendent, waking consciousness occurring, as Bucke alluded, somewhere in the middle, the purpose of which, James suggests in *The Varieties,* is the medium of bodily consciousness and the means by which the person accesses these other states of consciousness which somewhere have their field of application and adaptation.

Having established the domain of consciousness as essentially a dual state, where waking rational consciousness stands in relation to

---

[8] 'Hypnopompic' is the term now used to refer to the zone of imagery we pass through on waking in the morning.

the trance state, which itself reveals a variety of altered states of consciousness operating intelligently behind the scenes, lecture three focused on Myers' conception that hysteria was a disease of the hypnotic stratum, characterized by hyper suggestibility. James then introduced the psychogenic hypothesis — that ideas can cause physical symptoms by way of what investigators called the reality of the buried idea. Traumatic memories are stored in the subconscious in the form of an image to alleviate the suffering that lost memories create. One has to get down to the level of subconscious functioning where the image is being held and alter it in some way.

Lecture four further develops the idea that split off fragments of waking rational consciousness can float around in the subconscious, charged with energy, and operate according to laws of their own. A single traumatic experience could then attract subsequent traumatic experiences to it, appropriating their energy and growing in power. Finally, as the tension level rises, the buried idea, now a swirling complex, can burst forth into the field of waking consciousness in disguised form, either as a physical symptom or a full blown case of multiple personality. The important point of this lecture, however, is that James for the first time broaches a growth oriented dimension to personality. In certain individuals, he wrote, a secondary personality may emerge that is superior to the first and original lifelong identity. This secondary personality can dominate the field so pervasively that it becomes the individual's permanent personality from then on. These were Myers' views as well.

At any rate, we have revealed enough to suggest that Myers' theories were at the heart of James's conception of a dynamic inner life. The interested reader can consult the new second printing of *William James on Exceptional Mental States* for details on James's four remaining lectures (Taylor, 2010e).

Myers died before publication of *The Varieties of Religious Experience* and did not live to see the further use of his ideas made there. In that work James suggested the development of a cross-cultural, dynamic, and comparative psychology of mystical states, and mentioned the work of Janet, Morton Prince, Boris Sidis, particularly Myers, and also of 'Breur and Freud', as making head roads into these matters. He alluded to an event in 1885 which revolutionized psychology in this regard, but scholars are in disagreement as to whom or to what James was referring. The religious scholar Ann Taves, reviewing the work of Sonu Shamdasani and myself in her book *Fits, Trances, and Visions*, maintains it was the work of Pierre Janet on dissociation theory and his case of Leonié, first described in a paper before Charcot's *Société de psychologie physiologique* that year. On several occasions, James had alluded, however, to the great discovery in 1885 of the Belmont medium, Mrs. Leonora Piper, who showed clairvoyant powers but no morbid traits. There is also a case to be made for F.W.H. Myers, as that was the first year he unveiled his essays on a subliminal psychology, which James maintained was a revolutionary moment in psychology.

Myers died in 1901 and, as we have said, his unfinished work *Human Personality and Its Survival of Bodily Death* came out posthumously.[9] In his obituary tribute to Myers, James maintained he would certainly be judged as a man of the future, the contributor to an entirely new psychology.

There is one final anecdote to recount, written by a physician, Axel Munthe (1929). Munthe had been traveling on a boat in Italy in 1901 on which both William James and F.W.H. Myers were also aboard. Myers was quite sick and near-death. Munthe was called in to the deathbed as the practising physician, while William James had remained out in the hallway, too grief stricken to go in. At the same time he held with him a notebook, as James and Myers had made a pact that when either one of them died first, at the moment of supreme passing the other would be near-by to receive the all important evidence of a last message, indicating life after death. James sat there in a chair, notebook ready, pencil in hand, while Munthe attended to Myers in his last moments in the other room. Munthe reported that after a short period of time he pronounced Myers dead and left. On his way out he glanced over his shoulder and saw James sitting there in his chair, head hanging down, with his hands covering his face, and the notebook in his lap, the pages of which remained completely blank.

The Revival of Interest in Myers

Interest in Myers' life and work has been on the rise since publication of Henri Ellenberger's *Discovery of the Unconscious* (1970), a book that essentially brought the Freudo-centric era in the history of dynamic psychology and psychiatry to an end by showing a more accurate picture of the rise of depth psychology in the late 19th century, in which Freud was only one example. Numerous schools of

---

[9] James had written to Myers in January 1897, asking 'How goes the great book? The great book I mean on Subliminal Consciousness?' Ignas Skrupskelis, who edited James's *Letters*, thinks this later became *Human Personality and Its Survival of Bodily Death* (1903), but my sense is that James had a much greater and more important work in mind that he hoped Myers was working on than that (Skrupskelis & Berkeley, 1998, vol. 8, p 221).

depth psychology flourished that were not grounded in Freudian ideas, among them the systems of Pierre Janet, Paul DuBois, F.W.H. Myers, Boris Sidis, and Roberto Assagioli, to name but a few. As Ellenberger pointed out once in an interview, depth psychology began to flourish in the late 19th century along with other scientific bodies of knowledge, but with the normalization of all these developments that occurred in general science after 1900, only depth psychology was eliminated from the picture, yet it was later to become the primary focus of activity in clinical psychology and psychiatry for the next one hundred years. We must then add to that observation the fact that only psychoanalysis made it through the barriers erected by the hegemony of reductionist positivism thrown up by the basic sciences, so that in the US, no depth psychology has ever been taught in American medical schools except psychoanalysis.[10]

A school of historiography in psychiatry and psychology immediately sprang up following Ellenberger's lead that produced historical studies such as my own *William James on Exceptional Mental States* (1982), Mark Micale's *Beyond the Unconscious: Essays in the historiography of Henry Ellenberger* (1993), Fernando Vidal's *Piaget before Piaget* (1994), Mikkel Bork-Jacobson's *Remembering Anna O: A Century of Mystification* (1996); Sonu Shamdasani's *Jung and the Making of Modern Psychology: The Dream of a Science* (2003); and my recent work, *The Mystery of Personality: A History of Psychodynamic Theories* (2009a).

An entirely different line of investigation had also been launched by Michael Murphy's *Future of the Body* (1992). Murphy, co-founder of Esalen Institute in Big Sur, California, appears to be the primary contemporary author within the American psychotherapeutic counter-culture to have written extensively about Myers.[11] Murphy's project has been to develop the idea that the transformation of personality toward a higher, spiritual level of consciousness rests at the molecular level with the transformation of individual cells in the body.

---

[10] Nevertheless, these other systems have continued to exist, but at the periphery of the academy and mainstream definitions of science. Janet had a revival in the 1930s at Harvard Business School through the efforts of Elton Mayo, and again in the 1980s around the neo-dissociation theorists such as Bessel van der Kolk, Onno van der Hart, Earnest Hilgard, and others. Esalen Institue in California took up the system of Assagioli's psychosynthesis in the 1960s, while Jung has continued to flourish in the shadow of psychoanalysis and also in the American psychotherapeutic counter-culture.The recent post-Freudian era has also marked a resurgence of interest in Jung, demonstrating that, indeed, his complex psychology was unrelated to Freud's ideas. See Jung (2009).

[11] The pychiatrist Ian Stevenson, who developed twenty cases of reincarnation, was also a reader of Myers (Stevenson, 1974).

Bodywork, emotional and physical experience, sexuality, pure foods, and lifetime spiritual practice represent the cleansing and perfection of the body, which is not just a mechanical processor of food into waste, but a temple for the transformation of consciousness.

Reflecting on the history of Esalen and his own philosophy, Murphy drew a group of investigators into his circle such as Edward E. Kelly, Emily Kelly, Adam Crabtree, and others, who all had an interest in Myers from the standpoint of his contributions to psychical research, and the Era of Dissociation in the late nineteenth century, and they were keenly aware of Myers's relevance for modern parapsychology. Murphy's sponsorship was one of the key factors that led to their recent book, *Irreducible Mind: Toward a Psychology for the 21st Century*, which was dedicated to 'F.W.H. Myers: A neglected genius of scientific psychology'.[12]

Myers' Legacy

F.W.H. Myers, we can safely say, played a significant international role in the diffusion of dynamic psychology and psychiatry in the late nineteenth century through his investigations with the Society for Psychical Research in England. We may ask why, if psychical research has been totally debunked by reductionist science in the twentieth century, has psychical research, now called parapsychology, persisted? One historical answer is that it already established itself one hundred and twenty-five years ago as a player in the scientific study of consciousness by providing a foundation for what came to be known as experimental psychopathology and modern psychotherapeutics. That it drifted off into trying to pattern itself after physics and the physical sciences was logical, but not where we would predict it would have any effect alone by itself. We may also ask why there is a resurgence of interest in Myers' work? My suggestion is that particularly through the work of William James, his psychology was congruent with the humanistic implications of the modern neurosciences, which seek answers to the so-called Hard Problem in the scientific study of consciousness; namely the relation between the brain and the mind (Taylor, 2009b; 2010a–d). It is a problem which, in my opinion, the empirical reductionists, because of their antiquated epistemology, based as it is on Descartes, Newton, and Kant, have no preparation to answer.

---

[12] Kelly *et al.* (2007). See also Hamilton (2009).

References

Borch-Jacobsen, Mikkel (1996) *Remembering Anna O.: A Century of Mystification*, translated by Kirby Olson in collaboration with Xavière Callahan and the author, New York : Routledge.

Braude, A. (1989) *Radical spirits: Spiritualism and Women's Rights in Nineteenth-century America*, Boston, MA: Beacon Press.

Ellenberger, Henri F. (1970) *Discovery of the Unconscious: The History and Evolution of Dynamic Psychiatry*, New York: Basic Books.

Gurney, E., Myers, F. W. H. & Podmore, F. (1886). *Phantasms of the Living*, London: Rooms of the Society for Psychical Research; Trübner and Company.

Hamilton, Trevor (2009) *Immortal Longings*, Exeter, UK & Charlottesville, VA: Imprint Academic.

James, W. (ed)(1885) *Literary remains of the Late Henry James*, With an introduction by W.J., Boston, MA: James R. Osgood.

James, W. (1887) Consciousness of lost limbs, *Proceedings of the American Society for Psychical Research*, **1**, pp. 249–258.

James, W. (1890) *The Principles of Psychology*, 2 vols,

James, W. (1897) *Will to Believe and Other Essays in Popular Philosophy*, New York: Henry Holt.

James, W. (1902a) *The Varieties of Religious Experience*, New York: Longman.

James, W. (1902b) Frederic Myers's services to psychology, *Proceedings of the Society for Psychical Research*, **17**, pp. 13–23.

James, W. (1907) *Pragmatism: A New Name for some Old Ways of Thinking*, New York: Longmans, Green & Company.

Jung, C.G. (2009) *Liber Novis* [The Red Book], Edited and co-translated by Sonu Shamdasani, New York: Norton.

Kelly, E.F., Kelly, E.W., Williams, E., Crabtree, A., Gauld, A., Grosso, M. & Greyson, B. (2007) *Irreducible Mind: Toward a Psychology for the Twenty-first Century*, Lanham, MD: Rowman and Littlefield Publishers.

Micale, Mark S. (ed.) (1993) *Beyond the Unconscious: Essays of Henri F. Ellenberger in the History of Psychiatry*, introduced and edited by Mark S. Micale; translations from the French by Françoise Dubor and Mark S. Micale, Princeton, NJ: Princeton University Press.

Munthe, Axel (1929) *The story of San Michele*, New York : E.P. Dutton.

Murchison, C. (Ed.) (1930/1961) *A History of Psychology in Autobiography*, New York: Russell and Russell.

Murphy, Michael (1930/1992) *The Future of the Body: Explorations Into the Further Evolution of Human Nature*, Los Angeles, CA: J.P. Tarcher.

Myers, F.W.H. (1885) Automatic writing or the rationale of planchette, *Contemporary Review*, **47** [February], pp. 233–49.

Myers, F.W.H. (1886) Human personality in the light of hypnotic suggestion, *Proceedings of the Society for Psychical Research*, **4**, pp. 1–24.

Myers, F.W.H. (1891-1892) Review of William James's *Principles of Psychology, Proceedings of the Society for Psychical Research*, Supplement 1, **7**, pp. 111–133, London: Kegan Paul, Trench and Trübner.

Myers, F.W.H. (1903) *Human Personality and its Survival of Bodily Death*, New York: Longmans, Green, and Company.

Shamdasani, S. (1993) Automatic writing and the discovery of the unconscious, *Spring; Journal of Archetype and Culture*, **54**, pp. 100–131.

Shamdasani, Sonu (2003) *Jung and the Making of Modern Psychology: The Dream of a Science*, Cambridge & New York: Cambridge University Press.

Skrupskelis, I.K. & Berkeley, E.M. (eds) (1998) *The Correspondence of William James*, Charlottesville, VA: Univ. of Virginia Press.

Stevenson, Ian (1974) *Twenty Cases Suggestive of Reincarnation*, 2d ed., revised. and enlarged, Charlottesville, VA: University Press of Virginia.

Taves, Anne (1999) *Fits, Trances, and Visions*, Princeton, NJ: Princeton University Press.

Taylor, E.I. (1982) *William James on Exceptional Mental States*, New York: Scribner's Sons.

Taylor, E.I. (1984/2010) *William James on Exceptional Mental States: Reconstruction of the 1896 Lowell Lectures*, New York: Scribner's Sons.

Taylor, E.I. (1988) On the first use of psychoanalysis at the Massachusetts General Hospital, 1903–1908. *Journal of the History of Medicine and Allied Sciences*, **43**(4), pp. 447–471.

Taylor, E.I. (1996) *William James on Consciousness Beyond the Margin*, Princeton, NJ: Princeton University Press.

Taylor, E.I. (2009a) *The Mystery of Personality: A History of Psychodynamic Theories*, New York/The Netherlands: Springer.

Taylor, E.I. (2009b) *Déjà vu*: William James on 'The Brain and the Mind,' 1878. Paper for Div 32 symposium on 'Neurophenomenology and the enactive theory of Consciousness', Annual conference of the American Psychological Association, Toronto, Canada, Aug 7, 2009.

Taylor, E.I. (2010a) Could Radical Empiricism Guide Neurophenomenology as the Future of Neuroscience? Plenary address honouring the centenary of William James's death, Annual conference on 'Toward a Science of Consciousness', April 12–17, Tucson, Arizona.

Taylor, E.I. (2010b) William James and Neurophenomenology. Paper presented at the William James Centenial Symposium on 'In the Footsteps of William James', sponsored by The William James Society and Harvard University, Lamont Library, Harvard University, August 16.

Taylor, E.I. (2010c) William James and the Humanistic Implications of the Neuroscience Revolution: An Outrageous Hypothesis, *Journal of Humanistic Psychology, Special James centenary issue*, **50**, pp. 410–429.

Taylor, E.I. (2010d) William James on an Intuitive, Phenomenologically Oriented Psychology in the Immediate Moment: The True Foundation for a Science of Consciousness? Special issue on Consciousness in the Neurosciences, *History of the Human Sciences*. Fall issue. In press.

Taylor, E.I. (2010e) *William James on Exceptional Mental States: Reconstruction of the 1896 Lowell lectures*, Second printing, Portsmouth, NH: The Jetty Press.

Vidal, Fernando (1994) *Piaget before Piaget*, Cambridge, MA: Harvard University Press.

Paper received September 2010.

NEW IN PAPERBACK

Immortal Longings
F.W.H. Myers and the Victorian Search for Life After Death

By Trevor Hamilton

340 pages £14.95 / US$29.90

Imprint Academic

ISBN 9781845402488

The first full-length biography of Frederic W.H. Myers, leading figure in the Society for Psychical Research, and the friend and associate of Browning, Gladstone, Ruskin, Tennyson, Swinburne, Henry James, Prince Leopold and other influential Victorians. The book offers a fascinating insight into a key period in the development of Victorian thought.

> 'The life of F.W.H. Myers – a man of various and remarkable gifts – involved many of the most significant aspects and personalities of the Victorian intellectual scene, yet no full biography of him has hitherto been written. Trevor Hamilton has brought together a good deal of new information about him, and analyses his career and character with sensitivity and insight. He tackles the decades-long commitment to psychical research, for which Myers is now best known, in detail and with admirable balance and lucidity. Altogether a fascinating read!'
> **Alan Gauld**

> 'Frederic Myers was one of the great pioneers in the scientific exploration of consciousness. He was original, brave and prolific. In this well-researched book, Trevor Hamilton sheds new light on his life and shows how Myers' work was embedded in the rich social and intellectual life of late-nineteenth-century Britain. I read it with great interest.'
> **Rupert Sheldrake**

> 'No author before Hamilton has presented such a global and integrative perspective of Myers. Hamilton combines well the personal and intellectual aspects of Myers with his psychical and psychological work. Furthermore, he covers areas of Myers that have previously been neglected, or only briefly discussed. In fact, I would recommend that Hamilton's work must be the first step in obtaining a good panoramic view of Myers.'   **Carlos S. Alvarado**, *J. Soc. Psychical Res.*

Christopher Mole

The Content of Olfactory Experience

Abstract: *Clare Batty has recently argued that the content of human olfactory experience is 'a very weak kind of abstract, or existentially quantified content', and so that 'there is no way things smell'. Her arguments are based on two claims. Firstly, that there is no intuitive distinction between olfactory hallucination and olfactory illusion. Secondly, that olfaction 'does not present smell at particular locations', and 'seems disengaged from any particular object'. The present article shows both of these claims to be false. It shows that naïve subjects find it quite natural to draw a distinction between olfactory hallucination and olfactory illusion. And it argues that the phenomenology of normal olfactory experience is of particular objects as having smells. Two confusions are responsible for Batty thinking otherwise: (1) Batty's examples are cases of extreme pungency, and she mistakes a peculiarity of intense perceptions for a property of olfaction more generally; (2) Batty focuses on very short time slices and so confuses limitations on the information carried by a single sniff for a limitation on the logical form of all olfactory content.*

In an important contribution to a recent issue of this journal Clare Batty argues that the content of human olfactory experience is 'a very weak kind of abstract, or existentially quantified, content' (Batty, 2010, p. 21), and that: 'As a result, there is no way that things smell' (p. 19). Batty presents these conclusions as capturing certain manifest features of the phenomenology of olfaction. Her aim, she tell us, is to 'argue for a view about the nature of olfactory content that honors its phenomenology' (p. 11). But her conclusions' claim to phenomenological plausibility is surely quite dubious. Even after reflection on the nature of olfactory experience it seems phenomenologically accurate to say the sort of thing that Batty's view forbids us from saying: that there is such a thing as a way that things smell. It seems perfectly natural, for example, to say that my roses smell a certain way, that my compost heap smells a different way, and that my lawn clippings smell a third way. These claims seem obvious. They do not seem to be figurative. Nor do they seem to be exaggerations, or instances of loose talk. We should not give them up unless an argument proceeding from even more obvious premises forces us to do so.

The argument that leads Batty into a position that gives up such claims is based on an inference to the best explanation of two alleged facts. The first of these alleged facts is that, because 'the notion of an olfactory illusion is not something that resonates with us' (p. 12), 'the traditional distinction between illusion and hallucination does not apply to olfactory experience' (p. 24). The second alleged fact is that 'olfactory experience does not present smells in distinct locations' (p. 15) and so 'seems disengaged from any particular object' (p. 16), with the result that olfaction 'cannot solve the Many Properties Problem'; where this 'Many Properties Problem' is understood as being 'the problem of distinguishing between scenes in which the same properties are instantiated but in different arrangements' (p. 14).

Given the first of these two alleged facts as an explanandum the inference that leads to Batty's picture, as giving us the best account of olfactory content, is relatively straightforward.

The traditional difference between hallucination and illusion, as Batty understands it, depends on it being the case that in illusion, but not in hallucination, we are presented with a real object as having properties that it does not have. If olfaction presents no objects then, *a fortiori*, it does not present real objects as having properties, and so it never presents them as having properties that they do not have. But, equally, if it presents no objects then nor does it present us with objects other than those before us, and so it lacks a feature displayed by paradigmatic cases of hallucination. Batty's claim that no objects figure in the contents of olfactory experiences therefore explains why it should be that 'the notion of olfactory illusion is not something that resonates with us' (p. 12) and why 'the traditional distinction between illusion and hallucination does not apply to olfactory experience' (p. 24).

Batty's explanation for the second alleged fact — that olfactory experience cannot 'distinguish between scenes in which the same properties are instantiated but in different arrangements' — is somewhat less straightforward. It depends on more than just the idea that the content of olfaction is existentially quantified. This is because it *is* possible, while using only existentially quantified representations, to 'distinguish between scenes in which the same properties are instantiated but in different arrangements'. To represent such a distinction one needs to make use of more than one existential quantifier, and one needs to make use of an expression for non-identity. But Batty will not allow that the content of olfaction includes more than one quantifier. She writes that: 'while a characterization of the content of olfactory experience may be rich in terms of predicates (as rich as the situation we are in and our discriminatory abilities will allow), it will only ever need one quantifier' (p. 20). Batty's view, then, is that the content of an olfactory experience is an unstructured set of properties, represented as being instantiated at approximately the location of the subject. With that restriction on the contents of olfaction in place it would indeed be true that olfaction could not distinguish between scenes in which the same properties are instantiated, but in different arrangements. And so it would be true that olfaction cannot solve the Many-Properties Problem.

Batty's picture of the content of olfactory experience therefore provides explanations for both of the features that she claims are attributes of olfaction. Neither of those features, however, turns out to be a genuine one.

Consider first the claim that 'the traditional distinction between illusion and hallucination does not apply to olfactory experience'. This is simply mistaken. There are cases of olfactory misperception that it is natural to characterize as hallucination. There are cases of olfactory misperception that it is natural to characterize as illusion. And there is a clear, and perfectly traditional, difference between them. Batty herself accepts that there are examples of the first sort. 'We seem to have no problem', she says, 'with the idea of an olfactory hallucination' (p. 12). One such example is that of the phantosmia exhibited as an early symptom by some patients with Parkinson's disease. Basile Landis and Pierre Burkhard give the following account of such a phantosmia, as experienced by a 57-year-old Parkinson's patient:

> Since 2000, she has complained of abnormal olfactory symptoms characterized by the occurrence of brief, repeated, and stereotyped episodes of strong smell sensations without substrate. Odorant perceptions were difficult to describe precisely and did not correspond to known odors. When prompted, she compared them to perfumes, to a 'rainy day', or even to a 'wet dog', ascribing them a pleasant aspect. Episodes usually

lasted a few seconds, up to minutes, and could occur many times per day in an unpredictable fashion. Conversely, known odors were perfectly identified, and she denied any subjective smell loss. (Landis and Burkhard, 2008, p. 1237f)

It is surely quite natural to describe this patient as suffering from olfactory hallucinations. That is exactly how Landis and Burkhard do describe her. That is what sixteen of the students in my sample of twenty-two said was the natural description of the case.

It is much less natural to describe these unpredictable episodes of smells, experienced independently of whatever aroma substrates are present in the environment, as olfactory illusions. Only five of the students in my twenty-two student sample claimed to find 'illusion' a natural description of the case. Two students weren't sure how the case should be described.[1]

For an example of the second sort — an olfactory distortion that it is natural to describe as an illusion, but not as an hallucination — consider the following, from the notes accompanying the recipe for 'Cinnamon and/or Vanilla Ice Cream' in Heston Blumenthal's *The Fat Duck Cookbook*:

> If you smell cinnamon followed by vanilla-and-cinnamon, what you get is vanilla. And vice versa… Cinnamon and vanilla are particularly good at this…
>
> [A]n ice cream in a glass flanked by two plastic squeezy bottles with conical tops narrow enough to nudge into a nostril… worked really well, and the effect seemed both stranger and even more in need of an explanation when the mouth was involved as well as the nose. I tried it out on some of the regulars at the Fat Duck and it invariably provoked a powerful mixture of amazement that it happened, and curiosity as to why. (Blumenthal, 2008, p. 234)

It seems quite natural to describe the olfactory effect that this dish depends on as an illusion. Seventeen of the students in my sample said that they found that to be the natural description. It seems relatively unnatural to describe the dish as inducing olfactory hallucinations.

---

[1] Twenty-two undergraduates at the end of an 'Introduction to Cognitive Systems' course were asked to fill in a questionnaire. The course from which the students were recruited did not cover material related to olfaction, hallucination, or illusion. The questionnaire presented the two examples discussed here, lightly edited for readability (e.g. in the Parkinson's case, 'Odorant perceptions' became 'These smell perceptions', and in the cookbook case 'what you get is' was replaced by 'all you can smell is'). The two examples were each followed by the question: 'Do you find it more natural to describe this as a case of hallucination, or as a case of illusion?' Three answers were available to tick: 'Hallucination', 'Illusion', and 'Not sure'. Half the students were given the cookbook case first. Half were given the Parkinson's case first. In both cases the three possible answers were presented in the same order.

Only four students regarded that description as natural. One student was unsure. If we discard data from the three students who were unsure about how to categorize one or other of the cases then a chi-squared test reveals the trend in this data to be a statistically significant one ($\chi^2 = 11.359$, d.f.=3, P=0.0099).

The difference between the Parkinson's symptoms and the gastronomic trickery corresponds to, and is plausibly explained by, what Batty identifies as the traditional distinction between illusion and hallucination: in the illusory case we perceive a real object — the ice cream — as having properties that differ from those it really has. In the hallucinatory case no real object is being misperceived.

This is bad news for Batty's claim that the content of human olfactory experience is never a singular proposition, but only ever 'a very weak kind of abstract or existentially quantified content'. Batty would have us believe that that claim has the virtue of collapsing a distinction that, having no intuitive force, we ought to collapse. Instead her picture robs us of the resources that we need for the drawing of a distinction that *is* intuitively marked.

What, then, of Batty's second alleged explanandum — her claim that 'olfactory experience does not present smells in distinct locations', that smell 'seems disengaged from any particular object', and so that olfaction cannot solve 'the problem of distinguishing between scenes in which the same properties are instantiated but in different arrangements'? Again the consideration of examples calls this alleged explanandum into question.

It may be by smell that I identify that there are traces of garlic on my left hand and traces of ginger on my right. The experience by which I discern that this is so is *not* one in which I find an object-independent disengaged garlic smell to be around when raising my left hand to my nose, and an object-independent disengaged ginger smell to be around when raising my right. Such an experience would be possible, but it would also be peculiar. It is not what we experience in the usual case. In the usual case olfaction presents our two hands as, respectively, the bearers of the two smells.

Batty is led to the mistaken view that object-independent, non-localized content is what we always experience in olfaction because her preferred examples of olfactory experiences are cases in which the thing experienced is extremely pungent: they are cases where a whole room is filled with lemon air freshener and with the smell of fish, or where the smell of coffee pervades an entire space. In these extreme cases it may be that the content of our experience omits information about determinate location. But this is not a general feature of olfactory experience. Nor is the non-localization of extreme percepts peculiar to the sense of smell. The auditory experience of a fire alarm ringing somewhere in the street may present the sound as coming from one house in particular, but when we are in the corridor where the alarm is loudly ringing the experience is not of the sound as located in any particular location, but of the sound as filling the entire space. Even in the visual domain it may be that a bright strobe light somewhere in the visual field adds a general strobing content to the experience that is not exhausted by the experience of strobing that is tied to a determinate location. It seems, then, to be typical of intense percepts that they are experienced without determinate locations. In an imprecise modality, such as olfaction, the threshold at which localization gives out may be relatively low. Batty's choice of extremely pungent examples therefore leads her to mistake the non-localization of extreme perceptions for a general and peculiar feature of olfaction.

Despite the complication resulting from her focus on cases of extreme pungency, Batty is not wholly mistaken here. She is right to identify 'Many Properties Problems' as marking a point at which there seem to be constraints on the possible contents of olfactory experience. It *does* seem possible, *pace* Batty, to smell that a particular object has an olfactory property. But what does not seem possible is to have a purely olfactory experience that tells one *how many* objects have that property. One may see that two of one's fingers have been painted red, rather than one, or feel that two of one's fingers are being stroked, rather than one, or hear that two of one's fingers are tapping on a resonant surface, rather than one. What one cannot do is to smell, with a single sniff, that two of one's fingers are garlicky, rather than just one finger having received a double dose. If one wants to extract quantitative information from olfaction then multiple sniffs will be required.

To say this, however, is not to find an alternative way of getting to the conclusion that Batty wants. Batty's aim is to show that 'accounts of representational content cannot always be based on the visual model' (p. 11). But to say that olfaction does not give us quantitative information in a single sniff is not to identify a respect in which the content of olfactory experience is unlike the content of vision. In both cases we must accept that the information carried by a single sensory sampling is impoverished relative to the content presented in normal experience. That this is so even in the visual case is one of the less controversial lessons that has been taught to us by the very extensive literature on our inability to recognize changes that occur when we are attending to the wrong thing, or that occur between saccades, or under the cover of an appropriate mask (Grimes, 1996; Mack and Rock, 1998; Noë, 2002; O'Regan *et al.*, 1999). What is peculiar to the olfactory case is just that in the olfactory case the distinct sensory samplings occur at greater temporal intervals. Batty is therefore right to identify something unusual in the way in which olfaction puts one into sensory contact with the objects around one, but wrong in attributing this peculiarity to a restriction on the logical form of olfaction's content.

Acknowledgement

Thanks are due Kim Voll, for help with the analysis of data.

References

Batty, C. (2010) What the nose doesn't know, *Journal of Consciousness Studies*, **17** (3–4), pp. 10–27.

Blumenthal, H. (2008) *The Fat Duck Cookbook*, London: Bloomsbury.

Grimes, J. (1996) On the failure to detect changes in scenes across saccades, in Akins, K. (ed.) *Perception*, pp. 89–110, Oxford: Oxford University Press.

Landis, B.N. & Burkhard, P.R. (2008) Phantosmias and Parkinson disease, *Archives of Neurology*, **65** (9), pp. 1237–1239.

Mack, A. & Rock, I. (1998) *Inattentional Blindness*, Cambridge, MA: MIT Press.

Noë, A. (2002) Is the visual world a grand illusion?, *Journal of Consciousness Studies*, **9** (5–6), pp. 1–12.

O'Regan, J.K., Rensink, R.A. & Clark, J.J. (1999) Change-blindness as a result of 'mudsplashes', *Nature*, **398** (6722), p. 34.

Paper received April 2010.

CONSCIOUSNESS PUZZLE PAGE!

BY E. SUBITZKY

Graham Horswell

Nature & Human Nature

13th Annual Conference of the Consciousness & Experiential Psychology Section of the British Psychological Society at St Anne's, Oxford, 2010

'Mind is part of nature, not apart from it' was, according to the programme, the starting point for this year's annual conference of the Consciousness and Experiential Psychology section of the British Psychological Society. The conference organizers (John Pickering and Susan Stuart, ably assisted by Gethin Hughes, Emma Crofton, and Emma Shackle on behalf of Oxford University) had drawn together a collection of contributors whose interests include ecology, ecopsychology, neuroscience, eastern traditions, neuropsychiatry, philosophy, art, architecture, and artificial intelligence (amongst others). For this reviewer, such a diverse gathering gave a wonderful air of the multidisciplinary nature of consciousness studies in modern times, and fostered an atmosphere of good-natured debate throughout the weekend.

Apart from the keynote addresses, the conference was mainly structured in parallel sessions, which forced attendees to make some very tough decisions in terms of where to focus their attention. For my part, I decided to station myself arbitrarily in one room for each day in the hope that I came across some interesting talks that I might otherwise have passed up — and this was certainly the case. So what follows is not a blow-by-blow account of the whole conference, nor a comprehensive synopsis of individual talks, but one person's general experience of the weekend. I'll take the opportunity now to apologise to those who presented that I didn't get to listen to, or that I fail to

Correspondence:
Graham Horswell, Assistant Managing Editor, *Journal of Consciousness Studies*
Email: graham.jcs@gmail.com

mention herein, but unfortunately, physics being what it is, I am as yet unable to be in two places at once.

Let's start with the Keynote Speakers — a trio of leading lights in their respective fields:

First up was Peter Fenwick, who took the audience through a fascinating discussion of his research into NDEs, deathbed coincidences, and other phenomena related to human death. It was a great treat to hear a respected neuropsychiatrist candidly discuss his interest in such 'controversial' ideas, and the evidence he has gathered — impressive by its sheer magnitude — was persuasively presented.

Professor Fenwick posits a possible five-dimensional reality to explain phenomena related to dying, drawing on various ideas from the study of quantum mechanics. He also highlighted the possibility of 'fields' of consciousness — similar, as far as I could gather, to Rupert Sheldrake's concept of morphogenetic fields (another controversial theory) — but his preference was clearly towards the former explanation. His latest book, *The Art of Dying* (co-authored with his wife Elizabeth), draws together his evidence and ideas, and if the book is as entertaining and thought-provoking as his presentation, I can thoroughly recommend picking up a copy! He has an infectious enthusiasm for his research, hampered only by the comparative lack of funding available for investigations into death-related phenomena. One can only hope that more professionals of Professor Fenwick's standing lend their support to such endeavours in future.

On Saturday afternoon came David Abram, described in the conference programme as a 'cultural ecologist, philosopher, and performance artist' (and from what I gather, these are only some of the many strings to his bow). His talk focused on climate and consciousness, and how nature and landscape directly affect our feelings, emotions, and awareness. The speech was playful and poetic, but don't let that fool you into thinking that important issues were not being discussed — the themes addressed directly relate to some of the most pressing problems we face as a species.

Dr Abram highlighted Gaia theory (as proposed by James Lovelock) — the concept that the biosphere has a rudimentary agency; it is a subject as well as an object. His own ideas suggest that 'each land has its own psyche', each landscape directly influences its inhabitants, and thus one's state of awareness changes as one moves from one place to the next. Climate has a similar effect — changing individuals' moods, emotions, disposition, etc. — and Dr Abram proposes (implores) that, as a species, we need to reconnect with nature rather than trying to dominate it.

Finally, on Sunday morning we were treated to an enigmatic discussion of the eastern traditions from Matthijs Cornelisen. What this man doesn't know about traditional Indian psychology simply isn't worth knowing, and he spent the morning indulging us with a thoroughly coherent account of 'The' Indian view (i.e. the common themes running through Indian traditions, the 'broad consensus' of the many views available).

Firstly, Dr Cornelisen described how, in the Indian traditions, consciousness is *primary*, it does not 'arise' from brain function, or from anything else, it simply **is**. Consciousness is transcendent, cosmic, and immanent. It exists not only in humans, but in everything — we are just one manifestation of it (i.e. consciousness exists in many modes, one of them mind).

According to 'The' Indian view, the ordinary waking state of humans is enmeshed in the workings of the mind (or brain), so we (westerners) tend to equate consciousness with the brain as an organ, but there are many different types of consciousness (such as the habits of the form and function of matter) which pervade nature as a whole. So the universe remains in perfect balance because consciousness is in everything, and 'everything must know everything in order to behave in the correct way'.

As if these three talks weren't enough to be thinking about over the course of a weekend, conference delegates were also exposed to numerous thought-provoking discussions from other contributors:

Richard Stevens (one of the founding members of the CEP section, I believe) introduced us to his 'Trimodal Theory' of human nature. This theory suggests that we, as humans, have three 'modes' or 'bases' underlying human action — biological, symbolic, and reflexive — and that, potentially, mankind's 'recent' dissociation from the natural world could be explained as an imbalance between these 'modes'. The paper provided a fresh approach to man's apparent 'need' to command his environment, and how best to address the problems that derive from this propensity.

Adam Melinn talked about 'Consciousness in Objects and Animals'. This session was an introduction to panpsychism (which was clearly distinguished from animism or monism), and hinged on the idea that 'objects, as well as animals, may have memories or some type of conscious narrative attached to their existence as individual things'. For example, and to paraphrase Nagel's famous article, Adam wondered 'what is it like to be a baseball bat?' He focused on the idea that all objects have the ability to store information/'memories' about past events, and that in a way this information is a form of communication, and as such can be considered, on some level, to be a form of consciousness.

To give you an idea of the good-natured debates at the conference, in the Q&A session at the end of this presentation, one listener argued that there is a need to specify that there is a difference between *storing* information and *using* information — it could be argued that consciousness is the *use* of information rather than just the ability to store it. It is only because we (humans) have the capabilities to interpret the 'memories' held by objects, that the possibility of objects containing consciousness can even arise. Unfortunately, the session time out before this debate could really be fully concluded...

Paul Stevens spoke lucidly about ecopsychology. The view presented in this talk relates to the concept that we are integral to the environment, not separate from it (echoing the thoughts of David Abram). 'We are made of our environment,' Paul stated. 'The environment is not a scene through which we move, but the medium within which we are embedded.' Paul's presentation hinged on the idea of 'embedment' — the idea that 'our inclusion in an environment is an essential part or characteristic of ourselves' — and how we can potentially *use* this embedment to foster a more symbiotic relationship between nature and our individual selves. (As an aside, Paul presented a shocking statistic from the WHO: they suggest that depression will be the second biggest killer by 2020 — second to heart disease — so it seems obvious that we need to address issues of personal contentment and happiness sooner rather than later.)

Bryony Pierce's talk, she stated, was more of an initial airing of an idea she has been developing — that of panabstractism (**not** panabstract**ion**ism as people apparently repeatedly think — refer to it incorrectly at your peril!). Bryony playfully asked if we really need another -ism, given the veritable plethora of confusing -isms that exist today. She argued that there is, however, room for one more — panabstractism: the idea that abstract relations are part of everything, and physical things cannot exist without abstract relations. Could consciousness arise from abstract relations and not straight out of physical matter (as physicalism would have us believe)? Bryony didn't know, but she rightly suggests that this is a philosophically underdeveloped area of enquiry.

Rob Pepperell came at consciousness from a different angle still, claiming that mind creates the world we experience, and suggesting that there is powerful evidence and argument against a mind-independent reality. His talk focused on how art can be seen 'to contribute to questions about mind, nature and existence' — giving the audience an insight into how artists 'have explored many of the same essential problems as metaphysicians and scientists, even if they have done so by different means and with different outcomes.' Rob highlighted some of the works by Cézanne, Braque, etc. and interspersed his own insights with direct quotes from the artists themselves as to how they experienced reality.

In his talk, Peter Wyss argued that the notion of 'emergence' fails to hold any explanatory power. He asked, 'do we really explain anything when we say that something emerges from something else?' This type of question is likely to be received coolly (at best) by theoreticians that claim that consciousness will eventually be explained in terms of underlying neurological processes, but Peter was persuasive in his arguments: for example (and taken from the abstract of the talk), 'when we claim that mind emerges from matter, we mean to say that mind connects to matter in an unpredictable way. Hence, we express not only our confidence that mind emerges from matter, but also our ignorance about how this is possible.' As such is the case, Peter claimed, we should stop using the term emergence as some sort of explanation of the phenomenon of consciousness. Rather, we should accept that consciousness appears to be a thing in itself –– i.e. 'emergents are entities that are ontologically (or existentially) dependent on their bases, yet have a distinctive and independent identity as being of a new kind.'

As mentioned above, the presentations briefly described here make up only a fraction of what was on offer throughout the weekend. Other talks that I attended, but that space limits me from discussing in detail, included Aaron Sloman's discussion of virtual machines and whether Darwinian evolution can be successfully extrapolated to explain consciousness (or 'putting ghosts into machines'); Tristan Moyles' talk on conceptualism and animal perception; James Buchanan's presentation on Merleau-Ponty and object transcendence; Alex South on habit and Merleau-Ponty; Joulia Smortchkova's discussion of mental pointing/demonstration; Alfredo Martinez on Antonio Damasio's work on the mind–body problem; and Michael Braund's discussion of ecological psychology.

Even this list is not exhaustive — there were numerous other sessions that I simply could not attend, all of which would undoubtedly have been as thought-provoking as the others. Finally, there were also a number of workshops (of which I only made it to Keith Beasley's on Reiki healing), and these seemed to go down extremely well with the other delegates I spoke to throughout the conference.

All in all, the conference was jam-packed and highly successful. The theme was extremely well-received by everyone in attendance, and it was brilliantly organized. I can thoroughly recommend attendance at future events, especially if you're new to the conferences (as I am), because you will be warmly welcomed by a close-knit community of likeminded individuals.

Snow, P. J. *The Human Psyche in Love, War and Enlightenment*. Boolarong Press, Brisbane, Containing: 8 sections, 210,000 words, 247 quotations, 38 original figures.

"....at last the neurobiology of the human psyche..."

The *Human Psyche;* a far reaching exposé of human identity that seeks to unify the startling new insights gained from modern neuroscientific studies of higher consciousness, with perspectives gained from introspection and philosophy. In simple, straightforward prose and diagrammatic form it presents several new models of the generation of, and interactions between, the neural centers that are responsible for thought, emotion and mood. It will be of particular interest to neuroscientists, neurologists, biologists, mental health professionals, students of religion and philosophers and indeed all those fascinated by the foundations of human behavior, its origins in the animal world and its implications for our future.

The *Human Psyche* reminds us that we live in a time when science finally has significant answers about the true nature and origins of human behavior – a perspective that heralds a new era that will inevitably see the dissolution of many hallowed, though plainly stagnant institutions and the establishment of a new world.

"...invaluable reading for postgraduate students."

A$49.95

ORDERS:
www.boolarongpress.com.au

About P.J.Snow : http://en.wikipedia.org/wiki/P.J._Snow

Book Reviews

Michael Tye
Consciousness Revisited: Materialism without Phenomenal Concepts
Cambridge, MA: The MIT Press, A Bradford Book, 2009, 256 pp.
ISBN 978-0262012737

Reviewed by Bruno Mölder
University of Tartu, bruno.moelder@ut.ee

Michael Tye's latest book, *Consciousness Revisited*, is his fourth MIT Press volume dedicated to philosophical issues concerning consciousness. However, this one stands apart from his previous books, as here Tye significantly revises several of his earlier views. For instance, he now denies the existence of phenomenal concepts, rejects strong intentionalism, and has changed his views on how we know about the phenomenal features of our experiences. To my mind, the readiness to change and modify one's views in the face of counter-arguments is an admirable characteristic of a philosopher, since it supports the image of philosophy as a discipline where it is arguments that make people embrace or give up ideas. Clinging to a position even if it cannot be defended would turn philosophy into a boring and dogmatic subject.

The issues that Tye's book deals with are of interest not only to people working on consciousness, but also to philosophers specialising in the philosophy of mind, the philosophy of language, epistemology or metaphysics. The first chapter is of an introductory kind. In it, a central character steps onto the stage: the so-called 'phenomenal character' that is unpacked as 'what it is like to undergo the experience' (p. 9). The second chapter places the consciousness issue in the context of physicalism: the thesis that in the actual world, microphysical phenomena determine all other phenomena. Here, Tye outlines four puzzles for physicalism which are very well known. Indeed, for each there is a cottage industry in the philosophy of mind. These are, as Tye names them, 'the Mary puzzle', 'the zombie problem', 'the explanatory gap', and 'the hard problem'. In chapter 6, Tye presents his solutions to these puzzles, based on his new position. The third chapter brings us to the issue mentioned in the subtitle of the book — the devastating critique of theories of phenomenal concepts. From this, Tye moves on to discuss various views concerning the content of visual experience, and settles on a position close to disjunctivism. The fifth chapter is central for understanding the whole book, for here Tye outlines the Russellian distinction between two kinds of awareness or knowledge and presents his account of the phenomenal character of experience. As we will see below, this distinction helps him to answer the main objections to physicalism in the following chapter. The last two chapters extend Tye's account to further specific issues in the philosophy of mind. Chapter 7 deals with the interpretation of the change blindness phenomena. Here, Tye defends the position that one is not aware of every change in one's visual field. In chapter 8, Tye discusses our knowledge of the phenomenal character of our experiences and explicates the sense in which we enjoy privileged access to this character. The book closes with a defence of phenomenal externalism, the view that the factors internal to the brain do not determine the phenomenal character, or, in other words, that the phenomenal characters of experiences by identical brains could differ in some conditions.

The book is written in a fairly condensed style. In the course of arriving at his own position, Tye usually outlines a proposal or a theory, presents several versions of it, and then gives arguments against these versions. Possible replies are considered and arguments against those are offered as well. As a result, the book contains a host of arguments, most of them presented in quite a terse manner. I must confess that I got lost in several places, assuming (wrongly as it turned out) that the position under construction is the one that Tye is going to espouse, but soon learning that this is still meant for refutation (e.g., his construction of the Kaplanian account of the phenomenal character). In this respect, I sometimes wished that the presentation was signposted a bit more explicitly.

If I had to summarise the book in a sentence or two, then I would say that its central problem is how to account for the features of phenomenal consciousness and the puzzles it seems to generate for physicalism without relying on phenomenal concepts and qualities internal to the mind. Tye develops a view that treats consciousness as involving objects and properties in the world, a view in which a special kind of direct contact with perceived objects plays a crucial role.

More specifically, Tye puts a lot of emphasis on the distinction between 'thing knowledge' and 'fact knowledge'. With some modification, he thereby takes on board the Russellian distinction between 'knowledge by acquaintance' and 'knowledge by description'. Whereas fact knowledge is propositional, the thing knowledge does not require knowing any facts pertaining to the thing. This knowledge is provided by one's becoming conscious of that thing. What is required is 'an encounter in experience' with it (p. 101). In this usage, there is no distinction between knowledge and awareness. Tye notes that knowing a thing in this sense does not even require conceptualising the thing in any way (p. 100). That this is so follows from his condition for being conscious of an entity:

> If a phenomenally conscious state of mine is such that at a minimum it at least enables me to ask 'What is that?' with respect to some entity, and it does so directly on the basis of its phenomenal character alone, then I am conscious of that entity. But if a phenomenally conscious state of mine is not so situated, then I am not conscious of the relevant entity. (p. 14)

Besides such points, Tye does not really explicate the notion of thing knowledge much more, and perhaps this is one of those notions that we are supposed to grasp intuitively. This notion is then employed in resolving the familiar puzzles for physicalism. According to Tye, we can make sense of Frank Jackson's colour scientist Mary thought experiment by using the aforementioned distinction. Recall that Mary is supposed to know all the physical facts about colour vision, but she has not seen any colours herself. When she sees colour for the very first time, she supposedly learns something new that she did not know before. The task for a physicalist is to explain what it is that Mary finds out and how she could find anything out at all given that she already knew everything physical. Tye's solution is very neat and simple: originally Mary had complete fact knowledge, but she was lacking acquaintance with the phenomenal character of a colour experience. When she saw some colour, she acquired this knowledge by acquaintance. This solution is compatible with physicalism, for non-physical *facts* are not required to explain what Mary learns (presuming that a physicalist account of *thing* knowledge can be given). The distinction between two kinds of knowledge is also prominent in Tye's responses to the explanatory gap worry and David Chalmers' hard problem. (It is not involved in his response to the worry concerning the conceivability of zombies, where he argues that zombie scenarios fall short of being metaphysically possible.) Basically, the first problem is that even when we have a full physical account of consciousness at hand, we still do not understand why these physical phenomena produce this particular phenomenal feeling but not any other, and hence our account is still not complete. The second problem consists in the more general puzzlement as to why physical phenomena yield phenomenal consciousness at all. Tye's reply to both puzzles relies on the point that thing knowledge cannot be logically deduced from the knowledge of facts (p. 139). The knowledge of all the physical facts is thus not sufficient to yield acquaintance with a phenomenal character, and this feeds the impression that something crucial about phenomenal consciousness is left out from our best physicalist account. According to Tye, any gaps can be closed by simply postulating identities involving conscious states and physical properties, supported by *a posteriori* considerations.

In the past, Tye's strategy in responding to worries of that sort was to rely on the peculiar features of phenomenal concepts that we employ in introspection. Most crucially, phenomenal concepts are supposed to be special in the sense that they have no inferential connections to other concepts and, thus, claims involving them cannot be deduced *a priori* from truths involving physical concepts. Tye now rejects this strategy, partly because all theories of phenomenal concepts are prone to serious objections (as he shows in chapter 3) and partly because he does not think that phenomenal concepts are special in any required way. In his new view, many other concepts are also not *a priori* linked to physical concepts. He also argues that, like other concepts, concepts that we apply when we talk about our experiences can be applied and even possessed without 'full understanding', that is, can be applied also by those who have not even had the respective experiences (sect. 3.6).

Given the centrality of the notion of acquaintance in Tye's new account, it deserves a longer analysis than can be provided here. Let me record just some worries. Tye connects consciousness of a thing with wondering or asking about the thing. The way he presents it on p. 14 leaves the impression that what is offered to us is a necessary and a sufficient condition. I have two problems with this. First, it is hard to see the evolutionary advantage of connecting consciousness with wondering, given that the latter seems to be a more advanced ability than the capacity of being conscious of something. Or at least we would need to explain why, in creatures who can entertain propositional attitudes, consciousness has become so intimately related with the capacity to wonder. My second point is that it is hardly believable that the condition can be necessary. For imagine someone who is otherwise capable of entertaining propositional attitudes, but whose cognitive system responsible for forming relevant propositional attitudes has become temporarily faulty or isolated from the output systems. Due to the impairment, this person cannot ask or wonder about the things around her, but (at least intuitively) it seems to me that, because of this, that person has not yet become a zombie. It seems that she could still be phenomenally conscious of things around her; she is merely unable to wonder about them.

Tye claims that 'knowledge by acquaintance of an entity is a kind of non-conceptual, non-propositional thing knowledge' (p. 136). This non-conceptual state must play a certain functional role in one's cognitive system, namely, it should make it possible for one to form an attitude about that thing (p. 211). In this respect, Tye's approach relates to his earlier work (Tye, 1995; Tye, 2000). However, while Tye assumed earlier that the non-conceptual content is 'abstract' in the sense that it represents only general features, he now defends the view that the particular things 'enter' into the content of experience. For such an account, hallucinations can be a problem, as, in the case of hallucinatory visual experience, there really are no things that appear to one in hallucination. According to Tye, due to the lack of the respective object, veridical and hallucinatory experiences do not have the same content (even if they appear the same). These experiences instantiate both the same 'content schema', which in the case of veridical experience is filled with a particular thing, and in case of a hallucination, is left unfilled (pp. 81–82). But note that if the way things appear to one in the veridical and hallucinatory experience is impossible to tell apart (as might sometimes happen), then the appearances should involve also indistinguishable phenomenal characters. What makes it true that in the case of both experiences the appearances can be the same? Tye proposes to explain the appearing in terms of a disposition to believe:

> My visual experience has a gappy content — a content with a gap in it where a seen object should go along with such properties as blueness, roundness and bounciness. But this gappy content disposes me to believe that there is something blue, round and bouncing. This is what makes it the case that it appears to me that there is something blue, round, and bouncing. (p. 92)

Presumably Tye takes appearing to be constituted by being disposed to believe, given that we can read 'making it the case' as 'constituting'. If so, then what constitutes the fact that the hallucinatory experience appears to have a certain phenomenal character is that the unfilled or 'gappy' content disposes one to believe that there is something with such and such properties. Presumably, a similar story should be told about the case of veridical experience. In the veridical case as well, an awareness of the phenomenal character must be constituted by the fact that the content of the experience disposes one to believe that there is something with such and such features. This does not require that the veridical experience and the hallucination have the same content (in addition to the same 'content-schema'), although both contents could dispose one to believe the same thing.

Such an account allows that an object can appear to be present without actually being present. When combined with a nod to disjunctivism, this may lead to troubles concerning the role of objects in the veridical experience. If a mere 'gappy' content can generate an appearance of an object, it would create a redundancy in the account to assume that in the veridical case it is the very objects entering into the content that play a role in constituting how they appear to us. But an alternative position, which does not use the fact that an object is a part of the content in accounting for the object's appearance is not attractive either. In this view, the object would be only a peripheral addition to the theory, a device to tell veridical experiences apart from hallucinations.

As one can see from the issues I have brought up in this review, *Consciousness Revisited* is a thought-provoking piece, as one would expect from a good work in philosophy. It is a very refreshing contribution to the mainstream philosophy of mind, a field that has been spinning around the same old puzzles and conceptions for too long.[1]

References

Tye, M. (1995), *Ten Problems of Consciousness: A Representational Theory of the Phenomenal Mind* (Cambridge, MA: The MIT Press).

Tye, M. (2000), *Consciousness, Color, and Content.* (Cambridge, MA: The MIT Press).

---

[1] Work of this paper was supported by grant No. 7163 from the Estonian Science Foundation. I am grateful to Paul McLaughlin for checking my English.

Michael N. Marsh
Out of Body and Near-Death Experiences: Brain State Phenomena or Glimpses of Immortality?
Oxford University Press, 2010, pp. 309 + xxv. Price: £60.
ISBN 978-0-19-957150-5.

Reviewed by Chris Nunn

Professor Michael Marsh is a research physician who later took a theology degree — apt and interesting qualifications for anyone wanting to get to grips with what he terms Extracorporeal Experiences (ECEs). This book derives from his DPhil thesis in theology. Like many works with a similar origin, it isn't always reader-friendly, but that's not the only stylistic problem. The first section (chapters 1–9), which deals with the veridicality and origins of ECEs, is based on examination of the writings of 'five influential authors'.[2] The approach here is markedly *de haut en bas* and sometimes positively acidulous, especially in the earlier chapters. Even as late as p. 169, we get 'My account illustrates their [i.e. his 'influential authors'] defective evaluations in excluding much work regarding disturbed temporal lobe function…'. On p. 126, to give another example, he writes 'I can hardly believe that intelligent people can so obstinately continue to pursue such hopelessly insubstantial ends [referring to attempts to check the veridicality of OBE reports by concealing objects where they can't be seen by a patient's corporeal self]'. Marsh tells us that he has never himself interviewed an ECEer, relying entirely on accounts written by others. Armchair critics may legitimately criticize, but not denigrate, those who've done the spadework. As many of us know from our own experience, a writer can readily get swept along by the heat of argument into use of unwise language. That's why we need editors. Though the book looks nice, OUP have done a poor job on it.

The shorter, second section of the book (chapters 10–13) discusses Christian ideas about souls and the afterlife, and how ECEs might relate to them. It is quite different in tone from the first. Waspishness is (almost) entirely absent and assertions of the correctness of Marsh's own opinions, in contrast to the inadequacy of those espoused by other authors, are far less jarring. Let's move on from stylistic issues to discuss Marsh's views. The two separate sections of the book need to be dealt with in turn.

---

[2] Namely: Raymond Moody, Kenneth Ring, Michael Sabom, Margot Grey, and Peter and Elizabeth Fenwick (who are counted as one).

The aim of the first section is to show that ECEs are in fact not 'extracorporeal'; they are very much products of disordered brain function. Marsh points out that OBE reports are generally vague and lacking in detail compared to descriptions that could be expected from a 'real' eyewitness. The accounts by blind OBEers that have allegedly reported normal or super-normal vision while 'out of the body' are misleading, he avers; some were elicited through poor interview technique, while others (in cases of acquired blindness) may be attributable to memories of vision. The famous case alleged to have witnessed goings-on in an operating theatre while she was in 'suspended animation' for treatment of a cerebral aneurysm (Pam Reynolds) could have gathered the information by normal methods, while her experience may have occurred during the recovery phase following her operation.

When it comes to the 'out-of-this-world' aspect of NDEs, Marsh shows that the reported phenomenology is more varied and sometimes more dreamlike than is implied in some texts, especially those of Moody, Ring and Grey. He suggests that the schmaltzy, chocolate-boxy (I'm paraphrasing here) descriptions of paradise in many accounts are much more likely to reflect subjective fantasies than any 'objective' reality. He also has an 'anti-veridical' argument that I haven't come across elsewhere; namely, the fact that some NDEers who initially find themselves in hellish surroundings are often whisked straight to 'paradise' doesn't fit well with orthodox beliefs about the difficulties of escaping hell!

The next and most substantial part of the book is to do with an often interesting look at pathological and other states that can be associated with NDE-like experiences. Dreams, phantom limbs, temporal lobe glitches, endorphins, hypercapnia, hypoxia, migrainous auras and sleep disorders are all discussed. Mention of pharmacological agents is limited to nitrous oxide, ketamine and a brief reference to LSD — which is a pity since the overlap between NDE and ayahuasca phenomenology, for instance, is greater than that in any of the examples discussed.

While none of these factors individually is associated with a 'full house' of NDE experiences, the implication is that some combination of them would suffice to produce all the phenomena. Marsh suggests that NDEs occur shortly before recovery of 'normal' consciousness, and are divided into an early phase associated with vestibular disturbances and visual cortex re-oxygenation, followed by a late phase when 'higher' mental functions are re-establishing themselves. He emphasizes the possible significance of the fact that NDEs always terminate when a patient 'regains consciousness'.

Apart from its somewhat hand waving nature overall, there are problems with this formulation. One, for example, is that NDEs have occasionally been reported by people who have not obviously suffered any significant brain impairment. Another is that, from the NDEer's point of view, what Marsh calls 'regaining consciousness' following a brain impairment actually refers to *loss* of the subjective clarity, intensity and memorability of NDE experience in favour of very different qualities (i.e. confusion, haziness, etc.). The first problem can be dealt with by appeal to occult pathology. The Fenwicks, in particular, have called attention to the difficulty of accounting for the second; Marsh suggests that some sort of factitious memory may provide the answer.

Wearing his more consistently theological hat in the second section of the book, Marsh reiterates that ECEs in themselves are valueless by-products of brain malfunction. The picture of 'paradise' on offer simply doesn't fit the more sophisticated version of 'the afterlife' that he elaborates on the basis of Christian doctrine. However, he allows that one must accept the evidence pointing to spiritual benefit associated with the experiences. NDEers have consistently been reported to be changed after their experience, becoming less afraid of death, more loving and less selfish than comparable patients who have not had an NDE. NDEers are recipients of 'divine grace', he suggests; that, not the inherently worthless experience itself, is what benefits them.

Many of the difficulties with Marsh's account can perhaps be attributed to implicit aspects of his thinking. There's a sort of pervasive, 'clockwork universe' reductionism, which leads him to envisage a deep divide between material brains and spirits. Nevertheless, the 'afterlife' is often discussed as if it must incorporate something very like our familiar form of spatio-temporality. One is tempted to speculate that the early waspishness may have originated in disappointment that neither NDEers themselves, nor collectors of their stories, have provided believable evidence for a 'heaven' so conceived. But, although the general gist of what Marsh says about the neural correlates of ECEs is probably true if incomplete, it doesn't necessarily follow that the experiences have no inherent 'spiritual' value, or even that they are never in any sense veridical. If there is no deep gulf between matter and spirit, and if 'the afterlife' is in fact very different from anything we can readily conceive (as Marsh in places suggests), his 'divine grace' argument could be taken to indicate that NDEs are in fact important. Maybe they should be regarded as divinely inspired or allowed *parables*, expressing truths in a form that experiencers are able to understand. Indeed a parable analogy, with or without divine authorship, may provide a pointer to the possible meaning of NDEs that could interest many of us.

Maxine Sheets-Johnstone
The Corporeal Turn: An Interdisciplinary Reader
Exeter: Imprint Academic, 2009, 400 pp., ISBN 9781845401535

Reviewed by Steve Torrance

'Sheer physicality.' This is one pivotal notion around which the book circulates (if a book can circulate around several pivots at the same time, as this multi-dimensional work undoubtedly does!). The term 'sheer physicality' occurs in a discussion of 'existential fit', which is characterized as 'the felt body being felt as a *consummately* physical presence' (p. 79) — a presence, that is, that enables that body to be thoroughly at one with its physical world. The author gives some telling illustrative examples of existential fit: a young chimpanzee swinging back and forth between branches in a forest; two birds soaring on an upcurrent of air; a walker rolling herself down a grassy hill for the sheer joy of it (could this be the author herself?). These are all acts done, not to achieve some utilitarian goal, but as celebrations of animate corporeality. Other, more in-depth, explorations of sheer physicality ensue in the chapter — dance and love-making (which, here, as elsewhere in the book, are seen as closely linked, in their exemplification of the expressive sensory-kinetic dynamics of exuberant corporeal being).

Maxine Sheets-Johnstone (whom I have had the pleasure of meeting and spending time with on a couple of occasions) is physically small, very light on her feet, and, notwithstanding her advanced years, as happy to *dance* her philosophy as to state it in words (and indeed to have her audience dance it as well).[3] As a trained dancer, whose doctoral work was in the Philosophy of Dance, strongly grounded in Phenomenology, her physical agility is, I would judge, as important to her as her intellectual prowess. Philosophy is usually conceived of as

---

[3] I searched for an online link to a good video of Maxine Sheets-Johnstone, performing, in person, a practical exploration of dance. Nothing of exceptional quality appeared available. However I located, and strongly recommend, an excellent round-table discussion led by her, on 'Dance, Movement, and Bodies: Forays into the Nonlinguistic' held at the Philoctetes Center, New York City, in September 2007, available online at http://www.youtube.com/watch?v=-pTxptDPQzI (accessed 4/11/2010). Many of the central themes of *The Corporeal Turn* are featured in this discussion.

a cerebral, sedentary, activity; I mention these rather personal, physical, details of the author in order to emphasize how central animate physicality, in the sense of active engagement of the 'tactile-kinaesthetic body', is to her philosophical viewpoint and her conception of how philosophy is to be done.

This collection of essays arcs 30 years of the author's writing life, the first chapter republishing an essay of 1979, and the book itself appearing as a publication in 2009. Only two of the chapters are of previously unpublished material, but, as with many single-author collections, presenting them as a sequence within one cover provides an opportunity for the author to weave a pattern of interconnecting and revisited themes, and for the reader to reap the advantages of that rich, multiply-layered context when reading any particular chapter. In this case only a book-length presentation can do justice to the fecundity and complexity of the author's thought.

The author's very helpful introduction provides pithy summaries of each chapter, and also puts each of the chapters under one of four overarching *ur*-themes. But this thematic classification should not be taken too rigidly: most of the essays resonate with several themes at once, so the pigeonholing of one chapter per theme is at best a first pass at trying to characterize what the book deals with. Nevertheless, taking that first pass, here are these four super-topics: 'Living Bodies'; 'The Genesis of Consciousness'; 'The Primacy of Movement'; 'Evolutionary and Phenomenological Semiotics'.

Trying to give a more nuanced sketch of the book's concerns is harder, but one can start by stating what Sheets-Johnstone is *contesting* in her work, and then move on to her positive claims and inspirations. Mind, intelligence, what it is to be human, to be alive — are deeply misconstrued in mainstream cognitive science. Prevailing conceptions are anthropocentrist and 'adultist' (p. 365) — they fail to do justice to the deep evolutionary continuities between human-ness and nonhuman animal life, or to the importance of childhood and indeed neonate explorations in the formation of the whole human being. This phylogenetic and ontogenetic shallowness leads to a number of errors — the dominance of the linguistic-cognitive, cerebral, eye- and brain-based processes of animate activity over the more fundamental and primordial processes of tactile-kinaesthetic, dynamic corporeality. The very term 'cognitive science' is perhaps a misnomer, since it hijacks a whole collection of crucial questions (such as what is mind? how does it relate to the body? how special is the human species? how does language relate to meaning? how do concepts originate? how does consciousness originate?) and rebrands them as questions essentially about cognition, conceptualized as language-and-symbol-manipulation, and about the brain as a cognitive (or computational) engine.

Even the 'embodied' movement in cognitive science comes under Sheets-Johnstone's fire: she describes the term 'embodiment' as a 'lexical band-aid covering a three-hundred-fifty-year-old wound generated and kept suppurating by a schizoid metaphysics' (p. 215; see also p. 196). In place of a cognitivist science, she has developed a study (scientific and rigorous, to be sure, but hardly to be trapped inside the term 'science') of 'animate form' which sees thinking, emotion, consciousness, meaning as all emerging from our deep history as corporeal beings (where 'our history' here means not the history of humans and perhaps their hominid precursors, but the entire evolutionary unfolding of the living, animate world).

Sheets-Johnstone's method is multidisciplinary, drawing upon phenomenological, psychoanalytic, evolutionary, ethological, psychodevelopmental, literary, and aesthetic sources, alongside many other disciplines in the cognitive and biological sciences. One impishly titled essay illustrates the multiple layers and references that she considers essential in developing her textured theses: 'On Bacteria, Corporeal Representation, Neanderthals, and Martha Graham'. The text is a rumination on the origins of meaning-making, and issues a challenge to classical theorists of language who obsess about how language could suddenly arise with *Homo sapiens*. Sheets-Johnstone shows, using a variety of illustrative examples, how language, communication and meaning-making are not just tools of intellectual and verbal thought; on the contrary they emerge from the animate corporeality of the countless species that make up 'our' (humanity's) deep evolutionary history. This involves, *inter alia*, a reassessment of Neanderthal tool-making, as well as a defence of the need to recognize, alongside the sophisticated language forms that make up our human-ness, the deep communicative power of dance-forms such as Martha Graham's *Lamentation*.

The essentials of Sheets-Johnstone's approach are thus clear: to develop a composite, multilayered vision, which requires an uncompromisingly cross-disciplinary approach, combining many different sources, including phenomenological, psychoanalytic, natural-historical, developmental, dynamical-systems, literary, aesthetic perspectives, as well as those based on many other disciplines within the cognitive and biological sciences. Thus, to return to the four overarching themes mentioned above: some of the essays develop this composite vision by meditating on the nature of what it is to be a living body. Some — in particular her signature paper 'Consciousness: A Natural History', familiar to readers of this journal (and in this reviewer's view one of the best papers ever published in it) — propound a view of consciousness as essentially linked to movement, and thus as having a long evolutionary lineage that can even be traced back to the 'surface recognition sensitivity' of motile bacteria. Some articulate the centrality of movement and animate being to thinking, affectivity, learning, and to habitual, skilled action such as dance. And some centre upon language, meaning and 'semiosis' and propose an account of concepts, semantics and syntax that sees each of these as rooted in preverbal, bodily-kinetic activities and experiences that long predate the appearance of the word-wielding human species.

Clearly, with this book as with others, including her *Roots* trilogy, and *The Primacy of Movement,* Maxine Sheets-Johnstone has established herself as a key contributor to a growing critical tradition within the sciences of life, cognition, consciousness which develop an 'embodied', 'enactive' perspective which offers sharp challenges to the cognitivist, brain- and computation-centred approach which still dominates the mind sciences. Yet this critical tradition is one with which she seems strangely unwilling to declare a common intellectual alliance. Indeed she eschews, or rebuffs, terms such as 'embodiment', 'enactivism', and so on, and makes only scant references to works of other current authors who offer accounts which are congruent with her own views (exceptions to this include Shaun Gallagher, Daniel Stern and J. Scott Kelso; yet authors such as Francisco Varela, Evan Thompson and others, who might have been referred to more frequently, if only for friendly criticism, have few or no mentions). So the picture that emerges from reading her work is of an author who prefers to pursue a relatively lone path, and who seems often to find it easier to stress differences rather than harmonies with many of the authors that a reader might see as forming with her a common, vibrant, critical tradition.

Having said that, this book, and her work in general, mark her out as a truly original and enormously valuable thinker, whose influence will surely grow over coming decades, within the intellectual movement of which she is clearly an important part. In particular, her distinctive contributions to the understanding of consciousness in the context of its deep evolutionary history, and above all, her celebration and elaboration of its *sheer physicality*, offer a welcome alternative to the many anthropocentric, infocentric and neurocentric accounts that currently populate the consciousness field.

Charles Tart
The End of Materialism: How Evidence of the Paranormal is Bringing Science and Spirit Together
Oakland, CA: Noetic Books and New Harbinger Publications, 2009, xiii+397 pp., ISBN 978-1-57224-645-4 (hbk)

Reviewed by Charles Whitehead, www.socialmirrors.org

Charles Tart's latest book, judging by the quotes on the flyleaf, has already received a number of glowing reviews — but hardly the recognition it deserves. The launch of the book was not heralded by long extracts on the front page of the London *Times*, or a storm of publicity throughout the news media. Nor was it listed at number one on Amazon's Hot Future Releases Chart. These distinctions were reserved for the latest gospel of atheism, *The Grand Design*, by Stephen Hawking and Leonard Mlodinow, who claim that modern physics can explain Everything without the 'need' to believe in God. By Everything, of course, they do not mean consciousness or the paranormal phenomena reviewed by Tart. Like Richard Dawkins, they assume that religion is a primitive alternative to science — an attempt to explain the universe by people who lacked adequate information. Since they don't know any anthropology, they don't realise that they have reinvented a hypothesis first proposed by the British Intellectualists in the 19th century, and long since rejected by anthropologists because it is not consistent with ethnographic evidence. Hawking and Mlodinow are dismally ignorant of religion. They think it is sufficient to attack a straw man — Sir Isaac Newton's argument that order in the solar system testifies to a Creator God. Extra-solar planets, they say, make 'the coincidences of our planetary conditions ... far less remarkable and far less compelling as evidence that the Earth was carefully designed just to please us human beings'.

Charles Tart has written a far more important and compelling book than Hawking and Mlodinow. But modern physics gets the major accolades, whilst parapsychology remains a tiny, underfunded, and largely neglected discipline — even though its implications for our understanding of reality are vastly more profound than those of physics. Before his latest profession of atheism, Hawking suggested that a God *may* have created the cosmos and the laws that govern its behaviour — but He does not intervene by 'breaking the rules'. Others have argued that consciousness likewise cannot exert 'physical' effects, because that too would 'break the rules' (i.e. conservation laws). But the evidence reviewed by Tart shows that psychic phenomena do precisely that. If human consciousness can 'break the rules', then we cannot dismiss the possibility of a God who does the same.

Before reading Tart's book, my first thought was whether we really needed another disproof of materialism. There has been a 'quiet revolution'[4] going on for several decades, and many authors have exposed the logical contradictions within, and the empirical evidence against, materialism. But therein lies the rub. The vast majority of scientists continue to be incorrigibly materialistic despite all reason and disproof, and do so by denial, dismissing evidence incompatible with their beliefs, and never critically examining their most fundamental assumptions. The people who most need to read Tart's book — or so I thought — simply won't read it. The point I was overlooking here — so wonderfully clarified by Tart — is the extent to which materialism has invaded the unconscious minds of modern people, even including those who see themselves as leading spiritual lives and seeking spiritual growth. This means pretty well everybody needs to read this book.

Tart does an excellent job of trouncing materialism. He presents terminally conclusive arguments, and does so with leisurely calm and clarity which makes for very easy reading. I do not believe even Richard Dawkins could read this book and still declare himself to be a materialist, without doing grievous violence to his own integrity as a scientist and a human being. Tart is also refreshingly honest about his own possible biases and personal weaknesses. Without compromising his scientific rigour, he has set aside the conventional formalities of academic discourse. I have long believed that academic conventions, though ostensibly serving to ensure objectivity, are in fact a mask behind which academics conceal their human fallibility and buttress their own authority — rather like the masks worn by surgical teams, even though they have been proven to have no effect on hospital infection rates.

Tart has also written an excellent overview of psi research, the fruit of a distinguished fifty-year career in the field. What I am less sure about is whether paranormal research is necessary or sufficient to bring science and spirit together. It worked for him: the discovery of such research restored his belief in the spirit. But it didn't work for me: I always believed in psi because my mother had precognitive dreams; but that did not prevent me, as a boy, concluding that only morons believe in God.

---

[4] The phrase comes from a review by Larry Dossey, cited on the flyleaf of the book.

Tart opens his introduction with the classic account of a spiritual experience which occurred to the American psychiatrist, Richard Maurice Bucke, in 1872,[5] and which led to Bucke's belief in 'cosmic consciousness'. Tart returns to Bucke's experience in the final chapter of the book. So he clearly sees such experiences as of core importance to understanding human spirituality. But there is no chapter specifically addressing spiritual experiences. Rather, eleven chapters address eleven paranormal phenomena, which Tart divides into two groups — the Big Five (telepathy, clairvoyance, precognition, psychokinesis, and psychic healing) and the Many Maybes (postcognition, out-of-body experiences, near-death experiences, after-death communications, mediumship, and reincarnation). The Big Five are those for which meticulously controlled studies repeatedly provide such overwhelming statistical evidence that it would be preposterous to dismiss their results as due to chance (Tart also systematically dispatches alternative physicalist explanations). The Many Maybes are those which, though the evidence is impressive, Tart does not regard as so well supported.

In consigning phenomena to the status of a Maybe, Tart is erring on the side of caution. Ian Stevenson, for example, has investigated thousands of cases of apparent reincarnation. In many of these, birthmarks, congenital deformities, likes, dislikes, phobias, and addictions coincide with characteristics of the supposed reincarnated person. The sheer number of such cases is at least impressive, even though we may be unable to measure their statistical significance. However, dividing the average human skin area into 10 cm squares, Stevenson calculated that the chances of a person having two birthmarks in the same squares as the entry and exit wounds of a bullet would be 1 in 25,600 ($1/160^2$). Stevenson cites 18 such cases. One, Necip Ünlütaskiran, had seven birthmarks, six of which corresponded to the knife and bullet wounds that killed the alleged reincarnated person, as described in a medical document. The odds against this occurring by chance exceed two quadrillion to one ($1/160^6 = 1/2,684,356,560,000,000$).

Contrast this with the astronomical numbers associated with Tart's Big Five. A meta-analysis of 309 studies of precognition, for example, produced odds against chance of 10 septillion (10^{25}) to one. But do we really need to draw a line between a quadrillion and a septillion? This raises the question of who you want to impress. Is Tart writing for

---

[5] The original pamphlet version is quoted in William James's classic *The Varieties of Religious Experience* (p. 399 in the 1985 Penguin reprint).

materialists and the people he describes as 'pseudo-sceptics' (those who feign scepticism but actually are bigoted fundamentalists), or is he writing for those who are genuinely open-minded, but whose confidence, integrity, or spiritual aspirations may have been compromised by the prevailing dogmas of materialism? We know that scientism dismisses all contrary evidence on principle, no matter how many zillions of zeros follow the decimal point in the p value. There is really no point writing for such people. It is the honest doubters who need Tart's book.

In the chapter on mediumship, Tart mentions the Scole report, but does not go into details. This is a pity, because the report describes the most spectacular psi phenomena recorded for many decades. The Scole mediums claimed to have contacted a group of 'spirit scientists' who promised to provide proof that human personalities survive bodily death. The resulting phenomena were observed by some of the most senior and seasoned members of the Society for Psychical Research. I only have space to give one example. A tiny ball of light — such as often appeared during séances — besides passing through the table top and in and out of the bodies of the investigators, on two occasions descended into the base of a Pyrex bowl where it changed into the glowing image of a crystal. The investigators were able to pass their hands through this image. But then the image was transformed into a solid crystal, which could be picked up and replaced. There is no need to calculate statistical probabilities to know that this defies the laws of physics as currently understood.

Or again, in the chapter on near-death experiences, Tart does not mention prospective studies which in many ways carry more evidential weight. Pim van Lommel has described the incident which triggered his interest in conducting such a study — a cyanosed and comatose patient (who of course had his eyes closed) subsequently reported seeing van Lommel place the man's false teeth in a drawer at the time. When asked how he could possibly have seen this, he explained that he was floating above his body, and was able to observe everything that occurred. Again, statistical analysis hardly seems necessary to demonstrate the extreme improbability that the man could have imagined, invented, or subliminally perceived this event, including the ability to recognise van Lommel the following morning.

The main difference between Tart's Big Five and his Many Maybes seems to be one of measurability. The idea that science should only investigate those areas of human experience that can be counted, weighed, or measured originated with Galileo, and no one can figure out quite why he came to this conclusion. Measurability is itself a materialistic demand. The trouble is that only the Many Maybes hold the promise of providing useful information about the nature and meaning of human spirituality. The Big Five, on the other hand, tell us very little about spirituality *per se*. Research on these psi abilities merely disproves materialism — which is, of course, the main aim of Tart's book. But is that enough to 'bring science and spirit together'?

The Eastern spiritual traditions which Tart frequently invokes emphasize that paranormal phenomena will manifest as a result of spiritual practice, but these are peripheral and must not distract the seeker from the quest. Tart also mentions that psychic researchers frequently suspect that the phenomena they investigate are 'teasing' or 'playing with' them — furnishing enough evidence to justify belief, but too evanescent, transitory, and elusive to provide a fully satisfying analysis. He further presents evidence that psi effects are commonly unconscious. There must be a reason for all this. I think spiritual practices allow psychic phenomena to occur because such practices involve surrender of the self. Otherwise the paranormal has to be suppressed because of the dangers of inflation, or at least loss of an identity anchored in space and time. Paranormal phenomena are not in themselves aids to spiritual growth, though I agree with Tart that they are evidence of a dimension to reality that transcends space, time, and causality as currently understood.

Throughout his fifty-year career, Charles Tart has had to contend with resistance and ridicule from the pseudo-sceptics. Despite this, he refrains from polemic. Though his critique of materialism is ultimately devastating, his comments on the materialists themselves are always measured, courteous, and respectful. Being rather impatient with scientism myself, I cannot help wondering why he does not want to throw the money-lenders out of the temple. Tart's remarkable equanimity may be the result of his interest in eastern spiritual practices, notably mindfulness meditation, in which he has received tuition from Shinzen Young. But scientism does more than merely abuse human spirituality. It is also an abuse of science. Hawking and Mlodinow, for example, assert that there are 'almost certainly' many universes, not just one. The 'many worlds' hypothesis is bad science because it is not testable, and violates Occam's razor for no better reason than to 'explain away' the anthropic cosmological principle — which might otherwise be taken to support Newton's design argument. In *A Brief History of Time* Hawking considered any resort to the anthropic principle 'a council of despair'. Materialism creates bad science in many disciplines: biologists who believe that the fundamental principle of all life is a kind of capitalistic competition; cognitive psychologists who regard children as little-scientists-to-be, neglecting just about everything that makes us human; and neuroscientists who treat the brain as a stand-alone personal computer which evolved to accomplish work-like executive tasks. Insufficient attention is paid to the social significance of major human universals such as childhood play, song, dance, art, and imagination. Is it right that we should continue to tolerate the dehumanising dogmas asserted in the name of science, and directed at a public which, far too often, appears to lack adequate intellectual defences?

Scientists who hold spiritual beliefs often conceal them in order to protect their careers. I would like to see this situation reversed. Materialism should be recognised as a source of bad science, and the pseudo-sceptics obliged to conceal their beliefs. But then, of course, materialism itself would disappear, because it would lose its political function — the legitimation of scientific authority.

BOOKS RECEIVED

Mention here neither implies nor precludes subsequent review

Bayne, Tim, *The Unity of Consciousness* (OUP 2010)

Gangopadhyay, N., Madary, M. and Spicer, F. (eds), *Perception, Action, and Consciousness: Sensorimotor Dynamics and Two Visual Systems* (OUP 2010)

Krippner, S. and Friedman, H.L. (eds), *Debating Psychic Experience: Human Potential or Human Illusion?* (Praeger 2010)

Lorimer, D. and Robinson, O. (eds), *A New Renaissance: Transforming Science, Spirit and Society* (Floris 2010)

VOLUME 17 (2010) INDEX OF TITLES

For cumulative index see: www.imprint-academic.com/jcs

A Conference and a Question: Report on Consciousness and Spirituality II
R.K.C. Forman . . . . . . (5-6) 183

Acategorial States in a Representational Theory of Mental Processes
D. Feil & H. Atmanspacher (5-6) 72

alpha.tribe
E. Ayiter . . . . (7-8) 119

Analysis of Russell
T. Dace. . . . . (5-6) 41

Atomism and Atelic Conceptualization
F. Bothereau. . . . . . . (9-10) 221

Attention as Experience: Through 'Thick' & 'Thin'
R. Hine . . . . (9-10) 202

Beyond Scientific Materialism: Toward a Transcendent Theory of Consciousness
I. Baruss . . . . (7-8) 213

Blindsight in Monkeys, Lost and (perhaps) Found
S. Allen-Hermanson . . . . (1-2) 47

Book Reviews
Various . . . . (11-12) 188

Book Reviews
Various . . . . (9-10) 235

Book Reviews
Various . . . . (5-6) 220

Complex Experience, Relativity and Abandoning Simultaneity
S.E. Power . . . . (3-4) 231

A Conceptual Reorientation of Consciousness
C. Holvenstot. . . . . . . (7-8) 191

Consciousness Already There Waiting to be Uncovered: William James's Mystical Suggestion as Corroborated by Himself and His Contemporaries
J. Bricklin . . . . (11-12) 62

Consciousness Puzzle Page
E. Subitzky . . . . (11-12) 80

Consciousness, Attention and Commonsense
F. De Brigard . . . . . . (9-10) 189

ConsScale: A Pragmatic Scale for Measuring the Level of Consciousness in Artificial Agents
R. Arrabales, A. Ledezma & A. Sanchis . . . . (3-4) 131

The Content of Olfactory Experience
C. Mole . . . . (11-12) 173

Cosmetics, Identity and Consciousness
C. Power. . . . . (7-8) 73

Cultural Distortions of Self- and Reality-Perception
C. Whitehead . . . . (7-8) 95

Dennett's Theory of the Folk Theory of Consciousness
J. Sytsma . . . . (3-4) 107

Deprioritizing the A Priori Arguments Against Physicalism
R. Brown. . . . . (3-4) 47

Dissipative Thermofield Logic of the Tao Symbol
G. Globus . . . . (5-6) 125

Dissociation: A Natural State of Mind?
G. Garvey. . . . . (7-8) 139

Editor's Foreword
A. Combs. . . . . (11-12) 9

Editorial Introduction: Philosophers Facing Phenomenal Consciousness, Online
R. Brown . . . . (3-4) 6

The Epistemological Status of Transpersonal Psychology: The Data-Base Argument Revisited
H. Walach & A.L.C. Runehov (1-2) 145

The Essential Role of Consciousness in Mathematical Cognition
R.F. Hadley . . . . (1-2) 27

The Ever-New Flow of Time: Henri Bergson's View of Consciousnes
G.W. Barnard . . . . . . (11-12) 44

The Evolutionary Dynamics of Consciousness: An Integration of Eastern and Western Holistic Paradigms
M.G. Lockley . . . . (9-10) 66

Experiencing: A Jamesian Approach
S. Ginsburg & E. Jablonka (5-6) 102

Exploring Space Consciousness & Other Dissociative Experiences: A Japanese Perspective
O. Corazza . . . . (7-8) 173

Extra Ingredient: Consciousness Limerick
M. Lipkind . . . . (9-10) 230

Functional Sub-Types
P. Soom, C. Sachse & M. Esfeld
. . . . (1-2) 7

Getting Scientific with Religion: A Darwinian Solution... Or Not?
B. Morgan . . . . (3-4) 192

The Great Apostasy? William James's 1904 denial of the existence of consciousness
W. Lyons . . . . (9-10) 117

How to Improve on Heterophenomenology: The Self-Measurement Methodology of First-Person Data
G. Piccinini. . . . . (3-4) 84

How To Make Mind Brain Relations Clear
M.W. Jones . . . . (5-6) 135

The 'I''s Eye View of Its Consciousness
J.G. Taylor . . . . (1-2) 95

In Dialogue With the World: Merleau-Ponty, Rodney Brooks and Embodied Artificial Intelligence
R.L. Zebrowski. . . . . . (7-8) 156

Introduction to the Physics of Consciousness
W. Baer . . . . (3-4) 165

Is there Awareness Outside Attention? A Psychological Perspective
A. Combs, S. Krippner & E. Taylor
. . . . (11-12) 100

The Mind Is Not What The Brain Does!
H.P. Stapp. . . . . (1-2) 197

Minding the Developmental Gap: A Theoretical Analysis of the Theory of Mind Data
N. Dolcini . . . . (7-8) 37

Nature & Human Nature
G. Horswell . . . . . . (11-12) 181

Neurology & the Mind at the Turn of the Century
A. Combs . . . . (11-12) 93

A New Model for Consciousness Conferences
G. Yu . . . . (1-2) 209

Nineteenth Century Pioneers in the Study of Dissociation: William James and Psychical Research
C.S. Alvarado & S. Krippner
. . . . (11-12) 19

On Feeling (the) Present: An Evolutionary Account of the Sense of Presence in Physical and Electronically-Mediated Environments
J.A. Waterworth, E.L. Waterworth, F. Mantovani & G. Riva . (1-2) 167

The Other Person in Joint Attention: A Relational Approach
A. Seemann. . . . . (5-6) 161

Perceptual Modalities: Modes of Presentation or Modes of Interaction?
M. McGann . . . . (1-2) 72

A Psychological Commentary on the Essays
E. Taylor. . . . . (11-12) 11

Rethinking Reality
C. Whitehead . . . . (7-8) 7

The Role of Unconsciousness in Free Will
P. Droege. . . . . (5-6) 55

A Russellian Response to the Structural Argument Against Physicalism
B. Montero. . . . . (3-4) 70

Scientific Representation, Materialism and New Facts: A response to David Hodgson
E. Schier . . . . (1-2) 189

Simultaneity & Serial Order
J. Brown. . . . . (5-6) 7

The Singularity: A Philosophical Analysis
D.J. Chalmers . . . . . . (9-10) 7

Six Keynote Papers on Consciousness with some Comments on their Social Implications: TSC Conference, Hong Kong, 10-14 June 2009
C. Whitehead . . . . . . (1-2) 217

Transsexuals and Nontranssexuals Do Not Differ in Prevalence of Post-Penectomy Phantoms: Comment on Ramachandran & McGeoch (2008)
A.A. Lawrence . . . . . . (1-2) 195

TSC Tucson Tabloid: April 13-17, 2010, Tucson, Arizona
B. Faw . . . . (5-6) 189

Understanding Consciousness: A Collaborative Attempt to Elucidate Contemporary Theories
A. Pereira Jr., J.C.W. Edwards, D. Lehmann & C. Nunn . . . (5-6) 213

Wellbeing, Mindfulness and the Global Commons
J. McIntyre-Mills . . . . . (7-8) 47

What the Nose Doesn't Know: Non-Veridicality and Olfactory Experience
C. Batty . . . . (3-4) 10

'What the!': The Role of Inner Speech in Conscious Thought
F. Martínez-Manrique & A. Vicente
. . . . (9-10) 141

What's Missing in Episodic Self-Experience?: A Kierkegaardian Response to Galen Strawson
P. Stokes . . . . (1-2) 119

Who Was Frederic William Henry Myers?
E. Taylor . . . . (11-12) 153

Why the Neural Correlates of Consciousness Cannot be Found
B. Molyneux . . . . . . (9-10) 168

William James and the Search for Scientific Evidence of Life After Death
G.E. Schwartz . . . . . (11-12) 121

William James, Conversion and Rapid, Radical Transformation
A. Hastings . . . . (11-12) 116

Worldview Transformation and the Development of Social Consciousness
M.M. Schlitz, C. Vieten & E.M. Miller . . . . (7-8) 18

Zombies, Phenomenal Concepts, and the Paradox of Phenomenal Judgment
D. Beisecker . . . . (3-4) 28

VOLUME 17 (2010) INDEX OF AUTHORS

For cumulative index see: www.imprint-academic.com/jcs

Allen-Hermanson, S. . . . . . (1-2) 47
Blindsight in Monkeys, Lost and (perhaps) Found

Alvarado, C.S. & Krippner, S. (11-12) 19
Nineteenth Century Pioneers in the Study of Dissociation: William James and Psychical Research

Arrabales, R., Ledezma, A. & Sanchis, A. . . . . (3-4) 131
ConsScale: A Pragmatic Scale for Measuring the Level of Consciousness in Artificial Agents

Ayiter, E. . . . . (7-8) 119
alpha.tribe

Baer, W. . . . . (3-4) 165
Introduction to the Physics of Consciousness

Barnard, G.W. . . . . (11-12) 44
The Ever-New Flow of Time: Henri Bergson's View of Consciousnes

Baruss, I. . . . . (7-8) 213
Beyond Scientific Materialism: Toward a Transcendent Theory of Consciousness

Batty, C. . . . . (3-4) 10
What the Nose Doesn't Know: Non-Veridicality and Olfactory Experience

Beisecker, D. . . . . (3-4) 28
Zombies, Phenomenal Concepts, and the Paradox of Phenomenal Judgment

Bothereau, F. . . . . (9-10) 221
Atomism and Atelic Conceptualization

Bricklin, J. . . . . (11-12) 62
Consciousness Already There Waiting to be Uncovered: William James's Mystical Suggestion as Corroborated by Himself and His Contemporaries

Brown, J. . . . . (5-6) 7
Simultaneity & Serial Order

Brown, R. . . . . (3-4) 6
Editorial Introduction: Philosophers Facing Phenomenal Consciousness, Online

Brown, R. . . . . (3-4) 47
Deprioritizing the A Priori Arguments Against Physicalism

Chalmers, D.J. . . . . (9-10) 7
The Singularity: A Philosophical Analysis

Combs, A. . . . . (11-12) 93
Neurology & the Mind at the Turn of the Century

Combs, A., Krippner, S. & Taylor, E.
. . . . (11-12) 100
Is there Awareness Outside Attention? A Psychological Perspective

Combs, A. . . . . (11-12) 9
Editor's Foreword

Corazza, O. . . . . (7-8) 173
Exploring Space Consciousness & Other Dissociative Experiences: A Japanese Perspective

Dace, T. . . . . (5-6) 41
Analysis of Russell

De Brigard, F. . . . . (9-10) 189
Consciousness, Attention and Commonsense

Dolcini, N. . . . . (7-8) 37
Minding the Developmental Gap: A Theoretical Analysis of the Theory of Mind Data

Droege, P. . . . . (5-6) 55
The Role of Unconsciousness in Free Will

Faw, B. . . . . (5-6) 189
TSC Tucson Tabloid: April 13-17, 2010, Tucson, Arizona

Feil, D. & Atmanspacher, H.. (5-6) 72
Acategorial States in a Representational Theory of Mental Processes

Forman, R.K.C. . . . . (5-6) 183
A Conference and a Question: Report on Consciousness and Spirituality II

Garvey, G. . . . . (7-8) 139
Dissociation: A Natural State of Mind?

Ginsburg, S. & Jablonka, E. (5-6) 102
Experiencing: A Jamesian Approach

Globus, G. . . . . (5-6) 125
Dissipative Thermofield Logic of the Tao Symbol

Hadley, R.F. . . . . (1-2) 27
The Essential Role of Consciousness in Mathematical Cognition

Hastings, A.. . . . . (11-12) 116
William James, Conversion and Rapid, Radical Transformation

Hine, R. . . . . (9-10) 202
Attention as Experience: Through 'Thick' & 'Thin'

Holvenstot, C.. . . . . (7-8) 191
A Conceptual Reorientation of Consciousness

Horswell, G. . . . . . . (11-12) 181
Nature & Human Nature

Jones, M.W. . . . . (5-6) 135
How To Make Mind Brain Relations Clear

Lawrence, A.A. . . . . (1-2) 195
Transsexuals and Nontranssexuals Do Not Differ in Prevalence of Post-Penectomy Phantoms: Comment on Ramachandran & McGeoch (2008)

Lipkind, M. . . . . (9-10) 230
Extra Ingredient: Consciousness Limerick

Lockley, M.G. . . . . (9-10) 66
The Evolutionary Dynamics of Consciousness: An Integration of Eastern and Western Holistic Paradigms

Lyons, W. . . . . (9-10) 117
The Great Apostasy? William James's 1904 denial of the existence of consciousness

Martínez-Manrique, F. & Vicente, A. . . . . (9-10) 141
'What the!': The Role of Inner Speech in Conscious Thought

McGann, M. . . . . (1-2) 72
Perceptual Modalities: Modes of Presentation or Modes of Interaction?

McIntyre-Mills, J. . . . . . . (7-8) 47
Wellbeing, Mindfulness and the Global Commons

Mole, C. . . . . (11-12) 173
The Content of Olfactory Experience

Molyneux, B. . . . . (9-10) 168
Why the Neural Correlates of Consciousness Cannot be Found

Montero, B.. . . . . (3-4) 70
A Russellian Response to the Structural Argument Against Physicalism

Morgan, B. . . . . (3-4) 192
Getting Scientific with Religion: A Darwinian Solution... Or Not?

Pereira Jr, A., Edwards, J.C.W., Lehmann, D. & Nunn, C. (5-6) 213
Understanding Consciousness: A Collaborative Attempt to Elucidate Contemporary Theories

Piccinini, G. . . . . (3-4) 84
How to Improve on Heterophenomenology: The Self-Measurement Methodology of First-Person Data

Power, C. . . . . (7-8) 73
Cosmetics, Identity and Consciousness

Power, S.E. . . . . (3-4) 231
Complex Experience, Relativity and Abandoning Simultaneity

Schier, E. . . . . (1-2) 189
Scientific Representation, Materialism and New Facts: A response to David Hodgson

Schlitz, M.M., Vieten, C. & Miller, E.M. . . . . (7-8) 18
Worldview Transformation and the Development of Social Consciousness

Schwartz, G.E. . . . . . . (11-12) 121
William James and the Search for Scientific Evidence of Life After Death

Seemann, A.. . . . . (5-6) 161
The Other Person in Joint Attention: A Relational Approach

Soom, P., Sachse, C. & Esfeld, M.
. . . . (1-2) 7
Functional Sub-Types

Stapp, H.P.. . . . . (1-2) 197
The Mind Is Not What The Brain Does!

Stokes, P. . . . . (1-2) 119
What's Missing in Episodic Self-Experience?: A Kierkegaardian Response to Galen Strawson

Subitzky, E. . . . . (11-12) 80
Consciousness Puzzle Page

Sytsma, J. . . . . (3-4) 107
Dennett's Theory of the Folk Theory of Consciousness

Taylor, J.G. . . . . (1-2) 95
The 'I''s Eye View of Its Consciousness

Taylor, E.. . . . . (11-12) 11
A Psychological Commentary on the Essays

Taylor, E. . . . . (11-12) 153
Who Was Frederic William Henry Myers?

Various . . . . (11-12) 188
Book Reviews

Various . . . . (5-6) 220
Book Reviews

Various. . . . . (9-10) 235
Book Reviews

Walach, H. & Runehov, A.L.C.(1-2) 145
The Epistemological Status of Transpersonal Psychology: The Data-Base Argument Revisited

Waterworth, J.A., Waterworth, E.L., Mantovani, F. & Riva, G. . (1-2) 167
On Feeling (the) Present: An Evolutionary Account of the Sense of Presence in Physical and Electronically-Mediated Environments

Whitehead, C. . . . . (7-8) 95
Cultural Distortions of Self- and Reality-Perception

Whitehead, C. . . . . (7-8) 7
Rethinking Reality

Whitehead, C.. . . . . (1-2) 217
Six Keynote Papers on Consciousness with some Comments on their Social Implications: TSC Conference, Hong Kong, 10-14 June 2009

Yu, G. . . . . (1-2) 209
A New Model for Consciousness Conferences

Zebrowski, R.L.. . . . . . . (7-8) 156
In Dialogue With the World: Merleau-Ponty, Rodney Brooks and Embodied Artificial Intelligence

Colour Plates

from Gary E. Schwartz, 'William James and the Search for Scientific Evidence of Life After Death', pp. 121–52 above.

Figure 1 (see page 135 above)

Figure 2 (see page 137 above)